T0339196

MEMORIES OF TWO WARS

CUBAN AND PHILIPPINE
EXPERIENCES

BY

FREDERICK FUNSTON

INTRODUCTION TO THE BISON BOOKS EDITION BY
THOMAS BRUSCINO

University of Nebraska Press
Lincoln and London

⊚

First Nebraska paperback printing: 2009

Library of Congress Cataloging-in-Publication Data
Funston, Frederick, 1865–1917.
Memories of two wars: Cuban and Philippine experiences / Frederick Funston;
introduction to the Bison Books edition by Thomas Bruscino.
p. cm.
Originally published: New York: C. Scribner's Sons, 1911.
Includes index.
ISBN 978-0-8032-2289-2 (pbk.: alk. paper)
1. Funston, Frederick, 1865–1917. 2. Philippines—History—Revolution,
1896–1898—Personal narratives, American. 3. Cuba—History—Revolution,
1895–1898—Personal narratives, American. I. Title.
DS683.7.F8 2009
959.9'031092—dc22
[B]
2009006672

INTRODUCTION

Thomas Bruscino

When *Memories of Two Wars* first appeared in 1911, its author needed no introduction. By then Frederick Funston had been in the public eye in one form or another for nearly twenty years, and it is no exaggeration to say that he was among the most renowned living Americans. In the years since his early and sudden death in 1917, Funston's fame, to say nothing of his reputation, has been in a steady decline. The great and awful events of the crowded twentieth century just did not seem to leave room for Funston. Now it is unlikely that one American in a thousand or maybe one in ten thousand has ever heard the name.

That is too bad, because whether or not our modern sensibilities allow us to admire or like Funston, there can be no doubt that he *mattered*, and he did so at a time when his country began to matter too. Those two trends were not unrelated. The life of Frederick Funston says something about the times of Frederick Funston. That connection is an essential meter for gauging the historical importance of biography or, in this case, autobiography. What is more, and happily for the reader, Funston the man and Funston the writer were entertaining, regardless of any larger judgments about his lifetime of action and controversy.

And what a lifetime it was. He was born in Ohio to a Civil War veteran in 1865 and moved to Iola, Kansas, with his family two years later. As he came of age, he showed a restless spirit. He needed to do something, something big; the only question was what. His father, Edward Hogue Funston, had become a prominent Republican congressman, so politics was an option, but first he needed to make a name for himself independent of his father. He tried and failed to get into West Point—he was small at 5'4" tall, and his grades were only average—so the traditional military route was closed. For a time he went into teaching, but the reward from that sort of service takes years, and Funston could not stand to wait around. He went to the University of Kansas, where he made lifelong friends (including the famous journalist William Allen White), but he found structured studying not to his taste and never actually took a degree. Like his comrade White, he turned to journalism and worked for a short while as a newspaperman in Kansas and Arkansas. He never gave up writing, but the life of a small-town beat reporter grew stale after a few years, and he moved on to work on the Atchison, Topeka, and Santa Fe railroad as a collector, whiling away his time gathering tickets along the line (and occasionally fighting for them if necessary).

The opportunity that Funston first seized on his road to fame came in 1890—in the field of botany, of all places—when, through his father's efforts, he found employment on a government team that was to research the flora of Montana and the Dakotas. He did well enough to earn a spot on a far more perilous expedition through Death Valley the following year, where men and beasts alike succumbed to the brutal conditions. But not Funston, who came through only slightly the worse for wear. He turned the experience into more exotic adventures exploring the frozen reaches of Alaska. Over the next few years he traveled to Yakutat Bay, over Chilkoot Pass, down the Yukon River, and to above the Arctic Circle. His official reports for the Agriculture Department went no small way toward introducing interested Americans to their distant territory, and his experiences with natives introduced him to a variety of foreign cultures. Through it all he carried a typewriter with which he consistently recorded his tales, hoping all the time that he would make his fame and fortune by sharing his adventures in print and on the lecture circuit. As interesting and thorough as his botanical expeditions proved to be, they did not capture the imagination of an adoring public. Frederick Funston still strived to make his mark.

The allure of exploration, whatever its real dangers or accomplishments, had by the end of the nineteenth century dimmed from the heyday of Captain Cook and Dr. Livingston. Soldier-adventurers at the leading edge of empire would also be on their way out within a few decades, but in Funston's time they were at their peak—celebrated, for example, in the work of Rudyard Kipling, Funston's favorite author. As Funston closed his career in exploration and began struggling in his ill-fated attempts to build railroads in Mexico, quite a bit of work for soldier-adventurers became available to interested Americans. The story in *Memories of Two Wars* began in New York City when Funston learned of the chance to join Cuban revolution-aries in their fight against Spain. In a stunning piece of good timing that became a hallmark of the rest of his life, he inde-pendently entered into that war. Just as he finished in Cuba—nearly killed by disease, malnutrition, and various wounds—the United States was about to begin its work on the island. Funston had picked the right side, in the right place, at the right time, and as a result he got his regiment for the Philippines.

That choice gave him the opportunity; his natural abilities and relentless audacity took over. Whatever the initial enthusi-asm for the fight with Spain and America's entry into the im-perial scramble, the prolonged war in the Philippines became highly contentious—something most Americans would rather have just ignored. Funston himself would get caught up in the disputes, and he would draw the very public ire of no less a figure than Mark Twain. In that context, it is no small thing that he still emerged from the war as a genuine American hero. For reasons that this memoir makes clear, he became "Fighting

Fred" Funston, winner of the Medal of Honor and the man who almost single-handedly ended the war with the capture of Emilio Aguinaldo, leader of the insurrection.

He finally had fame, fickle though it may have been, and plenty of stories about which to write. And no doubt the end of his fighting in the Philippines marked a transition in his life. No longer would Funston search for his mission; he was now a brigadier general in the regular army. His calling had been found, and he took completely to the life of an officer. Indeed, the long dénouement from the Philippines led to an important test of his devotion to his new profession when the outspoken general learned that regular officers must curb their statements on politics and stifle critiques of political masters. A public jibe at a senator led to a reprimand from President Theodore Roosevelt (a friend and admirer, as it happens). Despite his strong opinions on all manner of subjects, Funston accepted the punishment, learned the lesson, and served in uniform the rest of his days.

The insurrection in Cuba and the counterinsurrection in the Philippines did not mark the end of his adventures. The vagaries of military life found him stationed in San Francisco in April 1906. Fate left him in charge on the 18th of that month, because the commander of his department was out of town. When the earthquake hit and the fires spread, the destruction and chaos nearly consumed the city whole. Funston took command as much as anyone could, stopped the looting (sometimes with force), helped the wounded, and knocked down buildings to contain the conflagration. Like much of the rest of his military life, these actions were not without controversy; not surprisingly, some accused him of acting too rashly. However, the weight of opinion eventually leaned in his favor, even if he probably did less than save the city, as some of his most ardent supporters claimed.

Still he was not done. After stints back in Cuba, then to

command at the staff school at Fort Leavenworth, Kansas, and then back to the Philippines, Funston took over the American occupation of the Mexican coastal city of Veracruz in the spring of 1914. Perhaps the years had begun to even out his temperament, or maybe the wealth of experiences gained at the fringes of American power had taught their lesson, but whatever the case, under Funston's guidance the occupation became a model, if there is such a thing, of imposed governance. In the midst of a charged and hostile environment, the Americans literally and figuratively cleaned up the town, providing sanitation and order throughout the affair. This stability did not last long after Funston and his men left in November, but the general had shown once again that he was an effective military commander, even while applying the policies of the Democratic administration of Woodrow Wilson.

Again fate put him where the action was. After Veracruz, he took command of the Southern Department, an area that included the bulk of the American border with Mexico. The revolutions that had led Funston to Veracruz also spilled over the border, and the general found himself managing yet another intricate conflict. As Mexican bandits struck over the border and stirred up trouble on the American side and as Americans in the border states began to run amok in response, his old temper returned but did not trump his sense of duty. He pleaded for permission to chase bandits across the border into Mexico but grudgingly obeyed his orders to cut off any hot pursuit. When Pancho Villa raided the border town of Columbus, New Mexico, in March 1916, the Americans finally got their chance. Funston's subordinate Gen. John J. Pershing became well known for his pursuit of Villa's band into Mexico, but lost in the clamor over the so-called Punitive Expedition was the effective manner in which Funston led the pacification of the rest of the border.

By 1917 Frederick Funston had been a bona fide American

hero living in the public eye on and off for nearly twenty years. With the war in Europe raging and everyone expecting American entry, it is no wonder his name came up as the leading candidate to command American forces in the upcoming fight. It was not to be. While Funston was attending a banquet in San Antonio in February 1917, less than two months before the American declaration of war, a sudden heart attack felled the warrior at the age of fifty-one. For all of his fighting and all of his accomplishments, he was denied the chance to prove his worth on a world stage, and the world was denied the chance to see what Funston's innate skills and uncanny good luck could have done in that most awful of wars.

Fortunately, Frederick Funston did not leave us empty handed. He always remained a prolific writer, and among his many works was *Memories of Two Wars: Cuban and Philippine Experiences*. First published in 1911, this book is a monument to that small slice of his life, its length a testament to six years of almost unbelievable adventure and drama. The first section, on Cuba, originally appeared as serialized articles in *Scribner's Magazine* beginning in 1910. Funston wrote the latter part, on the Philippines, during his return to the archipelago. Altogether it is a fascinating document, recounting a unique journey from beleaguered and desperate guerilla to confident and powerful counterguerilla, with a conventional fighting interlude for good measure.

As a memoir, this book is intriguing for what it is not. It is not an attempt at chest thumping. Funston felt no need to embellish his tale with wild claims of imagined feats; the truth was embellishment enough. If anything, he downplays too much, leaving out details of the horrible conditions under which he and the other insurgents labored for much of his time in Cuba, the specifics on the malaria he caught in the field, wounds he received in battle (he was shot through the lungs at one point), and the story of his capture by and escape from Spanish troops on his way off the island. Nor did he use this memoir to settle scores. While seeking to clear the air about any number of controversies in the Philippines—including church looting, killing of prisoners, and the manner in which he caught Aguinaldo—he took great pains not to engage in personal attacks on the individuals who levied the charges against him, even to the point of downplaying many of the disputes within the units he commanded.

Memories of Two Wars is even more worthwhile for what it is. It is at once an introduction to a slice of the Cuban Revolution, a peek into the motivation of Progressive Era filibustering Americans, a primer on the tiny but pitched battles and sieges of small wars, a look at the mindset and worldview of Americans at the turn of the last century, an account of the campaign north of Manila, an exposition on the eternal frustrations of fighting a counterinsurgency, a commentary on postwar amnesty and reconciliation, an apologia for crimes real and imagined, an honest look at the pain and humor to be found in war, and always, above all, a study of one of the most interesting and important people America managed to produce in its first 150 years. Rare is the autobiography that engages in so many fascinating historical themes. Even better, it is a riproaring good tale.

It is a great pleasure to reintroduce Frederick Funston to an audience that has too long forgotten him. And I can think of no better way to do so than to allow him to speak for himself about the events that made him so important and famous in the first place.

TO THE MEMORY OF

ARTHUR MacARTHUR FUNSTON

the little boy who in happy days gone by
often sat on my knees and, open-eyed and
wondering, listened to the story of the cruise
of the *Dauntless* and to accounts of midnight rides in the Philippines; but who now
sleeps forever in the national cemetery of
the Presidio of San Francisco, under the
shadow of the flag his childish heart so loved

THIS BOOK

IS AFFECTIONATELY DEDICATED

PREFACE

It seems to be expected nowadays that every one who writes a book, unless it is a society novel, will use up a page or more of valuable space in explaining why he did it. In this particular case the publishers are largely to blame, as they had not a little to do with hatching the conspiracy. At least, they are where the public can get at them, while the writer, being on the other side of the world, assisting in a small way in bearing the white man's burden, is safe; and before his return to within the jurisdiction of the courts of the home-land the statute of limitations will have thrown over him its protecting mantle.

If any person should start to read this book with the idea that he may find therein discussions of military strategy or tactics, or an elucidation of personal views on our recent incursion into the realm of world-politics, this would be an excellent moment for him to put on his hat and return the volume to the neighbor from whom he borrowed it. For this is nothing more than a contribution, such as it may be, to the literature of adventure. It has fallen to the writer to be brought into more or less close personal contact with some of the men who have had to do with the making of recent history in our own country, Cuba, and the Philippine Islands, and he has been an humble participant in some of the events of those few fateful years that changed us from an isolated and self-contained nation into a world-power. The last Cuban insurrection against Spain, the war between the latter country and the United States, and the subsequent insurrection of the Filipinos, are no longer matters of current interest, but have become a part of history—history, however, which does not deal with events so remote that it is devoid of all personal interest to people now living.

As certain as fate, some caustic critic, after hastily skimming through the pages of this book, will rise up, and with his typewriter smite the author for having presumed to refer to some of the military functions that he has attended as "sieges" or "battles." So let it be understood now that the writer is not altogether ignorant of history, and that he would be one of the last men in the world to compare Guiguinto with Gettysburg, or to speak of the sieges of Cascorra and Sebastopol in the same breath. The words "battle" and "siege" are terms that designate certain sorts of military operations, and they are not limited in their application by the numbers of men who participate in them. These words have been attached to many minor affairs in the histories of all countries, and habitually have been applied to clashes of arms that did not approach Jiguani, Las Tunas, Tuliajan River, or Calumpit.

Several of the chapters that go to make up this volume have already appeared in *Scribner's Magazine*. The original scheme was the publication in that periodical of four articles describing in detail several of the more important incidents of the Cuban insurrection in which the writer had participated, no attempt being made to write a complete history of personal experiences in that war.

After the articles referred to had been published there was planned a book which was to include them, and besides contain a complete and chronological account of what the writer saw in the Philippines. To fill out the breaks of many months that occur between the incidents of the Cuban insurrection that form part of this book would necessitate rewriting everything on that subject, besides a trip to Havana to consult official records; and the whole thing when finished would in itself be a volume. It is believed, however, that these four chapters will give the reader a fair idea of the conditions under which we marched and fought in those days.

It should be understood that this book is in no sense a history of the two small wars in which the author participated, being merely an account of what he saw, with just enough on general conditions to assist the reader in following the narrative.

In writing reminiscences it is difficult to avoid overworking the personal pronoun in the first person singular, without making the style so stilted that the account might be taken for an official report; but in this case an attempt has been made not to offend too deeply against the canons of good taste in that particular respect. Acknowledgment is hereby made of the fact that in the times described the writer was by no means the only person present in either Cuba or Luzon.

The author would scarcely advise a young man to follow in his own footsteps, and go into foreign lands looking for trouble merely because his own country did not furnish enough; as the chances are that he would finally rest in a forgotten grave, as was the case with not a few of our countrymen who assisted the Cubans in their struggle for independence, but whose very names are not now known by the people for whom they gave their lives.

After we have passed middle age the tendency of most of us is to live in the days that have gone by, and to give but little thought to the future. Whatever may happen to one later, if on many more than a hundred days of his life he has heard the popping of the bullets of the Mausers, he can congratulate himself on the fact that he is still alive; and can sit back in an easy chair and spend many pleasant hours thinking of the things that were. It is worth while if you win, but not if you lose. It is good to have lived through it all.

MANILA, *August*, 1911.

CONTENTS

CUBAN EXPERIENCES

PHILIPPINE EXPERIENCES

CUBAN EXPERIENCES

I

TO CUBA AS A FILIBUSTER

I HAPPENED to be in New York City in 1896, and one evening in the spring or early summer was strolling past Madison Square Garden, and impelled by curiosity dropped in to see the Cuban Fair then in progress.

This fair, promoted by resident Cubans and American sympathizers with the cause of Cuban independence, was held ostensibly for the purpose of raising funds for the purchase of hospital supplies for the insurgent forces in the field, but a subsequent acquaintance with what was being done on the distracted Island justifies a suspicion that more of the money was expended for dynamite and cartridges than for quinine and bandages.

The principal attraction at the fair on the occasion of my visit was a fiery and eloquent speech by General Daniel E. Sickles, well known to be one of the most valued friends of the Cubans in their struggle.

Since the outbreak of the insurrection I had taken considerable interest in its progress, and had indulged myself in a vague sort of idea that I would like to take part in it, I fear as much from a love of adventure and a desire to see some fighting as from any more worthy motive. Of course, I shared the prevailing sympathy of my countrymen with the Cubans, and believed their cause a worthy one. Whatever doubts I may previously have had on the expediency of mixing up in the rows of other people vanished after hearing General Sickles's speech, and I returned to my room that evening with my mind made up and spent a sleepless night, as befits one who has just determined on going to his first war.

The next morning, without credentials of any kind, I presented myself at the office of the Cuban Junta at 56 New Street, and inquired if I could see Mr. Palma, but did not succeed in doing so. Mr. Zayas, one of the attachés of the Junta, took me in hand and was most courteous, but assured me that they were sending no Americans to Cuba, and were confining their efforts in this country to raising funds and doing what they could to direct public sentiment in favor of their compatriots. I have since often wondered how I could have been so guileless as to expect them to receive me, a total stranger, with open arms. I could have been a fugitive from justice seeking a hiding-place, a worthless adventurer, or, worst of all, a spy in Spanish pay. It was evident that different tactics must be tried. Through a mutual friend I obtained a letter of introduction to General Sickles, and the next day called on the old veteran at his residence, and not only had a most pleasant chat with him, but left with a personal note to Mr. Palma in which the General stated that, though he did not know me personally, he felt justified in vouching for me on the strength of the letter I had brought him. Back to the Junta without loss of time, and now it was different. I was admitted without delay to the office of the kindly faced, honest old patriot who afterward became the first president of free

Cuba. Mr. Palma asked me if I had had any military experience and was told that I had not, but had read considerably along military lines and felt that I had it in me to make good. A question as to my knowledge of Spanish brought out the fact that I had a fair reading but not a speaking acquaintance with that language. Mr. Palma then stated that in order as much as possible to avoid violating the neutrality laws of the United States the Cubans could not receive applicants into their service in this country, but that I could be sent down on one of the first expeditions, and might, after my arrival, offer my services to whatever insurgent chief in the field I desired. My urbane but non-committal friend of the day before, Mr. Zayas, was now sent for and I was turned over to him.

This gentleman took my address and told me that as it was impossible to intrust the secrets regarding the sailing of filibustering expeditions to any one, I must not expect to be informed as to when I could leave, but must possess my soul in patience until sent for. In the meantime I was to call at the Junta once a week. On one of these visits Mr. Zayas told me that the Cubans were having indifferent success with their artillery in the field, largely because their people did not seem to know how to handle the guns, and suggested that if I were to acquire some knowledge on that subject before sailing it might add to my welcome. This struck me favorably, as my father had been an artillery officer in the Civil War, and I had been brought up on stories of fierce struggles in which the old brass Napoleons of that day had done their part. My own artillery experience consisted in once having seen a salute fired to President Hayes at a country fair in Kansas. The result of Mr. Zayas's suggestion was that I took a note from him to the firm of Hartley & Graham, the arms dealers from whom the Cubans purchased their implements of war, and had explained to me by one of their experts the mysteries of the Hotchkiss twelve-pounder breech-loading rifle, and was allowed to fondle that ugly looking instrument of death to my heart's content and take it apart and put it together again. A book of instructions as to its use and a lot of formidable tables of velocities at various ranges, etc., I all but committed to memory. My keen interest in this new subject so pleased Mr. Zayas that he suggested that I impart some of my valuable lore to some of his countrymen in New York who were presumably waiting in feverish anxiety for the sailing of the next expedition. This I agreed to do, though it struck me as a somewhat indiscreet performance in a city where Cubans were closely watched by Spanish spies, and where there were innumerable enterprising reporters looking for "scoops." But I kept my feelings to myself, and a few evenings later was conducted by one of the attachés of the Junta to a small hall over a saloon, well up on Third Avenue. All but a few of the lights were turned off and the window-shades were well drawn. Here we found about fifteen Cubans, callow youths in the main, the most of them, I judged, being students. These aspiring patriots chattered like magpies and smoked the most astounding number of cigarettes. In addition to this promising material, there were in the room several large and imposing-looking crates labelled "machinery." These were opened and turned out to be the various parts of a Hotchkiss twelve-pounder. My recently acquired knowledge, what there was of it, now became of use, and the gun was set up and taken apart a dozen times, and the breech mechanism, sights, and ammunition explained. As this gun is transported in sections on mule back, as well as dragged by a shaft, the various heavy pieces were lifted up to the height of an imaginary or "theoretical" mule and then let down again, a form of calisthenics that soon palled on the embryo artillerymen, the night being hot and the room close. Several times the pieces were allowed to fall to the floor with a noise that should have aroused the block, and I spent a good bit of time figuring out how I would explain to the police, if they came to investigate, what I was doing with such warlike paraphernalia in peaceful New York. But we were not molested, and for a month, once a week, went through this performance. But it was wasted effort. Whether any of these young men ever reached the Island to participate in the war, I do not know, but certain it is that there was not one of them in the artillery command of the "Departamento del Oriente," the only one that did any serious work with artillery during the struggle. But it was different with the gun that we trundled and knocked about on those hot summer nights above that Third Avenue saloon, for it had its baptism in that hell of Mauser fire at Cascorra, where it was served within two hundred yards of a trench full of Spaniards, until human endurance could stand the strain no longer, and the gun was dragged backward into a ravine by the survivors of the detachment. And later, at Guaimaro, Winchester Dana Osgood, Cornell's famous foot-ball player, fell across its trail, shot through the brain. It helped to batter down the stone fort at Jiguani and took part in the duel with the Krupp battery at Victoria de las Tunas, and I understand now rests in the Havana Arsenal and is pointed out to visitors as one of the relics of the War of Independence. Verily, the old gun had a career not to be ashamed of.

An interesting incident of the summer was a trip with several members of the Junta to the coast of Long Island to see a demonstration of the working of the newly invented Sims-Dudley dynamite gun, an instrument that looked more like a telescope on wheels than an implement of war. This gun was fired several times out to sea, to the evident consternation of an excursion boat which made the most phenomenal speed in getting out of the way. The explosions of its nitro-gelatine-loaded shells threw water and spray a hundred feet in air. Nearly a year and a half later I saw one of these guns, possibly the same one, at Victoria de las Tunas, reduce blockhouses and stone barracks to heaps of rubbish, wreck a Krupp eight-centimetre field-piece, and terrify hundreds of Spanish regulars into surrender.

So the summer wore along, but one afternoon in August came the fateful telegram, and after all these years I can quote its every word: "Be at Cortlandt Street Ferry at 7 P. M., ready to leave the city." My trunk was hastily packed and left behind, and with a few belongings in a small valise, and, I must acknowledge, with some sinking of the heart, I made my way to the ferry accompanied by an old friend of college days. Here I met Mr. Zayas and by him was introduced to a Mr. Pagluchi, a nervy-looking Italian of good address and appearance, who, I afterward learned, was a marine engineer and presided over the engine-rooms of the various steamers sent out by the Junta for the purpose of carrying reinforcements and arms to Cuba. Mr. Pagluchi was accompanied by four men, none of them Cubans, and not one of whom I had ever seen before. These were Charles Huntington, a fine-looking Canadian of soldierly bearing, who had served in the Northwest Mounted Police; Walinski, an Englishman of Polish descent; Welsford, a young man from New Jersey, and Arthur Potter, a former English marine soldier who had lived in the United States for several years. Huntington was one of the bravest men I ever knew, being, in fact, absolutely reckless. He served with distinction in the Cascorra and Guaimaro campaigns, and was finally killed in a fight with Spanish guerillas, his body falling into the hands of the enemy. Potter and Welsford were chums, careless, go-lucky young fellows; the former was terribly wounded at Desmayo, having both legs shattered, and spent nearly a year on his back in a "bush" hospital. He remained in Cuba after the war, and now lives in Camaguey. Of the final fate of Welsford and Walinski I know nothing.

On the ferry-boat the five of us tried to appease our boundless curiosity as to where we were bound by attempts to extract information from Pagluchi, but without success, as it was evident that one of the things that individual was paid for was keeping his own counsel, and he fully justified the confidence reposed in him by the Junta. He kept our tickets in his possession and said we would know all in due time. At Jersey City we took berths in a sleeper on the Pennsylvania, early the next morning passed through Washington, and in the fulness of time reached Charleston, South Carolina, where we were conducted to a hotel, and found among the guests about thirty Cubans, well-dressed, superior-looking men, standing about in little groups, conversing in low tones and worried about something. I recognized, among others, General Emilio Nunez, afterward governor of the province of Havana under the administration of President Palma, whom I had met at the office of the Junta, and by whom I was introduced to General Rafael Cabrera, a kindly and considerate old gentleman who was one of the veterans of the Ten Years' War, and who had lived in exile since its close. He was now returning to renew the struggle of younger days, but to lose his life without seeing the realization of his hopes.

Among other guests of the hotel were some fifteen or twenty well-groomed, quiet-appearing men whom we were at once warned against having anything to do with, as they were operatives of a well-known detective agency in the employ of the Spanish minister at Washington, with the exception of a few who were said to be United States Secret Service men or United States deputy marshals. It was the duty of these men to learn what they could as to our intentions in order that they might give to the proper authorities the information necessary to enable them to seize the vessel on which we were to sail. They had had no success with the wary Cubans, but their eyes brightened when they saw Pagluchi's five wards, and they lost little time in trying to get acquainted. Two of them took me in hand and suggested that there was nothing like a mint julep to make one forget Charleston's August climate. But I told them I was from Kansas, whereupon they suggested an ice-cream soda; there was a place a few blocks distant where were concocted cooling drinks that were the talk of the town. Would I not stroll down there? It was difficult to shake them off without retiring to my room and sweltering in the terrific heat. Finally, Huntington saw my plight, and coming over very genially offered to thrash both of them if they did not leave me alone. This had the desired effect.

Our curiosity as to how and when we were to reach Cuba was not yet satisfied. It was known that the steamer *Commodore*, famous as a filibuster, was lying in Charleston harbor closely watched by a revenue-cutter. She had been searched for arms, but none were found on board, and, as she carried no persons besides her crew and her papers were correct, there was no justification for her seizure. The vessel was merely under surveillance, and the arrival of the parties of Cubans in Charleston had added much to the importance of watching her. As will be shown later, the *Commodore* was merely there as a blind, and served her purpose well.

On the afternoon of the day following our arrival the Cubans, carrying their hand baggage, began to leave the hotel in little groups, each followed by one or more "sleuths." About half-past three Pagluchi told his flock to come with him, and we made our way to the station of the Plant Line system of railways, where we found one of the regular trains about to leave.

We were conducted to the rear car of the train, a day coach, where we found the Cubans who had preceded us from the hotel. Several of the detectives who attempted to secure seats in this car were told that it was a special chartered by a party of excursionists, and that we would be obliged to deny ourselves the pleasure of their company. So they found seats in the car ahead, and in due time the train pulled out of the station. As to the destination of the train to which our car was for the time being attached, I cannot say, but I know that we pounded along over the rails at a fair rate of speed until some time late at night, when we stopped at an obscure station in the woods; a locomotive backed up to our car from a siding, the car was quickly and quietly uncoupled from the train, which then proceeded on its way, while our car with its engine flew back on the track a few miles, was switched onto another line, and sped along for hours without making more than the few absolutely necessary stops. From a special car we had grown to be a special train, a small one, it is true, but none the less a special. The whole plan for escaping the men following us and throwing them entirely off the scent had been thought out by Mr. Fritot, the Charleston agent of the Plant Line, and worked to perfection. We had many a chuckle over the chagrin that must have been felt by our attentive mentors when they found how neatly they had been "sacked."

Just after sunrise we came to a stop at a little station in a region of pine woods. There was a small station building and possibly one or two other houses, and a good-sized sluggish river crossed by the railway bridge, under which lay a big tug, the *Dauntless*, soon to become famous as the most successful filibuster in the Cuban service, now making her first essay in the exciting work of dodging American revenue-cutters and outrunning Spanish gun-boats. On a siding near the river bank were three large freight cars, supposed to contain saw-mill machinery arrived two days before from New York. There was no longer any occasion for secrecy, and we were informed that the station was Woodbine, on the extreme south-eastern coast of Georgia, the river was the Satilla, the freight cars were laden with arms and ammunition, and the panting tug in the river was to carry us to Cuba. We alighted from the cars, stretched our cramped limbs, and looked over our surroundings with no little interest. Our engine and car pulled out, and the engineer, who evidently suspected that he was helping to make history, called out, "Good-by and good luck, don't let them Span-ions git you." We were served with a hasty breakfast of strong coffee and hard bread from the *Dauntless*, the freight cars were opened, we took off our coats and went to work, and work it was. The forenoon was sultry and the boxes heavy, but fortunately the carry was downhill and we returned up the river bank empty-handed. There were many among the thirty-five of us who had never done a stroke of manual labor in their lives, but we five were not in that class. Nevertheless, we were heartily

glad when the task was over, and all felt that we had qualified for membership in the freight-handlers' union. In
five hours there had been transferred to the hold of the
Dauntless the Hotchkiss twelve-pounder, with its pack-
saddles and other gear, and 800 shells, 1,300 Mauser and
Remington rifles, 100 revolvers, 1,000 cavalry machetes,
800 pounds of dynamite, several hundred saddles, half a
ton of medical stores, and 460,000 rounds of small-arms
ammunition. In truth, the Madison Square Garden fair
for the raising of funds for the purchase of "hospital supplies" had evidently been a howling success. I can testify
that the cargo of the *Dauntless* put many a man in the
hospital for every one it took out.

It was about noon when we were ready to cast off, and
the *Dauntless*, giving several defiant toots, as if in exultation, slipped down the river toward the sea. On the
bridge was her master, Captain John O'Brien, a noted filibuster, usually known by the honorary title of "Dynamite"
O'Brien, from some incident connected with one of the
Central American or West Indian revolutions that he had
been mixed up in. Blockade-running was an old story
with him, even before the Cuban insurrection, and during that war he had safely conducted a number of expeditions to the Cuban coast. He was an ideal man for the
perilous business, cool and resourceful, and a splendid
seaman. And all of these qualifications were needed for
filibustering in this particular war, for if there was one
thing well understood it was that every member of one of
these expeditions, if captured by the Spaniards, would get
the shortest shrift possible to give him. The Spaniards do

not fight revolutions with rose-water, and maybe they are right. Consequently, filibustering in those days was grim and terrible business, fit occupation for lion-hearted men. Insurrections with their attendant blockade-running are not so frequent as in the good times gone by. The industry is in the "dumps," and Captain O'Brien is now chief harbor pilot of Havana, the mild-mannered, thick-set man with iron-gray mustache who has conducted many a one of you on a passenger steamer through the narrow entrance past Morro Castle. I saw him ten years later, when he came out to bring in the vessel on which I was a passenger at the time of the second intervention, and we had a good embrace in Cuban style in memory of our hazardous voyage of former years. His present occupation must seem to him as tame as raising chickens.

Pagluchi had long before turned over his five members of the expedition to General Cabrera, doubtless glad to be rid of us, and was now in charge of the engines of the *Dauntless*. The crew consisted of just crew, and they look alike the world over. It seemed rather a shame to run these men, who probably did not know what they were doing, up against the chance of being blown out of the water by a Spanish gun-boat or of being lined up against that famous wall at the Cabanas fortress, the scene of so many pitiful tragedies. In a short time we were out of the river and on the Atlantic. A sharp lookout was kept before getting well out to sea, but not a wisp of smoke was in sight. As a part of the game to give us a clear field, the *Commodore* had left Charleston the evening before and steamed north, followed by the revenue-cutter, finally putting into Hampton Roads. So there was no danger to be apprehended from that particular vessel. Now followed four days of rolling and pitching on the broad swells of the Atlantic. How small and inconsequential the little *Dauntless* seemed on that wild waste of waters. She could have made the passage in two days but for the necessity of economizing her supply of coal for the return trip to some United States port, and to have enough fuel to enable her to speed up and make a run for life if the occasion arose. Always a victim to sea-sickness, even under the most favorable circumstances, I can never forget those four days of suffering as the little steamer labored through the sea, rolling and pitching, our only home, the deck, swept from time to time by clouds of spray, with an occasional wave for good measure. We lay about day after day in our water-soaked blankets, getting such snatches of sleep as we could, and now and then staggering to the rail to make the required contribution to Neptune. We certainly were as unhappy and as unheroic-looking a lot of adventurers as ever trusted themselves to the sea.

On the afternoon of August 16 we were told that we were approaching the north-east coast of Cuba. The wind and sea now moderated somewhat, and the worn and harassed filibusters began to come to life. All realized that this was the most critical period in our voyage, as the coast was patrolled by gun-boats and armed launches, and capture meant death, swift and inevitable. We five had among ourselves talked over such a possibility, and it was pretty well understood that if worst came to worst we were to take Kipling's advice,

> "Just roll to your rifle and blow out your brains,
> And go to your God like a soldier."

But not without making a fight for it, for the Hotchkiss twelve-pounder, the same gun at which I had drilled for the perspiring patriots in New York, was now unpacked and mounted on the deck forward and several boxes of ammunition opened. This was a task of great difficulty, a gun on a field-carriage mounted on the deck of a rolling vessel being about as dangerous to those serving it as to any possible target. But the brake ropes were adjusted and the piece anchored as securely as possible by means of other ropes, the wheels being also blocked by timbers. The muzzle pointed over the port bow, and if a necessity had arisen to train the gun in any other direction it was intended to accomplish the purpose by turning the vessel accordingly. As I was the only one on board who understood this weapon, General Cabrera placed it in my charge, and I had my four companions to assist in setting it up and in serving it in case of need. There were known to be two classes of vessels patrolling the Cuban coast—several gun-boats of rather low speed and a considerable number of fast, large launches, each carrying a crew of about a dozen men and armed with a Nordenfelt rapid-fire gun of small calibre. It was intended, in case we encountered a gun-boat, to depend entirely on the speed of the *Dauntless* to escape, but if our antagonist was a launch we were to let her get as close as possible and then open on her. We had no doubt that we could drive off any launch, and even hoped that we might frighten the crew into surrender. A tarpaulin had been placed over the gun as soon as mounted, in order that it could not be seen until needed for action. It is interesting to know that some months later, while attempting an expedition on the south coast of Cuba, the *Dauntless* had a gun mounted in this fashion and was pursued by an armed launch, whereupon she fired one shot, missing the target about half a mile, but the launch could hardly be seen for the spray she tore up in getting out of the way. This incident created much amusement, being spoken of as the first and only "naval battle" of the war.

We made out in time the low mangrove-covered coast, and could see far away the dim outline of the hills of the interior. We stood on deck with beating hearts and tense faces as the little steamer drew near the inlet known as Las Nuevas Grandes, a short distance east of the entrance to Nuevitas harbor, on the coast of the province of Puerto Principe or Camaguey. No vessel was in sight, but we were troubled by the appearance from time to time of a bit of smoke along the shore line far to the eastward. All who were supplied with glasses kept them trained on that part of the horizon. It was plain to be seen that Captain O'Brien and Generals Nunez and Cabrera were anxious, as they held several whispered consultations on the bridge. The smoke might be from a fire on shore or from a vessel bound eastward, the latter supposition being in favor from the fact that it was not seen for the last half-hour before darkness settled down over land and sea.

As night came on we could plainly see the flashes of the Maternillos light to the westward. And so, minute by minute, we drew nearer to our goal. A man was now taking soundings, and his voice and the throbbing of the engines were the only sounds that broke an oppressive silence. We five would-be Lafayettes and Von Steubens were grouped about the gun on the bow; the weapon had been loaded and the primer inserted, and the only thing that remained to be done, in case a necessity arose, was to remove the tarpaulin, get her pointed in the general direction, and pull the lanyard. We were taking no chances on nervousness and confusion at a critical moment cheating us out of one shot, at least, in case an inquisitive launch should poke her nose around the point that we had now passed. If I must tell all, our teeth were chattering, and not from cold, but from the terrific strain and from trying to force ourselves to be calm and cool.

Las Nuevas Grandes is merely an indentation in the coast and in no sense a harbor, and when we were about half a mile from the surf the engines were stopped. The *Dauntless* carried two regular sea boats, but these were not used in landing our cargo. Instead, she had brought, piled up on her deck, eight broad, flat-bottomed skiffs, each with two pairs of oars and a steering oar. A seaman would scorn to be seen in such a craft, but they were quite well suited to an aggregation of land crabs like ourselves, and owing to their flat bottoms could easily be hauled through a moderate surf. Each of us five "Americans," as we were called, to distinguish us from the Cubans, was put in charge of a boat, while the others were intrusted to three of our Cuban fellow-voyagers. The boats were lowered by hand over the rail without difficulty, but once in the water pounded about in a way that was most disconcerting. The crew of the steamer went below deck and passed up the cargo, which was tossed into the boats with feverish haste, no attempt being made to stow it properly. As no one was now left on board to serve the gun, it was dismounted and the various parts lowered, after much difficulty, into my boat. I was able to get away first, and with a crew of four at the oars pushed toward the surf, which, owing to the darkness, could not be seen, but was distinctly audible. About half-way to the shore we could dimly make out the line of breakers. Years before, I had had some pretty stiff surf work in Indian canoes on the Alaskan coast and thought I knew something on that subject, but the prospect before us was not alluring. The greatest drawback was the darkness, which made it impossible to see whatever rocks there might be, as well as to estimate the height or violence of the surf. But it was too late to turn back, and in we went. There was a lot of pitching and bucking, and a wave or two broke over us, but as soon as we struck, oars were dropped and overboard we went, up to our waists, caught the boat by its sides, and ran up onto the beach with it on the next wave. Fortunately, it was a perfectly clean, shelving, sandy beach, and we got through with nothing worse than a superb ducking and a boat half full of water. The gun with its wheels and carriage was carried beyond reach of the tide and thrown down in the grass, and the boat overturned to get out the water it had

shipped.   Just as we were preparing to launch, in order
to go for our next load, we heard excited voices near us,
and knew that the second boat was coming in.   We ran
down the beach to assist, but arrived too late to be of
service.   The boat was caught on one quarter, turned
broadside on, and hurled onto the beach.   The air was
literally full of *Jesus Marias*, interspersed with the impressive type of English cuss words in the use of which
one of my companions was no mean artist.   But the boat
was dragged out, and the next day at low tide its cargo was
recovered.   Both boats were now launched and started on
their return to the *Dauntless*.   On the way we met several
others, and gave them the information that the beach
was a good one but the surf troublesome.   All lights on
the steamer had, of course, been screened or extinguished,
but a lighted lantern had been hung over the shore side
for the purpose of guiding returning boats.

As it was deemed inadvisable to build a fire on shore,
there was no guide in that direction, with the result that
our cargo was scattered along about seven hundred yards
of beach.   So the work went on far into the night, an occasional boat upsetting, but without loss of life.   Luckily,
the excitement kept away all feeling of fatigue or hunger.
The wind was rising and the sky had become overcast,
and there were occasional squalls of rain.   My boat was
nearing the *Dauntless* for its sixth load, when we heard
an excited exclamation from the bridge, and saw to the
northward, over the mangrove bushes on the point, a
peculiar white light sweeping the horizon.   The steamer
had not anchored, but was keeping her approximate

position by means of her screw, and had had on a full head of steam ever since approaching the coast, ready to do her best in case she had to run for it. At this time two boats were loading alongside, but their crews piled into them and pulled clear, under some sulphurous orders yelled down from the bridge. There were a few tense moments in which we lay on our oars and awaited developments. Nearer and nearer came that cursed light, but the vessel itself could not yet be located owing to intervening land. But there was no time to lose, as to be caught in this little pocket of a bay meant disaster. The engine bell rang viciously, a black column of smoke poured from the funnel of the *Dauntless*, and the race for life began. It was known that this could be no launch, as launches—at least those at that time in the Spanish navy—do not carry search-lights, but must be a cruiser or a gunboat of some size.

The *Dauntless* plunged through the water, and for a couple of miles we could trace her by the smoke and sparks from her funnel. In order to clear the point she had to run straight out to sea, at first in the direction of the enemy. The search-light wavered here and there on the shore line and over the surface of the water, and finally fell on the *Dauntless*. There was a painful moment for those of us watching, and then came the distant booming of the guns; but finally these sounds died away and both pursuer and pursued faded from sight. With heavy hearts we rowed ashore, and the members of the expedition gathered about the piles of cartridge boxes and bundles of rifles on the beach, shivered in their wet clothing, and in subdued tones discussed the situation. All were present, but only about three-fourths of our cargo had been landed. Our position was not an enviable one, as we felt morally certain that the Spaniard would return after daylight and deal with us. We could, of course, escape into the bush, but all our war material would be captured. The hours dragged along, but finally morning came and ushered in a windy and sodden day, the trees and grass dripping moisture, and everything seemingly conspiring to depress our spirits and harass our worn bodies. On the supposition that the gun-boat would honor us with a visit during the day, search was made as soon as it was light for a suitable position for the gun, with the intention of doing our best to beat her off. An almost ideal natural gun-pit was found near the beach. In some violent storm a large log had been hurled beyond the ordinary high-tide mark, and had fallen across the mouth of a little gully, where sand to the thickness of several feet had been blown up against it. The gun was set up in the gully, its muzzle pointing over the log which served as a revetment for the sand. The position was most satisfactory, so far as protection was concerned, but had the disadvantage that the muzzle could not be depressed sufficiently to use the piece at short range. From fearing that the gun-boat would come in, we now began to worry lest it should not. We reasoned that the advantage was all on our side, as we had good protection and a steady platform, which the gun-boat could not have, the *Dauntless* having demonstrated how a small vessel could roll on that shallow and exposed coast. We would have a good, clear target, while to harm us the gun-boat must make hit on the muzzle of the gun, the only portion of it exposed. We knew that she must be an unarmored vessel, and that our shells would reach her vitals if our marksmanship was equal to the occasion. We even chuckled as we thought of the possibility of a lucky shot disabling her machinery, after which we could deliberately bombard her into a surrender and then go out to her in our small boats, thus beautifully turning the tables on our pursuer.

In the meantime a fire had been built and coffee made and bacon broiled, and this with some hard bread refreshed all greatly. It was thought best to carry our tons of military stores, piled helter-skelter along the beach, to some place concealed from view, and this slavish task consumed the greater part of the forenoon. Advantage was taken of low tide to recover those articles lost from the boats overturned in the surf on the previous night. Fortunately, boxes of cartridges and bundles of rifles are not easily swept out to sea, so that eventually the only shortage was one bundle of ten Remington rifles. The small-arms ammunition was not injured by its immersion, the boxes being tin-lined, but several cases of cartridges for the twelve-pounder were practically ruined, as we were to learn to our cost at Cascorra a few weeks later.

While carrying out these tasks many anxious glances were cast seaward, and about eleven o'clock a film of smoke was noticed far to the north. Closer and closer it came, until we could make out the hull of the vessel, but we were kept in a fever of uncertainty as to its identity.

If we could have had a broadside view our doubts would have been dispelled. It was considered unlikely that the *Dauntless* would return, and if not that vessel it must be a gun-boat. The Cubans, armed with Mausers, were scattered in groups along the beach to resist a landing party, and we five went to our gun-pit, loaded the piece, and made all preparations to open the ball. Considering our excitement when in danger the night before, all were remarkably cool and self-possessed, which probably arose from our conviction that if the gun-boat came close enough to open fire with effect she was "our meat." I was already sighting the gun and estimating the distance for a trial shot, when the vessel suddenly swung her broadside to, and we recognized the *Dauntless*. Captain O'Brien, fearing that we might use him as a target, had swung around purposely in order that we might identify the vessel. There was a wild run for the boats by all except a small guard left on shore, and we were soon out to the steamer. No time was lost in landing the remainder of the cargo, a task of a couple of hours. As to the adventures of the past night, we were told that the *Dauntless* had led the gun-boat a straight chase to the north for several hours, and, outdistancing her pursuer, had finally made a wide circuit and come back to get rid of the remainder of her cargo, being aided in her escape by the thick and squally weather. Months afterward we were informed, and I presume correctly, that the vessel that had given us such a close call was the torpedo gun-boat *Galicia*. It is almost certain that it was either the *Galicia* or the *Jorge Juan*, as they were said to be the only naval vessels, other than launches, on that portion of the coast at the time of our landing.

As the last boat load pulled away, the *Dauntless*, brave as her name, gave three defiant blasts from her whistle as a parting salute and steamed away, leaving us to our own devices on a strange and inhospitable coast. As we silently watched her fade from sight we realized that we had burned our bridges behind us and were in for the war. We made ourselves as comfortable as possible under the circumstances, keeping a lookout for any gunboats that might drop in on us. It has always been a mystery to me why the Spaniards at Nuevitas were not informed as to our landing by the gun-boat that discovered us. An expedition could have been sent against us with success at any time within the next four days. Although we could have kept a vessel off with our gun, fifty men landing out of its reach could have captured all our material, though we could have escaped into the jungle. It was, of course, impossible for thirty-five men to attempt to move our tons of impedimenta for any distance from the beach, and immediately after the final departure of the *Dauntless*, four men had been sent into the interior to get in touch with the rebel forces. Four anxious days passed, but finally a man was sighted coming along the beach, and two of our party went out to meet him. We heard them, when within calling distance, give the insurgent challenge, "*Alto! Quien va?*" and the reply, "Cuba," and knew that the new arrival was a friend. The man was one of the scouts of the advance guard of General Capote's portion of Maximo Gomez's command.

He was a ragged, unwashed individual, armed with a Remington rifle and machete, and was so glad to see us that he insisted on bestowing on each one of us the *abrazo*, a form of embrace much in vogue in Cuba. I took my medicine along with the rest, but not with noticeable enthusiasm. Soon came the advance guard, and then the main body, in all six hundred men, with a large number of pack-animals. It was too late in the day to begin the march into the interior, but the next morning all were on the move, every horse and man loaded to the limit. By nightfall we had covered thirty miles, and we new arrivals, being "soft," were about done for. We went into camp along a beautiful *potrero*, or pasture, with about a thousand men under General Maximo Gomez, who had marched thither to meet us. Before morning I had found in this force four fellow-countrymen, Walter M. Jones, a native of New York State, who had lived in Cuba for ten years, and who died after the war as chief of the harbor police of Havana; Arthur Royal Joyce, of South Egremont, Mass., who, a few weeks later, was to be terribly wounded in the grim work at Cascorra; William Smith, second in command of Gomez's personal escort, and James Pennie, of Washington, D. C., who afterward had the doubtful pleasure of contributing a leg to the cause of Free Cuba. We sat late around the camp-fire that night, exchanging experiences with these already seasoned campaigners. The next morning I was presented by General Cabrera to the grizzled and silent old chieftain, Maximo Gomez, veteran of the Ten Years' War, and had a good opportunity to see something of my future comrades in arms.

It was a rather impressive-looking force, the men, though very, very ragged, being well armed and well mounted. Much to my surprise, fully nine-tenths of them were white men, which was accounted for by the fact that these troops were raised in Camaguey, which has a smaller percentage of negroes than any other province in Cuba. Later I was to see organizations from the southern part of Santiago province, consisting almost entirely of negroes, but, take it through and through, there were many more whites than blacks in the insurgent forces. The next morning we were on the march, and in due time we new arrivals had our first taste of war, but that is another story.

II

CASCORRA, THE FIRST CUBAN SIEGE

THE day after reporting at the always shifting head-quarters of Maximo Gomez was spent by the *expedicio-narios*, as all recent arrivals from the United States were called, in resting after the trying march from the coast and in accustoming themselves to strange surroundings and to a manner of life entirely new even to those who had seen no little of rough life in the open. All day long there arrived trains of pack-animals laden with the cargo of the *Dauntless*, and before nightfall there was a stack of boxes and bundles that looked decidedly larger than the hull of that vessel.

During the day I had an occasional glimpse of our chieftain, whom I had met the previous evening. He was seated in a canvas hammock swung between a couple of small trees, and spent most of the day going over his mail that we had brought with us from the New York Junta, the only means of communication with the outside world enjoyed by the insurgents in the field. He dictated a few letters to his secretary, and after the noon-day meal took a nap. Upon awakening he swore roundly about something, addressing his remarks to his *asistente*, or personal servant. I did not at that time understand Spanish, but judged from his gestures and tone of voice that he was not complimenting that individual on his accomplishments. Shortly after this he sent for me, and having but recently witnessed his outburst, I approached with some misgivings. A member of his staff, Major Miguel Tarafa, in times of peace a Matanzas banker, acted as interpreter. The general began by expressing his appreciation of the spirit which had impelled us foreigners to leave our homes and cast our lot with a people struggling for independence, and then bluntly asked me what I knew about artillery. I told him frankly that my accomplishments were limited, to which he replied by saying, "Well, you cannot know any less than another American who came down here and said he knew it all." He then stated that he would place me in charge of the gun brought down on the *Dauntless*, and also of another and smaller Hotchkiss, one of 1.65 inch calibre, that he had with him, and said further that I would have the status of an officer with the privileges pertaining thereto, but that I would not actually be commissioned until after "making good." Then passing from weightier subjects, he asked me if I had ever eaten sugar-cane, and I had to confess that my acquaintance with the edible properties of that plant were about on a par with my knowledge of artillery. "Well," he said, with a grim smile, "you cannot be a real rebel until you know how to eat sugar-cane"; whereat he took one of several joints from the ground under his hammock, and with the fine Moorish scimitar which he carried in lieu of the omnipresent machete, showed me how to strip off the tough bark and get at the juicy pulp. He then had me try it with my own machete, and was no little amused at my awkwardness.

From that time he always took a great interest in me, and if we came in contact when there was an interpreter at hand he would inquire how I was getting on and how I liked being a "mambi," the uncomplimentary term by which the Spaniards usually referred to the insurgents. He always called me "Capi," an abbreviation of the Spanish word *capitan* (captain).

He was a stern, hard-hearted man, with a violent temper, but had in his nature some streaks of human kindness that shone luminously by contrast. He resembled exactly the many pictures of him that were published while he was in the public eye. He was a thin, wiry man with snow-white mustache and goatee, and was of pure Spanish descent, having the swarthy complexion of most Latins.

The officers of the force that we were now with were, as a rule, planters, cattle-raisers, farmers, or professional or business men from the towns, and were as a class the best men of the native Cuban population. Scores of them spoke English, having been educated in the United States or having lived there. At this period of the war they were well mounted, and were dressed neatly in white duck, which, being the clothing of the country, really constituted the uniform of the insurgents, so far as they could be said to have any. All were provided with appropriate insignia of rank, and wore on their hats the tricolored Cuban badge. The rank and file consisted mainly of employees of the plantations and cattle-ranches, and scattered among them a good many small farmers and cattlemen, with also clerks, mechanics, and laborers from the towns. They were ragged, and some, though not many, barefooted. They were armed with Mauser and Remington rifles and had well-filled cartridge pouches. Their rifles were badly cared for, nearly all being not only rusty, but fouled from not having been cleaned after use. All mounted officers and men carried the long or cavalry machete, with a blade about two and one-half feet in length. These were formidable weapons for hand-to-hand work, and had all been brought to the island on filibustering expeditions, having been especially manufactured for military purposes by a firm in Providence, R. I. Dismounted troops carried, in addition to their rifles, the short machete, used mainly in times of peace in cutting cane and brush. Earlier in the war, before the insurgents had been supplied with an adequate number of fire-arms, there had been a number of occasions when small Spanish detachments had been surprised and overwhelmed by superior forces of Cubans rushing them with the machete and cutting down all who did not surrender. The principal object of these attacks was to obtain the fine Mausers with which the Spanish troops were armed; but at the time of our arrival, the Cubans having been well supplied with rifles, and the Spaniards operating in larger columns and taking greater precautions to prevent surprises on the march, the machete had fallen from its high estate as a weapon of war and was relegated to such prosaic work as digging sweet-potatoes, chopping firewood, and cutting up beef.

Every officer and man carried a hammock made of canvas or gunny sacks, and immediately on going into camp swung it between a couple of trees, using it by day as a chair and by night as a bed. Nobody except newly arrived foreigners ever slept on the ground, and they only once, the various brands of ants and other insects that thrive in Cuba being particularly industrious and pestiferous.

The second morning after our arrival the whole force assembled at this place started on one of those aimless marches that were the chief weakness of the insurgent leaders. The cargo of the *Dauntless*, except some ammunition and medical stores that had been distributed, was left behind under guard, to be removed a few days later and stored under sheds constructed for the purpose at a point more distant from the coast.

Reveille sounded at three o'clock, hours before daybreak; the few provided with coffee had some prepared, horses that had been grazing throughout the night tied to picket-pins were saddled, another bugle-call sounded through the darkness, we fell into column of twos, and the cavalcade started.

We new arrivals, all of whom except General Cabrera had marched on foot from the coast, had been provided with mounts, and I drew the first of the nineteen horses that I was to lose in one way or another. We were following a narrow country road leading in a southerly direction. Daylight came in due time, and then flankers and scouts were thrown out from the column. We foreigners were in ecstasies over the beautiful scenery, now that we had left behind the savannas and mangrove swamps of the coast, and were crossing the rolling uplands of the interior. A large part of the country was primeval forest, with here and there little clearings in which were grown corn, beans, sugar-cane, squashes, sweet-potatoes, yucca or manioc, and other vegetables. There were also great *potreros*, or prairies, of thousands of acres of guinea grass from three to six feet high, on which grazed herds of fat, sleek cattle, at this period the principal source of the food supply of the insurgents.

In this motley band winding its way across country we of the *Dauntless*, in our New York clothes, seemed strangely out of place and looked about as ridiculous as we felt. At eleven o'clock the bugles blew "halt," and we scattered out along the margin of a wood. Horses were unsaddled and picketed to graze, hammocks swung, and fires started. A detail of men rode out to the most convenient herd and drove in a number of beeves, which were killed and dressed and the meat distributed in less than an hour. During the forenoon, as we had passed the numerous houses with their little clearings, toll had been taken in the form of such vegetables as were to be had. Also, some men had ridden a mile or two out on the flanks of the line of march and had come in with their pack-animals laden with vegetables. The beef and vegetables were cut up and placed in small iron kettles to boil. These kettles, which would hold, as a rule, enough for four or five persons, were carried on the march on the backs of men or strapped onto saddles, to the great discomfort of the unfortunate beasts concerned. Those who had been unable to procure kettles roasted their food before fires.

A negro had been assigned to attend to the wants of the five foreigners who had come on the *Dauntless*, so that we were spared the hardships that would have been our lot if we had been compelled to hustle for ourselves in the midst of such strange surroundings. At one o'clock the first meal of the day was ready. We were fiercely hungry, and had no fault to find with the food set before us, it being very satisfying to healthy men with good appetites. Some weeks later we began to make deprecatory remarks about this "aijacco," or everlasting stew of meat and vegetables, and to long for the wheaten bread and mutton chops of other days. Luckily for our peace of mind, we could not look into the future and see the days when the whole country should have been desolated by war, when the cattle were all gone and we had to live almost exclusively on fruits and vegetables, and mighty few of those. When the lean times came and we rode for days fairly faint from hunger, when a piece of meat of any kind was a luxury, we looked back longingly to those days of comparative plenty in Camaguey and wondered how we ever could have been dissatisfied.

After the meal had been finished, all stretched out in their hammocks and slept for a couple of hours. Then the camp livened up, there were visits back and forth, card games, and some singing by those who had accomplishments in that line. The newspapers that we had brought down from New York were passed from hand to hand and read and reread until they were worn out. Just after dark came the second and last meal of the day, exactly like the first. Then groups gathered about campfires and talked until late at night. Then tattoo and taps, blown by a superb bugler, whose equal I have never heard in the United States service, and we stretched out in our hammocks to sleep. Again at three o'clock came reveille and the beginning of another day's march. This march and camp have been described somewhat in detail, as they were typical of those features of our life for the next two years. Unless chasing Spaniards or being chased by them, the Cubans rarely made more than one march a day, and this began two hours before daybreak and ended before noon. But there arose occasions when we tore through the country regardless of this custom. The first day's march of the column had been through a part of the country not yet touched by the war, but on the second day there was a decided contrast. As we approached the great Camino Real, or Royal Road, leading eastward from Puerto Principe, we saw on all sides the ruins of burned houses, and barb-wire fences had been cut until there was but little of them left but the standing posts and tangled meshes of wire in the grass. Before the war was over Spaniards and insurgents had clashed on nearly every league of that road from Puerto Principe to historic Guaimaro, a distance of seventy miles. We passed through the potrero of La Machuca, where a few weeks later we were to "mix it" with a column of the enemy under General Castellanos, and marched through the ruins of the little town of Sibanicu, and had pointed out to us, three miles to the eastward, the church tower of Cascorra, that obscure village so soon to add to the glory of Spanish arms, every survivor of its heroic garrison to receive the coveted "Cross of San Fernando," the Spanish equivalent of our Congressional Medal of Honor and of the Victoria Cross of Great Britain.

At ten o'clock we passed to the southward, and an hour later went into camp at the abandoned cattle-ranch known as La Yaya. The owner's house had not been burned, and General Gomez's staff established themselves in it, but the "Old Man," as we had learned to call him behind his back, ordered his hammock swung from a couple of trees across the road.

About two miles distant was the humble home of a very decent Cuban family, and soon there came an invitation for Huntington, Potter, Welsford, and myself to stay with them until we could be suitably outfitted for life in the field. Walinski did not accompany us, having gone to the westward with General Cabrera, and we never saw him again. The invitation to visit this family was no doubt the result of an intimation from some member of the general's staff, but nothing could have exceeded the kindness and courtesy with which we were treated during our stay. We chafed at the delay, but finally there arrived our outfits—white duck suits, heavy shoes, leggings, and Panama hats—and we were ready for war. While we were being rigged out, General Gomez had gone on one of his usual aimless marches and had returned to La Yaya. He sent for me, and through Major Tarafa stated that he was going to attack the town of Cascorra, but with small hope of success, as it was known that the commandant was a man of exceptional resource and courage, and that the garrison, a part of the Fourth Battalion of Tarragona, was made up of Catalonians, those northern

Spaniards famous for the desperate courage with which they usually defend any post intrusted to them. I told the general frankly, that so far as the artillery was concerned, it could do no more than batter down the block-houses and fortified buildings with common shell, the only form of projectiles other than canister with which we were provided, and that without shrapnel but little damage could be done to the defenders after they had taken to their trenches, which would be as soon as we began to blow the buildings about their ears. The result of this observation was a round cursing of the Junta for having sent no shrapnel. General Javier Vega, Gomez's chief of staff, was present at this conversation. He was a silent sort of man, and apparently knew as little as did his chief regarding the limitations of the small guns that we were to use.

After a few days we started on a long, roundabout march. I do not know where we went except that our course was generally to the eastward. We passed around the town of Guaimaro and saw the Spanish flag floating defiantly from the head-quarters building, little dreaming that in a few short weeks it was to be lowered after desperate and prolonged fighting, and that the entire garrison would become our prisoners. On this occasion a group of us, including the general and his staff, sat on our horses on a ridge only eight hundred yards from the nearest Spanish work. With us was the insurgent flag carried by head-quarters, so that our character was known to the garrison, but there was no exchange of shots. A well-directed volley at this time might have rid Spain of the fiery old guerilla who through two wars had been a thorn in her flesh. After leaving Guaimaro, the general concluded he would like to try out his two guns, the target being a rock in a pasture, distant about eight hundred yards. It was the first time I had ever had anything to do with firing a cannon, and my shooting was not good, but the shells when they struck the ground burst with a lively bang and much smoke, and the onlookers were very much impressed. From here we marched back to La Yaya, passing north of Guaimaro. A day or two later the general announced that he was ready to try Cascorra, and sent General Vega and myself to select positions for the artillery. We set out accompanied only by a few orderlies, and leaving these finally in charge of the horses, crawled on our hands and knees all about the town, a task that consumed the entire day. The town was a small one, having under normal conditions a population of only a couple of hundred, but there were now but very few noncombatants left, they having either fled to Puerto Principe for the protection of a larger garrison or taken to the field with the insurgents. The garrison consisted of one hundred and sixty men, all infantry, and having no artillery. These troops occupied three defensive positions as follows: At the western or Puerto Principe side, at the point where the Camino Real enters the town, a brick building strengthened by bags of earth extending to the loop-holes, which were about five feet above the floor. In times of peace this building had done duty as a tavern. About five hundred yards to the south-east, and lying directly south of the centre of the village, was a strong stone

church, which like the tavern was loop-holed and strengthened by bags of earth. Both the church and the tavern
were surrounded by standing trenches. On the east side
of the town was a strong earthen redoubt defended by
about half the garrison. This, as well as the fortified
buildings, was surrounded by a maze of barb-wire entanglements, while the three works, which formed an
almost equilateral triangle enclosing the town, were connected by closely built barb-wire fences. It was plain,
even to a layman in the art of war, that we had a big job
cut out for us. It would not be difficult quickly to render
the church and the tavern untenable, but this would result only in driving their defenders to the trenches, where
they would be in but little danger from shell fire, while the
destruction of the small but substantial redoubt was a siege-
gun job. Artillery positions were hard to find. It must
be remembered that this was before the day of indirect
fire, and even if it had not been, there was among us no
one who could have made use of it. We would have to
be able to see our target. There was a low ridge fifteen
hundred yards to the eastward of the redoubt, and I
favored this position, knowing that from it we could destroy
the church and tavern, and that we could not seriously
damage the redoubt at any distance. It was believed
that with these buildings battered down, the infantry
could rush the trenches surrounding them, and then might
be able to work up closely enough under cover of the
houses of the town to stand some chance of getting into
the redoubt. In the opinion of General Vega, the position preferred by me was entirely too far from the two

most vulnerable defences, which it was desired to attack first. We had crawled through the grass to within four hundred yards of the tavern, and at this point the general selected the first position for the artillery. I was horrified, but kept my views to myself. The intervening ground was level, and covered with a growth of bushes and of guinea grass about four feet high, with here and there a few scattered trees of good size. During the day spent in spying out the environs of Cascorra we had not seen a Spaniard, but had heard the soldiers laughing and singing. Little they foresaw the storm that was soon to break upon them.

We returned to La Yaya late that night, and then things began to happen more rapidly. The next day Gomez and his eight hundred men marched over to the town and went into camp in several positions, completely surrounding it. That night a detail of men under the engineer officer attached to head-quarters constructed a typical Cuban *trinchera*, a sort of parapet, at the position selected for the artillery. As we were to make use of this type of defence on many subsequent occasions, this one merits a brief description. Two rows of stakes about six feet high and three feet apart were driven into the ground and the space between them filled in with tightly tamped earth, which was held in place by a revetment of poles and fence rails, laid one on top of the other inside the two rows of stakes as the earth was filled in. A gap about the size of an ordinary door was left for the gun to be fired through. There was thus protection for a few of the infantry support and for the ammunition and the men handling it, but those actually loading and aiming the piece would be completely exposed. We Americans watched the work for a while and then walked over to camp in no particularly hilarious frame of mind. While a detail of Cubans had been provided to attend to the transportation of the guns and their ammunition and do other heavy work, we were expected to do the actual loading, aiming, and firing, and realized that we were up against it good and hard. We lay down in our hammocks, but I for one could not sleep a wink. At four o'clock we rose and walked over to the position. The parapet was practically completed, and soon the infantry support of about a hundred men arrived. A few of these found cover behind the parapet, but the majority were deployed on its flanks and lay down flat on their faces. The insurgents had surrounded the town so quietly the day before that it is doubtful if the Spaniards had suspected their presence. It must be taken into consideration that it was impossible for so small a garrison to send out patrols, as they would quickly have been cut up by the ever-watchful Cubans. The noise made in building the parapet must have been heard, however, although it was no doubt difficult to estimate the distance from their position. As a matter of fact, if a hot fire had been opened and maintained, keeping the bullets well down to the ground, the work would have been materially interfered with. The two hours remaining until daylight dragged heavily. It had been resolved not to use the smaller gun at this time, but the Hotchkiss twelve-pounder, that had begun its warlike career over the Third Avenue saloon, was placed in position, the wheel ropes, sight, and other paraphernalia put on, a number of boxes of shells were brought up, and we sat down and waited for daylight to lift the curtain. It was to be the baptism of fire for four of Pagluchi's wards, and a sizzling, red-hot one. Except for the calls of the sentries and the occasional howl of a dog, the little town was as quiet as death itself.

At last the suspense was over, the darkness began to give way, and we could make out the upper part of the tavern, the view of the lower part and of the surrounding trenches being obstructed by the brush and grass. It had been left for me to decide when to open fire, and now I gave the word. The veterans, Jones, Joyce, and Pennie, rolled and lighted fresh cigarettes, Welsford sought solace in an unusually large bite from the remnant of his last plug of "store tobacco," Joyce handed an ugly looking shell to Huntington, who slipped it into the breech as Potter opened the block, Pennie took the lanyard, and I squatted behind the gun with one hand on the elevating screw and aimed at that part of the building visible, while Jones, behind me, moved the trail to left or right, as I indicated. In a few seconds I was satisfied, gave the screw a turn to lower the muzzle, and stepping from the piece, climbed on top of the parapet to the windward of the gun in order to observe the shot, yelled "Fire!" to Pennie, and the ball had begun. I had forgotten to place my hands over my ears and was almost deafened by the crash within a few feet of my head. A fraction of a second later I saw a burst of flame and smoke from the upper part of the building and saw the bricks come tumbling down. Jumping down at once from my exposed position, I landed on the back of a Cuban patriot who was lying behind the parapet and put him out of that battle, the first casualty in the siege of Cascorra. My shot had been a bit higher than was intended, but had done its work. As the gun had roared out and the smoke was seen pouring from the building, the Cubans all about the town raised a great yell of "Cuba Libre!" We rushed to the gun and soon sent in another, a centre shot that blew a lot of earth-filled bags to smithereens and made a fine hole. We had begun to wonder whether there was to be a fight or not, as not a shot had been fired in reply, but now the storm broke, and a fine blizzard it was. The air was suddenly full of those peculiar popping noises that we were soon to know so well, leaves dropped from the trees, there were odd movements in the grass, a patter against the opposite side of our shelter was distinctly audible, and a bullet struck the tire of one of the gun wheels with a sound like a blow from a hammer. The nervousness of waiting was over, the fighting blood in us mounted quickly, and with yells and cheers and amid the enthusiastic "Bravos!" of the near-by Cubans, we sprang to the gun and for a short time loaded and fired so rapidly that the barrel of the piece became badly heated. The parapet afforded excellent protection for those who were behind it, but the exact position of the gun was indicated by its smoke, so that an uncomfortable number of bullets came through the gap left for it. We could see only the roof of the church, and could not easily bring to bear on it on account of its angle from the parapet, but the men in the trenches around it made out our exact location from the smoke and soon began to take an interest in the proceedings. We were partially protected from their fire by the right wing of the parapet, though the ground all about us was made exceedingly dangerous. Less than a minute after the enemy had opened fire, a Cuban infantryman standing near us had his attention called to blood trickling down his once white trousers, and sank to the ground, calling on most of the saints in the calendar. The man had received a flesh wound, being shot through the thigh, but was so excited that he did not know it, thinking that some one had accidentally struck him. I have known of several similar cases. As I was aiming the gun for about the twelfth shot, I felt a hard blow on the sole of my left foot and made a fall that afterward cost me no end of chaffing and inquiries as to whether or not I had at some time been one of the ornaments of the theatrical profession. A bullet had split the sole of my left shoe and knocked off the heel, but had inflicted no more severe injury than a considerable bruise. Occasionally a man was hit and carried away, but despite all the uproar there were but few casualties. And so this strange little battle went on for an hour, now fast and furious for a few moments and now almost dying out for a like time. So far it had been a contest between about eighty Spanish infantrymen and a handful of men with a cannon. The Cuban infantry had not yet opened fire, as there was no satisfactory target for them and there was danger of hitting their comrades scattered around the town; and the Spaniards in the redoubt could do nothing but listen to the sound and fury, as the tavern was in a direct line between them and our position. The building which had at first been our target had been almost reduced to rubbish, and we were firing low in order to make hits on the trenches around it, but it was unsatisfactory work, as there was no way to ascertain the effects of our shots owing to the intervening grass. Several times we dragged the gun from behind the parapet and took shots at the church, with no other effect than to damage the building somewhat and to draw an increased fire from its defenders.

We had accomplished all we could from our present position, so I walked over to General Gomez's headquarters, distant about four hundred yards, and suggested that we keep up a slow fire during the remainder of the day and that at night a new parapet bearing on the church be built. This was agreed to, and I started on my return to the gun. On the way I walked over to where our ammunition mules were standing to see how they were getting on. A couple of them had been slightly wounded, and while I was looking them over, one big fellow received a Mauser bullet through the nose. He was cropping grass at the time, and for a few seconds shook his head vigorously and then went on eating. We Americans took a great interest in those mules, having been told by the Cubans that they were "countrymen" of ours, as they had been taken from a sugar plantation the owner of which had bought them in the United States.

The gun had become so heated by a rapid spurt of firing toward the last, that the breech-block had expanded to such an extent that it could not be worked. The mechanism was taken apart and thoroughly oiled, but we finally had to resort to pouring water on the affected parts, a very slow process, as the supply had to be brought from some distance, and naturally was not cool. The Spanish fire had died down to an occasional volley, and our "battle" was beginning to drag. We sat around behind the parapet discussing the incidents of the day, and about every half-hour sent in a shell just to let our friends the enemy know that we were still on the job.

At dark we returned to our camp, near head-quarters, and I had a long talk with the general, who expressed his keen appreciation of the way we had done our work. He was apparently in doubt as to the next step to take. I took the liberty of telling him that he would never take the town unless he was willing to throw in his infantry just so soon as we had destroyed the church. It must have seemed abominably cheeky for a man just out of his first fight to be giving advice on military matters to a man who had been under fire before he was born, but no offence was taken. The general explained that while his men had captured some small towns by surprising and rushing the garrisons, they had never yet made an assault on men on the alert in good trenches, protected by entanglements, and he feared that they were not equal to it. A repulse, he said, would badly demoralize them. He felt that they could take the church and tavern positions, but with the redoubt bearing on both still in the hands of the enemy, no advantage would be gained. His men could not successfully assault this, the real key to the position.

It was evident that the promised parapet bearing on the
church would not be built that night.

The second day was a repetition of the afternoon of
the first—a shot about every half-hour at either the tavern
or the church and an occasional volley from the trenches
in reply. That evening we Americans talked the matter
over, and Jones and I were delegated to say to the general
that if he would have a good position constructed that night
from which we might effectively shell the church, and give
us an hour in the morning in which to destroy that building, we would gladly lead an assault on that and the tavern
positions, fixing two hundred as the number of men required for the enterprise. It was our theory that if we
made the dash the Cubans would follow us, and that once
in the shelter of the trenches we could not be driven
out by fire from the redoubt, and if the eighty men in the
latter made a sortie against us, which was unlikely, their
works would quickly be occupied by a force kept in hand
for the purpose. In view of the successful assaults made
subsequently by the Cubans at Guaimaro and Las Tunas,
I have not the slightest doubt that we would have succeeded, though at heavy cost. Several Cuban officers,
hearing of our proposal, volunteered to assist in leading
the attack. At one time the general came near yielding,
but finally came out with an abrupt "No!" telling us that
we were madmen. He gave us the cheering information,
however, that he was going to order the construction of
another parapet for the gun, much nearer to the trenches
around the ruins of the tavern, where our view would be

unobstructed by grass and brush, and that he expected us from this new position literally to blow the dons out of the ground. Jones and I maintained a discreet silence until out of earshot, and then made a few unprintable remarks about the turn affairs had taken.

Among the officers serving with the insurgents was General Avelino Rosa, a Colombian, exiled for political reasons from his own land. He was a man brave almost to rashness, but exceedingly unpractical. General Rosa was in direct command of the force of infantry and dismounted cavalry surrounding the town, and had worked some of his men nearer and nearer to the tavern position by taking advantage of inequalities of the ground, and during the second day of the bombardment had livened matters by exchanging shots at short range with its defenders. He had reported to General Gomez that by taking advantage of the cover afforded by a ravine we could obtain a position within two hundred yards of the tavern, where we would be in full view of the trenches and could undoubtedly destroy them. He was ordered to construct the necessary parapet that night. This in itself was an extremely ticklish operation, but the material was prepared at a distance and placed in position as quietly as possible. The work had to be carried on intermittingly, as at the slightest noise the Spaniards opened up with volleys. The parapet was completed just before dawn, having cost the lives of several men. It was very short, extending only about eight feet on each side of the opening left for the gun. The upper part had been built across the top of the opening with a hope of affording some protection to those actually handling the piece. Before day-light a detail dragged the much-abused Hotchkiss quietly into the ravine and along it until we were directly opposite the new position, when it was hoisted out, the unavoidable noise drawing a fire that killed one man. I felt morally certain that we could never serve the gun from here, but it was agreed among us that whatever might occur, we were not to show the white feather or ask to be allowed to get out. Months afterward Pennie and I, visiting the ruins of Cascorra, paced the distance from our parapet to the trenches and found it to be two hundred and sixteen yards. Here we were protected from the fire of the church by intervening buildings, but, to the dismay of all concerned, it was found after it was too late to remedy the defect that we were exposed to fire from one corner of the redoubt. So far, the smaller gun, the two-pounder Hotchkiss, had not been used, but on this same night a position was constructed for it about two hundred yards to our left rear and placed under charge of Jones.

We waited in our new posts until it was thoroughly light before opening fire, but not so with the enemy. With the breaking of day the Spaniards made out the exact location of the little parapet, the construction of which had drawn their fire during the night, and opened on us hotly, but without result, as we were in the ravine a few yards to the rear of the gun, where also was a strong infantry support under General Rosa. When it was thoroughly light we crawled out of the ravine on all-fours and sent in a shell that landed squarely on the low line of earth-filled bags that capped the low parapet of the

Spanish trench, exploding with a bang that sounded almost as loud to us as the report of the piece itself. The men at the two-pounder were awaiting the cue, and almost immediately we heard its sharp crack, and a shell whistled past us. We had fastened a rope to the trail of our gun, and immediately dragged it behind shelter to be reloaded. Again it was pushed up to the gap and fired. The Spaniards were replying furiously, and the worst of it was that their bullets were all coming close down to the ground, and were aimed at the gaping port-hole which they could so plainly see. It has fallen to me to participate in a good many fights in Cuba and the Philippines, but never anywhere have I seen the equal of what was poured into us during the hour that we held this position. The air was fairly alive with the sound of bullets, and their patter against the side of the parapet was so incessant that it would have been impossible to count them. The bark on near-by trees was cut to ribbons, and small bushes on our front were destroyed. After a few shots from our gun, the head cover connecting the tops of the two wings of the parapet was blown to pieces, a result that should have been foreseen, as the barrel of the piece was not sufficiently long for the muzzle to clear the parapet. Under such circumstances, aiming the gun, the only part of its service which was required to be done while it was exposed, was enough to try the nerves of any but a wooden man. Fortunately this was the work of but a couple of seconds, the target being so plain and so close at hand. In an attempt to keep down the Spanish fire, our infantry supports opened vigorously and added to the racket and confusion, but under the circumstances could not be expected to accomplish much, the enemy being too well sheltered. We were in a bad box, and I am sure all hoped to be ordered out of it soon. We were tearing up the tops of the Spaniards' trenches, but their fire was not diminishing, and they were constantly repairing the damage by filling bags of earth in the trenches and placing them in position without exposing themselves.

The fight had lasted about three-quarters of an hour when I noticed some thirty Spanish soldiers, the first I had ever actually seen, leave the redoubt and dash for the tavern trenches. They covered the ground by short rushes, throwing themselves prone about every sixty yards. At first it was thought that they were going to attempt to rush our position, improbable as such an enterprise seemed, but it was merely a reinforcement for the worn-out men who were making such a gallant fight against us. I attempted to take a shot at them, but the gun missed fire.

I was aiming the fifteenth shell when a bullet struck one of the trunnions almost at my nose. My nerves had been getting pretty shaky from several narrow escapes in sighting preceding shots, and I must confess that I threw myself flat on the ground and rolled to cover. Joyce jumped over me, quickly sighted the piece, and sprang from the gun. The imperturbable Pennie, lying on the ground and smoking a cigarette, jerked the lanyard and fired the last shot from this terrible death-trap. General Gomez had delegated to General Rosa the necessary authority to discontinue firing from this position whenever he thought best, and the latter, who was near at hand, ordered us to take cover in the ravine, abandoning the gun for the time being, although it was in no danger of capture, owing to the proximity of strong supports. Now that they had put the gun out of action, the Spaniards concentrated their fire on the Cuban infantry and inflicted several casualties. It was necessary to recover the gun, so in about half an hour three of us crawled stealthily out of the ravine and wriggled our way to it. Taking the trail-rope, we made a quick run, and despite a hot fire, reached the ravine and tumbled down the bank with little ceremony, pulling the gun after us with such haste that it landed upside down in the bottom. The two-pounder, being in a less exposed position, continued to fire at intervals during the day, but with practically no effect, owing to the small size of its projectiles.

I reported to our chief, and half expected a wigging because we had been unable to slaughter all the Spaniards in the trenches, but, on the contrary, was very kindly received, General Rosa having made a somewhat glowing report of what we had done.

That night two Cuban non-combatants, despite the vigilance of the Spaniards, succeeded in escaping from the town and came to our camp and were brought before the general, who abused them roundly for having remained under the protection of the enemy while their countrymen were undergoing the dangers and privations of the field. They were a very abject pair, and told all they knew about conditions in the town, and some besides. The garrison were badly worn out by the constant vigilance imposed, but apparently were well supplied with provisions and ammunition, and were improving their defences every night. They also stated that an assault was momentarily expected. There had been about twenty casualties so far, all except one from shell fire, whereupon we amateur artillerymen patted ourselves on the back at the first opportunity. The first shell of the fight, taking them by surprise, had killed three men in the tavern.

Early the next morning, the fourth day of the siege, the general sent me with General Vega to look for a position from which we could fire on both the redoubt and the church. For the time being he was through with fighting his artillery at long pistol-range, and quickly approved when informed that we had chosen the low ridge east of the town, this being about fifteen hundred yards from the redoubt and eighteen hundred from the church. It had the further advantage that a shell clearing the redoubt would almost certainly land in the much-battered tavern position.

The two-pounder was left where it was to amuse our friends in the tavern trenches, and I was ordered to take the larger gun around the town to the ridge. The distance was so great that it was not considered necessary to construct cover. About noon we opened, landing the first shell squarely in the centre of the works, and until dark fired slowly, as our ammunition was now running low. Occasionally, just to vary the proceedings, we paid our respects to the church, though I managed to miss it a couple of times, the end instead of the sides being toward us. The Spaniards were not inclined to expend much ammunition on us at this distance, and kept up a slow fire, evidently using their best shots for the purpose, as their shooting was fairly accurate. We suffered no casualties here during the two days that the ridge was occupied, though the gun was struck once. Our infantry support, which had had the unhappy faculty of catching bullets meant for us, was some distance to the rear and flank, and consequently out of danger. A portion of the Cuban infantry still held on to the ravine near our old artillery position, and kept up a useless fusillade.

The next day, for the first time, the general visited the gun while it was in action. On one occasion, just as it had been laid, he looked through the sights and jokingly remarked that we must be trying to shoot over the target, and said he would try his luck. He gave the screw a sharp turn, lowering the muzzle, and then himself pulled the lanyard. The shell ripped up some of the scenery about three hundred yards short of the redoubt, but the reader can rest assured that nobody thought of laughing. I relieved the strain by assuring the general that the cartridge must have been defective.

About the middle of the afternoon he came again, accompanied by his entire staff, and we realized from the looks on the faces of all that something was about to take place. The general, sitting on the ground a few paces from us, dictated a letter to his secretary, and after it had been copied, signed it; a Porto Rican major in the Cuban service, a gallant fellow whose name I cannot now recall, mounted his horse and, holding aloft a white flag, trotted toward the redoubt. Some time previously instructions had been sent to all the Cuban detachments to cease fire. The appearance of the Porto Rican in the open was the signal for a hot fusillade directed at him, despite the flag of truce. For a time it seemed inevitable that he must be hit, but he never faltered. We had about concluded that the enemy would not recognize the flag, when his fire died out, and we saw two officers leave the redoubt and proceed on foot to meet the bearer. They met about four hundred yards from the Spanish works; the plucky officer delivered his letter, and was compelled to sit on his horse with his back to the enemy's position until a reply from the Spanish major could be delivered, when he galloped toward us. That night a member of the general's staff showed us the correspondence. General Gomez's letter was a brief and courteous communication complimenting the commander of the garrison on his heroic defence against such great odds, and suggesting that he had done all that duty demanded of him in that respect, and ended by demanding his surrender, assuring him that he and his officers and men would be as well treated as the limited resources of the Cubans would permit. The Spaniard's reply was equally courteous, but stated that he would defend his post to the last extremity. A short time later firing was resumed, but this sort of fighting had become pretty monotonous to all concerned, and not much spirit was shown on either side.

One of the bits of information brought to us by the two non-combatants who had escaped from the town, was that the garrison of the church position, with the exception of those actually on duty in the trenches, slept in the building at night, taking it for granted that we could not then use our artillery. The result was an order for me to sight the gun at the church very carefully before nightfall, station a guard over it, and have the piece fired at ten o'clock. I did not exactly like this task, as it savored somewhat of assassination, but carried out my instructions. It was subsequently learned that this shell killed and wounded four men.

The siege had now lasted five days, and practically nothing had been accomplished except to kill some Spaniards, damage their works considerably, and all but wear out the garrison. There were only about thirty shells left for the twelve-pounder, and a hundred shell and canister for the smaller gun. A supply for both guns had been sent for to a *deposito* far away in the woods of Santiago province, but could not arrive for some days.

The next four days the artillery was out of it, but the infantry kept the town closely invested and denied sleep and rest to the harassed defenders. During this time one of the few Cubans remaining in Cascorra was caught trying to sneak through the insurgent lines at night. The next day he was tried and condemned. As the trembling wretch was led through our camp to die it made us sick at heart, as did many an event of like nature afterward. But any American who will read of the cheerful manner in which his ancestors hanged each other during the fighting between patriots and Tories in the Carolinas and Georgia in our Revolution can throw mighty few stones at the Cubans or any one else. Another tragic incident was the trial and execution of an insurgent officer. We could never get the straight of this, as our comrades were very loath to discuss the matter with foreigners, but it was rumored that he was found to have been in correspondence with the Spanish authorities in Puerto Principe.

In the early days of the investment, without our knowledge, the Spanish commander had sent a sergeant through our lines at night, and this man, by the greatest resource and courage, travelling by night and hiding in the woods by day, had succeeded in reaching the railway line north of Nuevitas, whence the news that Cascorra was undergoing siege was telegraphed to General Castellanos, the commander of the district of Puerto Principe, in the city of that name. The result was that one day a mounted messenger dashed into our camp and brought the news that a large column was en route from Puerto Principe, and was being observed and harassed by a small force of cavalry. During the siege various organizations had joined us from near-by parts of the island, and the general now had about fifteen hundred men. He ordered us to expend at once all the remaining artillery ammunition on the town, not with any hope of taking it, but to do as much damage as possible before its impending relief. We begged that we be allowed to save what little we had left and use it in the fight with the advancing column, but he would have none of it. So that night a parapet, the best we had yet had, was constructed at the astonishingly short distance of one hundred and eighty-three yards from the tavern trenches. The brief fight there the next day until we could expend our thirty shells was in a milder way a repetition of the third day. The Spanish fire was hot, but not so well directed. Nevertheless, at such short range it was serious work. Three men were killed behind our short parapet, and toward the last I heard a bullet strike Joyce, and turned around just in time to hear him say with the utmost self-possession: "Well, this reminds me of a little story." A man who can make such an off-hand remark as a bullet tears a big hole in his thigh probably deserves the palm for self-possession. We had a hard time carrying him out under fire. He was sent to one of the lonely hospitals in the bush, and so missed our great victory at Guaimaro, but was back to duty long before Jiguani. A few more shots and the twelve-pounder was through. That night the rain poured in torrents, the Cubans were drawn from about the town and concentrated a mile to the westward, all except a small escort for the two-pounder, which enlivened the night by fighting until its last cartridge was gone. The next day we remained in a sodden camp. The siege of Cascorra was over, but every hour couriers raced madly into camp with news of the whereabouts of the column of two thousand five hundred men with ten guns under General Castellanos. The next day was an eventful one, but is not a part of this story. The guns were sent away under escort, but we artillery-men at our request were allowed for the time being to join the cavalry as volunteers, and were provided with car-bines. Couriers came in faster and faster, and finally we heard the crackle of rifle-fire to the westward as the Span-ish column came on, brushing aside the tormentors hang-ing on its flanks. Then came the clash, the battle of La Machuca. There was no hope of preventing the relief of the town, but the general was determined to make the

Spaniards know that they had had a fight, and he certainly accomplished that purpose. The day was a perfect one and the entertainment of the best. For three hours the Spanish volleys and the rattling irregular fire of the Cubans made a pandemonium, added to by the booming of the Spanish batteries. A thin film of smoke drifted above the tree tops, and all was excitement and noise. But the Spaniards broke through and entered the town. Certainly visitors were never more welcome. They camped there that night, and the Cubans fired on them incessantly. It is a safe guess that not one of them had a wink of sleep. The garrison was increased, the ammunition supply replenished, and the defences improved; and on the evening of the next day the Spaniards issued from the town on their return, and the Cubans were promptly upon them. They made a few miles before nightfall and bivouacked, peppered all night by their tormentors. The next morning about three o'clock they resumed the march. The whole fifteen hundred of us were drawn up on both sides of the Camino Real to give them another fight, but the column turned to the north-westward, passed our left flank before our dispositions could be changed, and headed for the railroad between Las Minas and Nuevitas. Our infantry followed and attacked their rear-guard repeatedly, while five hundred of us mounted men, under the general himself, hung on to their left flank. It was a lively and exciting day. A few shots would grow into a heavy roll of fire, to die out in a few moments and begin again in another quarter. And so we swept along all of a beautiful day. Just after dark, as they were going into bivouac, the last clash with the rear-guard occurred. The next morning our mounted men made a savage attack on the enemy's advance-guard, and a lively scrimmage ensued in which we had three killed and sixteen wounded. Poor Potter, one of Pagluchi's wards, had both legs shattered and had his horse killed under him, and spent the next year on his back in one of the lonely hospitals. He never returned from Cuba, but became a resident of Puerto Principe, where he lives to-day.

The Spaniards reached the railroad on this forenoon, and we marched eastward to meet General Calixto Garcia, and in combination with his force to more than wipe out the failure of Cascorra.

III

THE FALL OF GUAIMARO

AFTER the brief but exciting Cascorra campaign, General Maximo Gomez and his force, reduced by casualties and the detaching of various organizations to about one thousand men, infantry, cavalry, and artillery, with two guns, had marched to the eastward, and in a few days was encamped alongside the force of General Calixto Garcia, about two thousand men, that, after a forced march made in obedience to orders from Gomez, had just arrived from east of the Cauto River. We Americans, having learned that General Garcia also had a few guns officered by our countrymen, proceeded to look up these latter without delay, and found several likable and interesting men who were to be our comrades through many months to come. These were Major Winchester Dana Osgood, who had won fame as a foot-ball player at Cornell and the University of Pennsylvania; Captain William Cox, of Philadelphia; Lieutenants Stuart S. Janney and Osmun Latrobe, Jr., of Baltimore, and James Devine, of Texas, and Dr. Harry Danforth, of Milwaukee. All except the latter, who served as a medical officer, belonged to the artillery, with Osgood in command.

As General Garcia, like General Gomez, had but two guns, it will be seen that the artillery of both forces was considerably over-officered. But this fault extended throughout the whole insurgent army, the number of officers, especially those of high rank, being out of all proportion to the number of men in the ranks.

We were soon presented to General Garcia, and were most kindly received by him. As the future service of the most of us was to be under his command, as he was one of the most prominent chieftains not only in this war, but in the ten years' struggle, a few words regarding his personality will not be amiss. He was a man of most striking appearance, being over six feet tall and rather heavy, and his hair and large mustache were snow-white. What at once attracted attention was the hole in his forehead, a souvenir of the Ten Years' War. On September 3, 1874, being about to fall into the hands of the Spaniards, and believing his execution to be a certainty, he had fired a large-calibre revolver upward from beneath his lower jaw, the bullet making its exit almost in the centre of his forehead. It is safe to say that not one man in ten thousand would have survived so terrible an injury. He was taken prisoner, and owed his life to the skill of a Spanish surgeon, though he remained in prison until the end of the war, four years later. To the day of his death, nearly twenty-four years later, the wound never entirely healed, and he always carried a small wad of cotton in the hole in his skull. General Garcia was a man of the most undoubted personal courage, and was a courteous and kindly gentleman. His bearing was dignified, but he was one of the most approachable of men. He seldom smiled, and I never heard him laugh but once, and that was when on one occasion he fired every one of the six shots in his revolver at a jutea, a small animal, at a few yards range without disturbing its slumbers. With him life had been one long tragedy of war and prison. He lived to see his country free from Spanish rule, but not yet a republic. Those of us Americans who had served under Gomez always regarded him with something akin to awe or fear, but all who came in close contact with Garcia had for him a feeling of affection. He was always so just and so considerate, and though some of us must have exasperated him at times, so far as I know he never gave one of us a harsh word. When the provocation was sufficient, however, he could be terribly severe with his own people.

General Garcia's staff consisted of about a dozen young men of the best families of Cuba. All of them spoke English, a great convenience for us foreigners who were constantly under the necessity of communicating with them. The chief of staff was Colonel Mario Menocal, a graduate of Cornell, and a civil engineer by profession. Declining a commission at the beginning of the war, he had entered the ranks, and was with Gomez on his memorable march from eastern Cuba to the very walls of Havana. He was a most capable and daring soldier, and his rise had been rapid. He was the nominee of the Conservative party for the presidency of Cuba at the last election. Another member of the staff was Colonel Carlos Garcia, a son of the general, and the present Cuban minister to the United States. He was a great friend of all of us American *mambis*, and we usually went to him with such troubles as we had.

General Garcia's force, having been raised in the province of Santiago, had a much larger proportion of negroes than the one that we had been with. With him here were several well-known negro chieftains, among them Rabi and Cebreco, the former one of the most striking-looking men I have ever seen. Some of the negro officers were quite capable in guerilla warfare, while others were mere blusterers and blunderers. Although the color line is drawn in Cuba in social matters, white men of the best families did not hesitate to serve under negro officers, and sometimes on their staffs. The Cuban negroes in the insurgent army were to me a most interesting study. They seemed much more forceful and aggressive than our own colored population as a rule, probably the result of most of the older ones having served in the Ten Years' War. And then, too, they had lived a more out-door life than the majority of the negroes of our Northern States, being plantation hands and small farmers, and had not been weakened and demoralized by city life. A surprising fact was that not a few of the older negroes of Cuba were born in Africa. Although the foreign slave-trade was abolished by law many years ago, it is a matter of common knowledge that up to as late as 1870 small cargoes of slaves from the west coast of Africa were run into Cuba. Juan Gonzalez, the man who served for more than six months as my "striker," or personal servant, told me that he distinctly remembered his capture, when about ten years of age, by Arabs on the Congo, his sale to the Portuguese, and the journey in a sailing-ship across the Atlantic. He ran away from his master and served in the Ten

Years' War, and so gained his freedom. These African negroes often conversed among themselves in their native dialect, nearly all of them having come from the same region on the Congo.

After a few days in camp to allow the men and horses of both forces to rest, the three thousand of us marched toward doomed Guaimaro, and drew our lines about the town. The combined forces were under the command of General Gomez, he being the insurgent commander-in-chief. General Garcia had with him two guns, a Hotchkiss twelve-pounder and a two-pounder of the same make, they being identical with the two guns that Gomez had used at Cascorra, and that we had brought with us. So we now had four pieces of artillery, all steel breech-loading guns, using fixed ammunition.

The little town of Guaimaro, in the extreme eastern part of the province of Camaguey, and sixteen miles east of Cascorra, has figured largely in Cuban history. Here convened on April 10, 1869, the first Cuban legislative body, which framed the constitution that served during the Ten Years' War, and which adopted as the Cuban flag the beautiful banner that to-day waves over the Presidential Palace in Havana, but was first seen on Cuban soil when the unfortunate Narcisso Lopez landed to start a war for independence in 1850. Practically all the Cuban population of Guaimaro had left the town months before, and the resident non-combatants consisted almost entirely of a few Spanish store-keepers and their families. The garrison, about three hundred men of the Second Battalion of Tarragona, was commanded by a major, whose name I have unfortunately forgotten, and was distributed among eleven defensive positions, mostly large two-story blockhouses, called *fortines*, though the strongest positions were the brick church with stone tower and the barracks, the former in the south part of the town and the latter at its south-west corner. All of these had earth banked up around them to the lower tier of portholes and were surrounded by barb-wire entanglements. All except the church were also surrounded by standing trenches. The key to the situation was the *Fortin* Gonfu, an isolated blockhouse on a low hill due north of the centre of the town and seven hundred yards from the circle of blockhouses surrounding it. The nearest support was the *Fortin* Isabella. Once established in the Gonfu blockhouse, the Cubans would completely dominate the town, which lay in easy artillery range on the level ground to the southward. The blockhouse in question was neither large nor strong, and its isolated position made its capture certain if a vigorous attack were made.

On the night of October 16th Gomez and Garcia with their staffs and personal escorts were encamped about a mile to the north of the Gonfu position, and we Americans with our four guns were near them. I had been commissioned a captain immediately after the Cascorra campaign, but Osgood being a major, I was ranked by him, and he was very properly placed in command of all the artillery. On the night referred to, General Gomez was in a somewhat irritable mood. One of the insurgent officers had sung in grand opera in Europe, and was entertaining a number of us within earshot of where our chief was trying to rest. The grim old fellow stood the Italian airs as long as he could, and then sent word to the offender that he had a horse that sang considerably better. But he did not interfere when General Garcia's fine band struck up, and played for a couple of hours. The Cubans were making no attempt to conceal their presence from the garrison, and the wind being favorable, the music must have been heard in the town. It no doubt gave the Spaniards a creepy feeling when they heard the Cuban national hymn, the *Bayames*, and listened to the cheers and the shouts of "*Cuba libre!*" that followed its playing.

At three o'clock the next morning I was startled from a sound sleep by a leathern-lunged bugler blowing reveille within a few feet of my hammock, and it is a peculiar and to me inexplicable fact that though I have certainly heard reveille several thousand times since that occasion, it invariably to this day brings to mind that depressing, chilly morning that ushered in the siege of Guaimaro, and calls up for the moment those stirring days that now seem so long ago. As the call was taken up by a score of bugles all about the town, I could not help wondering as to the feelings of the brave little garrison, so soon to begin their struggle against overwhelming odds. Completely isolated from the outside world, except when every three months a convoy reached them with supplies, they had for nearly two weeks in September listened to the booming of guns in the fighting about Cascorra, but could have had no inkling as to the result. Now they must have realized that their time of trial had come.

It had been determined to use but one gun in the attack

on the Gonfu blockhouse, and this was the twelve-pounder that belonged to Garcia's command. During the night a short parapet had been constructed for it about four hundred yards to the westward of the blockhouse, and practically on a level with it, though separated therefrom by a grassy swale. The piece was in position before daylight, with Osgood in personal command. For the time being, Gomez's artillerymen were to be but spectators, so Pennie and I took our post about a hundred yards on the left flank of the gun and about equally distant with it from the blockhouse, and awaited developments. After it was fairly light we saw a flash of flame and smoke from the shrubbery behind which the gun position had been constructed, and almost simultaneously a shell struck the ground a few yards short of the blockhouse, but on the ricochet went through it without exploding. The sixteen Spaniards in the little fort were on the lookout, ready for business, and in a few seconds came their fire, a continuous crackle, as they were using their magazine rifles at top speed. At first they fought from the lower story of the blockhouse, but after the structure had been hit a couple of times they abandoned it, and took to the trenches outside. At Guaimaro there were not the bags of earth in front of the trenches that at Cascorra had given us something to shoot at, the enemy having instead deep standing trenches. A man's head would be exposed for only the few seconds that it took him to empty his magazine. As soon as he saw no more fire coming from the blockhouse itself, Osgood confined himself to attempts to make hits on the top of the trench in the hope of landing a shell in it, but it was practically impossible to do so at such short range, the trajectory being so flat. And then, too, the ammunition that General Garcia had brought with him had been some months on the island, exposed to all sorts of weather and treatment, and many of the shells failed to burst. Our people shot slowly and carefully, but did not succeed in diminishing the enemy's fire to any great extent. Pennie and I, animated by a desire to get a little closer to the fireworks, made a run over to the gun, and reached there just in time to see the Hotchkiss on its recoil knock a Cuban senseless. These twelve-pounders, very light guns for their heavy powder charge, were nearly as dangerous toward the rear as toward the front. Despite the brake ropes, which were adjusted before every shot, I have seen them kick down a slope or along slippery ground for twenty feet, so that we soon learned to have the deepest respect for the ground in rear of one of these guns. The only time we attempted to limit these antics was by means of a bank of earth, and this experiment resulted in a broken carriage. Pennie and I stooped down beside the gun detachment and watched our perspiring and powder-begrimed countrymen work. The protection was scarcely half as high as the parapets behind which we had fought at Cascorra, and becoming somewhat careless in our anxiety to see the results of the shots, we were warned by Osgood to be careful, as the Spaniards were shooting well. The bullets were coming in steadily, and keeping well down to the ground. Osgood had just remarked to me that he had accomplished all he could, by driving the Spaniards from the blockhouse to the trenches outside, and that the infantry must do the rest, when a staff officer arrived to state that the Cubans were going to charge from the foot of the slope to our left, and to give directions that a lookout should be kept, in order that the fire of the gun might cease at the proper time. This was refreshing after what we had seen at Cascorra, where failure to use the infantry at the proper time had thrown away a victory. Of course, however, assaulting this isolated blockhouse was no such proposition as going against the much stronger and better-supported positions of the other town. Anxious to see the charge, Pennie and I hastened back to our old stand, and had hardly got settled down when a bugle rang out in the edge of the woods a hundred yards to our left, there were a number of briskly given commands, some faint cheering and a rattle of shots, and a company of men, mostly negroes, led by Garcia's chief of staff, Colonel Menocal, began to climb the grassy slope. Ordinarily chiefs of staff do not lead charges, but no chances were being taken on some bungler making a mess of this job. The slope was so steep and the grass so high and dense that the attack was made at a walk, the men in single line, firing and yelling excitedly. Pennie and I watched for a few seconds, when he said, "Me for this," and we started for the blockhouse, and at the same time saw Janney, Latrobe, and one or two others cutting across from the gun position, with revolvers drawn. When about half-way to the top we two stumbled over a negro, who as soon as he saw us began to writhe and moan, calling out that he was wounded. Desirous of rendering assistance, we turned him over, but could see no blood. "The damned coward is flunking," yelled Pennie, and twisting the fellow's Remington out of his hands, gave him the butt of it several times, thus making his lamentations more realistic. This man was the only one of the fifty who fell out, the others facing the music gamely. The first man through the wire entanglement and into the trench was Janney, who had joined the attacking company just before it reached the summit. Owing to our delay with the supposedly wounded man, the blockhouse was taken before Pennie and I reached it. The Spaniards had not waited for the Cubans, but had bolted out of their trench on the opposite side when the latter were about half-way up, and were doing a Marathon for the Isabella *fortin*, distant seven hundred yards. The victors fired on them from around the captured blockhouse, and killed one man about a hundred yards down the slope. The infantry company had lost its formation, and had dissolved into a mob of men, yelling and firing, until Menocal restored some semblance of order by knocking down several of the worst with the flat of his machete. Not one of the men making the assault had been hit, as the garrison of the blockhouse had not fired after they came in sight, and the enemy in the other forts could not see the attacking party until it reached the summit. The mob of men about the captured position now made a fine target, however, and from every blockhouse, the church, the barracks, and other points came a most terrific and well-sustained fire. There must have been some peculiar atmospheric or other condition that redoubled the sound, as these comparatively few rifles made for the time an almost unbroken roar, reminding us of the racket at La Machuca, where four thousand men were in action. The summit of the hill rapidly became too hot. Colonel Menocal screened some of his men in the trenches, and others behind the blockhouse, but sent about half of them down the hill, not, however, until several of them had been hit. Of course something ridiculous had to happen. A chicken, which the late garrison had evidently hoped to add to their next bill of fare, escaped in the confusion, and ran cackling around the blockhouse half a dozen times, pursued by Pennie, who finally killed it by throwing his machete at it. As all the remaining Spanish works were on a lower level than ourselves, the fire from them was necessarily directed upward, with the result that thousands of bullets, clearing the hill, spattered over the country for nearly two miles to the north. An aged colonel of Gomez's staff, lying peacefully in his hammock a mile and a half from the nearest Spanish work, was shot through the body, but recovered, and several other casualties in the camps resulted from this fusillade. In the meantime a number of us had entered the blockhouse and were exploring it. The lower story was littered with broken timbers, and a barrel of drinking water had been pierced at about its middle by a shell, but without destroying it or knocking it over. The remaining half-barrel of water quenched many a thirst that day. In the upper story we found a number of boxes of hard biscuit and some other food, and after filling our pockets began pitching the balance out to the men hugging the lee side of the building to escape the storm of bullets still sweeping the hill. A

Spanish soldier, wounded by a shell, had fallen across one box of biscuits and had bled there so profusely that half of them were saturated, but it was no time to be fastidious, and we emptied the upper part of the box and threw the uninjured contents to the hungry men outside.

In the meantime several officers of General Garcia's staff had reached us, and called attention to the fact that the Spanish flag was still floating from the pole on the blockhouse. This would never do, and it must come down. But it could not be lowered, being nailed to the staff. One of these officers, Lieutenant Luis Rodolfo Miranda, said he would bring down the flag, and several of us went out and from the safe side of the structure watched the operation. With assistance Miranda reached the roof, and slowly and painfully began drawing himself up the pole, which was about eighteen feet high and four inches in diameter. Every Spaniard in Guaimaro could see him, and I believe to a man tried to bring the gallant fellow down. Bullets hissed and crackled all about, and beat a constant tattoo on the blockhouse. The pole above or below him was hit several times. For a few moments that seemed endless we looked on in an agony of suspense, expecting every moment to see him come crashing down on the tile roof. We begged him to give it up and wait for night, but he kept on, reached the flag, cut it loose with his pocket-knife, slid down the pole with it, ran to the eaves, and leaped to the ground fifteen feet below. It would be difficult to imagine a feat of more reckless daring, and yet I have heard some of my own countrymen damn the whole Cuban people as a race of cowards.

We re-entered the blockhouse, and Osgood and I were discussing the possibility of getting the gun into it under such a fire, when Devine spied a magnificent saddle-horse tied to a long rope in a little swale about two hundred yards to our left front and about five hundred yards from two of the Spanish blockhouses. The horse, being out of the line of fire, had not been hit, but was prancing about, snorting with terror. "That horse would suit my style of beauty," remarked Devine, and before any one could stop him he had got out and started down the hill on a run. Once at the foot of the slope he was out of view of most of the Spaniards, but was in plain sight from three blockhouses, two of them quite close, and every man in them did his best to get him. He reached the rope, untied it, and tried to lead the animal, but the terrified beast declined to follow, and was soon brought down. Devine, having no use for a dead horse, started back up the hill. Osgood and I were breathlessly watching him from adjoining port-holes, when we saw him pitch forward into the grass. Osgood cried out, "My God, he is hit! I am going after him," and started down the ladder to the lower story, the only way to get out. I followed with no very definite idea as to what I was going to do, but in my haste slipped on the top round of the ladder and fell into the lower story, taking Osgood with me. Both of us were well bruised but not disabled. Reaching the outside, we found that Janney was running down the hill, racing like mad. The enemy now concentrated their fire on him, as they had on Devine. Janney was a power-ful man, and half carried and half dragged the wounded man up that slope under a fire that it would seem impossible a man could live through, it being especially severe after he had got half-way up, and was exposed to nearly all the Spanish positions. Several of us assisted him to lower Devine into the shelter of the trench. He was shot in the hip, a very severe wound from which he did not recover during the war, though he returned to duty after a couple of months. In our service Janney's act would have brought him the Medal of Honor, or in the British army the Victoria Cross, but the Cubans had not yet reached the stage of distributing decorations for gallantry.

After this incident the garrison apparently became somewhat tired of sweeping the hill with their fire, and gave us a respite, simply sending in an occasional volley. In the meantime General Garcia, accompanied by several officers of his staff, had reached the hill for the purpose of examining the captured position, one of his orderlies being killed at his side shortly after his arrival on the summit. Owing to the inevitable loss of life involved in the undertaking, the general determined to wait until nightfall before attempting to install a gun in the blockhouse. We artillerymen recognized the wisdom of this decision, though, maddened by the action of the Spaniards in trying to kill Janney while he was rescuing a wounded man, we could scarcely possess our souls in patience until we could have a chance to blow them out of their blockhouses.

During the remainder of the day nothing was done except to move some of our infantry closer to the captured hill lest the enemy should attempt to retake it by a sortie. We Americans went down to our camp for supper, but a few hours later returned to the position. Not having had enough excitement during the day, Captain Jose Estrampes of Gomez's staff and I crawled down in the darkness to the point between the Gonfu and Isabella blockhouses where the Spanish soldier had been seen to fall in the retirement from the former, and came back ahead an excellent Mauser rifle. The task of the night was to get a gun into the captured position, from which we could bring to bear on every one of the remaining Spanish works. Because something had gone wrong with its breech mechanism, the piece used during the day was not utilized, but we brought up the other twelve-pounder, the old veteran of Cascorra. A hole was broken through the north wall of the blockhouse, and the gun taken in through it. A port-hole was made on the opposite side bearing on the town, and before daylight we were ready for business. Just as the sun came over the horizon Osgood landed a shell squarely on the Isabella *fortin*, and for a couple of hours deliberately shelled that work and others in the vicinity. As always when these fragile blockhouses were under artillery fire, the enemy left the structures and fought in the trenches around them, where only by chance were they liable to suffer casualties from our shells. Here, however, our slight elevation above the town gave us some advantage in this respect. During most of the bombardment of this morning I remained outside, some forty feet east of the blockhouse, calling the shots for Osgood, as none of those in the structure could observe the effects of their fire owing to the smoke. I spent a part of the time in the building, however. Our infantry supports were well covered in standing trenches on the flanks of the block-house, these having been constructed during the night, so that there were no groups on the hill to draw the Spanish fire. The result was that the enemy apparently paid but little attention to us. It was finally noticed, however, that about once a minute a bullet would come through the port-hole, or strike very near it. The regularity of these shots and their accuracy convinced us that some exceptionally fine sharp-shooter was giving us his attention. On one of my runs to the blockhouse to announce the result of a shot, one of these bullets came in the port-hole just as I entered the gap in the rear, missing me only an inch or two. Several of those serving at the gun had had narrow escapes, and everybody was keeping as much as possible out of the danger zone, though a certain amount of exposure was unavoidable. Partly owing to our defective ammunition, and partly to a brisk wind blowing across the line of fire, several unfortunate shots had been made, and Osgood stooped over the gun to make on the sight a correction for wind. He had adjusted it satisfactorily, sighted the piece, and made the remark, "I think that will do," when all those near by heard a bullet strike him with a sound like a base-ball being thrown against a building. The few words just spoken were his last on earth. He sank across the trail of the gun, unconscious, and was lifted from it by his horror-stricken comrades and hurried down the hill to one of the dressing-stations. He did not recover consciousness, and in four hours was dead. The bullet had gone through his brain, and he passed from the vigor of early manhood into the long sleep in the fraction of a second. He could never have known that he had been hit. A year and a half later, it fell to me to recount the circumstances of Major Osgood's death to his father, Colonel, afterward Brigadier-General, Osgood of the United States army. The latter knew that his son had been killed, but was ignorant as to the attendant circumstances. The little group of aliens, fighting in a strange land for a cause not their own, were sore stricken. It was the first time one of our own number had been killed. Bound together by ties of race and language, and sharing the daily dangers and privations, we had become closer to each other than men ordinarily do in years of acquaintanceship under different circumstances, and now felt that the war was coming home to us. For a time we did nothing but sit in the blockhouse, well back from the fatal port-hole, and gaze in awe at the spatter of blood on the gun trail and note the devilish regularity with which the missiles from the sharp-shooter's rifle whistled past us. A staff-officer who was in the blockhouse with us had hastened to head-quarters with the news of Osgood's certainly fatal wound. We had asked him to obtain instructions as to who was to take command, Cox or myself, both being captains. It was General Garcia's desire that the former, having served directly under him, should be designated, but Gomez overruled him, and I was from that time in command of the artillery of the *Departamento del Oriente*. Cox, like the good soldier that he was, served under me faithfully and loyally until the end.

It was rightly guessed that the sharp-shooter was stationed in the church tower, distant eleven hundred yards, and I determined to make it my special business to kill him if I could. It was subsequently learned that he was an officer using a rifle with telescope sight. As the gun had not been touched since Osgood had sighted it, I ordered the lanyard pulled, and a shell smashed its way through one of the blockhouses. The poor fellow's last work had been well done. But hit the church tower I could not, owing to the defective ammunition and strong gusts of wind, though I struck the roof of the building within a few feet of it several times. If we could have had the deadly Driggs-Schroeder that we afterward used at Jiguani and Las Tunas, one shot would have done the work. But the fact that the tower was being fired at caused the sharp-shooter to abandon it for the day. Until nightfall our shots were distributed impartially among the three or four works nearest us, with an occasional shell for the church or barracks just to keep from hurting the feelings of their garrisons. During the afternoon we witnessed a futile and ridiculous charge made upon the badly battered Isabella blockhouse. The officer in command of this enterprise was a negro lieutenant-colonel of Cebreco's brigade. He had a battalion, and instead of deploying his men out of sight, under cover of the woods, he rushed them in column into the open within four hundred yards of his objective, and attempted to form line under a withering fire from the trenches around three blockhouses. His men huddled up, became panic-stricken, and fled, leaving their numerous killed and wounded on the ground, whence they could not be removed until nightfall. We poured shells into the Isabella during this performance as rapidly as we could load and fire, in order to confine the enemy to his trenches and keep him from reoccupying the remains of the structure. General Gomez witnessed this fiasco, and was wild with rage. That night the blunderer was tried by court-martial and sentenced to death, but this was commuted to reduction to the ranks, and the next day we saw the doleful-looking man carrying a Remington in the battalion that he had so recently commanded.

During the night of this day we brought up one of the two-pounders, cut a port-hole for it to the left of the larger gun, and placed it in position. The projectiles fired by this piece were too small to do much damage, but its accuracy was wonderful, and it had ammunition that had not been damaged. The next morning our friend in the church tower resumed operations, and we promptly went for him. Every shot fired at the tower from the little gun struck it, one shell, as we subsequently ascertained, striking within a foot of the small window from which the officer was firing. All the shells from this gun burst on the outside, however, the masonry being too strong for them. But they had the desired moral effect, and we had no more trouble with the tower sharp-shooter. During the day we used first one gun and then the other, as owing to the confined space it was not practicable to serve both at the same time.

All this while the Cuban infantry had the town closely invested, and from time to time there would be lively fire fights between them and the defenders of the trenches. October 20, the fourth day of the siege, was largely a repetition of the preceding day. We were firing slowly, as ammunition was running low, when we met with quite a serious misfortune. I had just given the order to fire the twelve-pounder, when, instead of the usual loud report and re-bound to the rear, the gun remained motionless, while for half a minute a stream of flame and gas poured from the vent. A shell had stuck in the barrel, half-way to the muzzle, the powder in the charge having become so dam-aged that it would not force it out. The removal of this loaded shell, with no special appliances for the purpose, was a most delicate and dangerous operation, and re-quired several weeks, the work being done by a Cuban mechanic. The piece was not permanently damaged, and fortunately we had with us another of the same calibre. The next day we fired but few shots, as we were all but out of ammunition for the twelve-pounder. An additional supply in a deposit many miles to the eastward had been sent for, but could not arrive for some time. It looked as if we were going to have another Cascorra fiasco. We had been considerably exasperated because of being com-pelled to fritter away our precious ammunition in a des-ultory bombardment of ten separate positions, instead of placing all our guns in action at one time and concentrat-ing their fire on some one of the more important works for half an hour, as a prelude to an infantry assault. The good work of the first day was not being properly followed up. The guns were taken to the rear, though the infantry held on to all their positions and from time to time ex-changed shots with the enemy. The question of the sub-sistence of so large a force had become a serious one. Large herds of cattle were driven in, but the surrounding country had been denuded of vegetables. The question of camping-grounds was also an embarrassing one. For sanitary reasons the Cubans moved their camps to new ground every few days, but not much more shifting could be done without taking the main body of troops so far from the line of investment that it could not be properly supported.

Time hung heavily on our hands, but we had some diversions. One night Huntington made a lone-hand raid on the town. He crawled through the Spanish lines, roamed unchallenged through the streets, and came back with a fine turkey. Inspired by this feat, Colonel Carlos Garcia's negro servant, who had known the town well in times of peace, begged his chief for permission to enter and endeavor to obtain a supply of Spanish delicacies from some of the abandoned stores. Permission was reluctantly given, and the plucky fellow set out on his perilous errand. He wormed his way through the grass, crawled under the barb-wire entanglements, reached the centre of the town, and effected entrance into a general store. Inside it was pitch dark, and he dared not strike a light, but by feeling about found a lot of promising cans, and deposited them in a sugar sack that he had with him. Handicapped by his heavy load, the return was slow and painful, as well as dangerous, but finally after an absence of five hours the exultant negro deposited his cargo at the feet of his waiting and appreciative master, whose friends promptly gathered about to see the result of this raid, and mayhap to partake thereof. By the light of a campfire the sack was emptied of its contents, eighteen cans of house paint. If there was any one thing that nobody had any use for in those days it was house paint. The subsequent proceedings were appropriate to the occasion. Last year when I had the pleasure of entertaining the present Cuban minister to the United States at my quarters at Fort Leavenworth, and we were going over the tragedies and comedies of the long-ago days in the bush, we dwelt long and lovingly on this incident.

One night about this time a very tall negro, one of the few Cubans left in the town, was caught trying to get through the Spanish lines. A rigid search of his person resulted in the discovery of a letter from the commandant to General Castellanos in Puerto Principe informing him that the town was undergoing siege. There was also found the sum of two hundred dollars in Spanish gold, which the unfortunate man confessed was his pay, given him in advance. He was promptly tried, and as promptly hanged, and the commander, unlike his brother officer besieged in Cascorra, waited with sinking heart as the days passed, listening for the sound of guns to the westward, and hoping for the relief that never came.

At last on the 28th, the eleventh day of the siege, the pack train arrived with the longed-for cartridges for our guns. General Garcia gave me instructions to bombard every position on the next day, and stated that under cover of darkness a general assault would be made. I was given entire discretion as to what use to make of the guns, and so that night had a small shelter constructed outside the Gonfu blockhouse and had installed in it one of the two-pounders, while the remaining twelve-pounder was placed inside in the old position, the extra port-hole being blocked up.   It was desired to find a position for the remaining two-pounder close to the church, as that building, except its tower, was of brick, and consequently not proof against the shells of the smaller gun.   An excellent location was found four hundred yards from one of the rear corners, approach to it being afforded by a shallow draw. The intervening ground was perfectly level, and bare of grass or bush.   Half-way from this position to the church, and a little to the right of our line of fire on that building, was one of the badly battered blockhouses with some twenty brave fellows hanging on to the trenches about it. This was a serious disadvantage, as we were subject to their fire at two hundred yards range and could not harm them, but there was nothing better to be had.   An excellent parapet with overhead cover was constructed at this point.   I had become heartily tired of the Gonfu position, and so placed Cox in charge of the two guns there and myself took the two-pounder near the church.   Cox had Janney, Latrobe, Jones, and the majority of the Cubans with the artillery, while I had Huntington, Pennie, and the remainder of our enlisted men.   Everything went off smoothly, and when daylight came on the 29th all the guns were in position.   I took the first shot, and sent a shell through the wall of the church on the line of port-holes just above the surface of the ground.   The Spaniards in the church, instead of having their port-holes about five feet above the floor, had torn a part of this up and dug standing trenches all about the inside of the building. So they were covered by the natural ground up to their shoulders, and above this were protected from infantry fire by the brick wall. It was an excellent arrangement, and I have never seen its like elsewhere. The enemy lost no time in replying, and all day gave us so hot a fire that the service of the gun was exceedingly difficult. Half a mile to our right we could see the discharges of the guns in the Gonfu position. All along the north and east sides of the town were heavy lines of infantry lying down and not firing. Just a few yards to the left of my position, down in the hollow, Dr. Danforth had his dressing-station, with instruments and bandages laid out for use. The fighting all day was pretty hot, and at times the fire on my position would compel us to delay for a time. All of our guns fired very slowly and deliberately. The newly arrived ammunition was much better than that we had been using, and there were practically no misses. It had been ordered that before darkness came on one of the guns in the Gonfu position should be sighted at the church tower and left until nine o'clock, when it should be fired. This was to be the signal for the assault. In order to avoid a misunderstanding all the guns were to cease some time before that hour. I kept up with my two-pounder until a little after dark, firing most of the time at the church but giving the pestiferous blockhouse on my right front an occasional compliment. The walls of the church had been well perforated, and the little shells had burst inside, inflicting casualties, but they were not heavy enough to shatter the walls or make breaches, so that the building retained its shape. At last an ominous silence fell over all, contrasting strangely with the turmoil of an eventful day. The last hour dragged with leaden feet. All were at high tension, as it was realized that the crucial hour was at hand. Was it to be a victory, or were the plucky Catalans to hurl us back in a bloody repulse? Every moment we would strike matches down behind the parapet in order to consult our watches. At last the hour came. There was a tongue of flame from the Gonfu position, and for an instant the church tower was lighted up by a bursting shell. A second later we heard the crack of the two-pounder. At the start there was no blowing of bugles and no yelling to draw the Spanish fire. Colonel Menocal had personal charge of the assault, but was at all times in communication with Generals Gomez and Garcia. He had systematized everything and left nothing to chance. Every unit had its objective indicated in advance, and it was pretty well understood that if there should be any serious blundering there would be some executions the next day. In order to avoid confusion and possible accidental encounters in the streets in the darkness, the attacking force was limited to five hundred men. It was thought that even if the job could not be completed during the night such advantages of position would be gained that it would not take much of daylight to finish it.

The echo of the gun had scarcely died away when a few low commands were given just to the right of my position, and about fifty men, deployed in a single line and without firing, rushed for the nearest blockhouse, the one that had warmed us up so persistently during the day. As there would not for some time be any use for the guns, I gave Huntington and Pennie permission to join the attacking party. This had covered half the distance before being discovered. There was then a lively popping from the blockhouse, and the Cubans raised a yell and covered the remaining hundred yards at a run. A few moments later those of us who had remained at the position saw a group of men coming out of the darkness. It was a detail bringing back the captured garrison of the blockhouse. About this time quite a furor broke out in the direction of the Isabella, but lasted only a few seconds. I did not propose to stay by a cannon that could not be used in this mix up, and knew that nobody would carry it off and that it could be found when needed, and so went in. Afterward in the town I came across all of my brother artillery officers. We were a fine lot, having run off and left our guns to take part in an infantry attack. In any other service we would have gotten into serious trouble, but the Cubans were lenient with us, apparently regarding this as the American way of doing things. I do not believe that any one can give a correct and detailed account of the events of this stirring night. There was a series of detached fights, some of them of short duration and others exceedingly brisk. The darkness was intense. Bullets were whistling in all directions, and one was in about as much danger from friend as from foe. The church was a hard proposition, and it was some time before we made progress against it. Dynamite was brought up, and Captain Estrampes and Huntington made an attempt to breach the walls. They got into the ditch outside with about fifty pounds of the explosive and the necessary fuse. The men in the church could not get at them where they were, and divining what was up, asked if quarter would be given. Being answered in the affirmative, they surrendered and were sent to the rear. By midnight everything except the barracks had fallen, and the firing had died down to an occasional sputter. There was now much yelling and cheering, and the Cubans were busy looting the captured positions, buildings, and shops of food, clothing, and cooking utensils. Many of those that had not taken part in the assault now broke away and entered the town, in order not to be left out in gathering in the spoils. The confusion became great, and it was evident that formations could not be restored until daylight. Colonel Menocal and I, as soon as it became light enough to see, made a reconnaissance of the barrack by getting into buildings in the vicinity. It was a one-story brick structure, about one hundred feet long, loophooled, and surrounded by the most effective barb-wire entanglement I have ever seen. I doubt if a dog could have crawled through it. It was evident that we must use a gun from one of the near-by houses, and I went back for the two-pounder that during the day had shelled the church. We selected for it a building at an angle across the street and forty yards distant from the nearest portion of the barrack building. As we did not dare expose ourselves in the street in view of the barrack, the gun was placed in position by breaking through the walls of several brick houses. From the inside of the house a few bricks were removed from the wall, and the muzzle shoved through within a stone's throw of its intended target. Ammunition was brought in, and infantry supports placed in rear of the row of buildings. We now waited for daylight. The yelling and the occasional shots had died out and the town was perfectly quiet. Hundreds of exhausted and hungry insurgents had thrown themselves down in the débris-littered streets and gone to sleep. It was now discovered that the Spanish hospital, full of wounded, was directly across the street from the barrack and only two buildings from where we had the gun. This was a nasty complication, and about five o'clock Menocal and I went in to discuss the situation with the surgeon in charge. This officer pointed out that a fight for the possession of the barrack must involve the hospital, and that there would be great danger of a conflagration. Menocal desired him to remove the wounded, offering assistance, but was informed that many of them were so terribly injured by shell wounds that it was out of the question. But we could not give up the advantages of our position. Menocal promised that in case of a fight he would not occupy the hospital, and in this way it might not be brought under fire. As soon as it was light Menocal, holding aloft a white handkerchief, boldly walked into the middle of the street and waited a moment. In the meantime I had the gun pointed to partially rake the building, and Huntington stood with lanyard in hand to fire in case he should be shot down. In a short time a captain emerged from the building and informed Menocal that he was in command, the commandant having been disabled by a shell wound during the day. The chief of staff replied by demanding his surrender, assuring him that all would be treated as prisoners of war. The captain replied that while he realized his position to be a desperate one, he still felt that he had a chance to repulse an assault. Menocal pointed toward the building that we were in, and the Spaniard saw for the first time the black, lean muzzle of the Hotchkiss. He seemed thunder-struck, realizing that the flimsy brick building would be but a death trap, as the shells would explode all through it and rake it from end to end. About this time a number of insurgent soldiers impelled by curiosity to see what was going on came out into the street within full view of the barrack, and some fifty yards from it. At this juncture a very lean pig escaped from somewhere, and dashed across the street, followed by a dozen laughing Cubans. They caught the animal within twenty yards of the wire en-tanglements, and were not fired on. In fact several cheers and "bravos" came through the Spanish port-holes. It was evident that it was about over. Menocal came back to the building where we had the gun, slapped me on the shoulder, and said: "They give up." In a few moments the door of the barrack opened and a white flag was hung out. The Cubans crowded about the entanglements, and the Spanish soldiers and some store-keepers who had taken refuge with them began to throw out packages of cigarettes. Generals Gomez and Garcia arrived and found the job completed. A number of us officers now entered the barrack, escorted by the Spanish captain. The men still had their Mausers, and were standing at the port-holes, evidently uneasy as to the treatment they were to receive from the ragged and motley crew outside. Their commander told them it was all over, and Menocal assured them that they were in no danger. They seemed glad that the end had come, being completely exhausted by the constant vigilance imposed by the thirteen days' siege. They laid down their arms and marched out, and soon were mingling with the men whom they had been fighting but a few hours before. For the time no restrictions were placed on their movements, and they were allowed to roam about at will. The most of us had reached the limit of physical endurance, having been without sleep since the morning of the second day before, and sank down anywhere in the shade, letting the war take care of itself for a few hours.

All the stores and dwellings in the town were thoroughly looted. It was not a pretty sight, but men in such desperate straits as were the Cubans could not be expected to spare the property of the enemy, either soldiers or noncombatants. Considering the fact that the Spaniards waged a war of absolutely no quarter, even murdering the wounded who fell into their hands, it was a matter for congratulation that not a single one of the prisoners taken at Guaimaro was in any way injured. In fact the Cubans seemed to bear no hatred whatever against the Spanish regulars, knowing that they had no option either as to their participation in the war or the methods of carrying it on. But the Spanish volunteers, made up of Spanish residents of Cuba who had of their own volition gone into the struggle, often fared badly at their hands, while for the hated guerillas, Cuban mercenaries in the Spanish service, it was certain death to fall into the power of the insurgents. It was these wretches who in that war committed many of the horrible atrocities that brought a stain on the Spanish name. Fortunately there were neither volunteers nor guerillas in Guaimaro, so that we were spared a painful sequel to the victory. The spoils of the siege were considerable, about four hundred Mauser rifles, several hundred thousand rounds of ammunition, and subsistence and medical stores.

As soon as we had had a few hours' sleep we started out to explore the town, being especially interested in the church. The interior was a scene of almost indescribable confusion. In addition to being the strongest fort, this building was the commissary storehouse, and the floor was littered several feet deep in flour, peas, broken hard bread, and boxes of sardines, our shells on the last day having ploughed through or exploded in this mass for hours. Blood was spattered everywhere, but the most grewsome sight was as much as a handful of brains mixed with fragments of bone sticking to the south wall several feet above the floor. Prisoners told us that on the previous day, while the commandant was trying to cheer up his men by calling their attention to the fact that the shells that were exploding all over the room were of small size and could not bring down the building, his orderly standing at his side was beheaded, his shattered cranium being hurled clear across the church against the opposite wall. The next shell, exploding almost in the face of the officer, had given the gallant soldier his death wound, three fragments striking him in the chest. In fact, had it not been that the garrison of the church was fairly well protected by the standing trench inside the building, the place would have been a veritable slaughter pen, as the wall offered just enough resistance to the shells to burst them immediately after penetrating.

During the day Gomez wrote to General Castellanos, Spanish commander at Puerto Principe, a letter that must have given the old man the keenest satisfaction. It was to the effect that he had taken the post of Guaimaro after thirteen days' siege, and that every man of the garrison not killed was a prisoner in his hands. He would not follow the precedent set by the Spaniards, but would give them the best care possible. He wished, however, to be rid of the wounded, and if General Castellanos would send the necessary number of ambulances, escorted by unarmed men and carrying the Red Cross flag, to the cattle ranch, "El Platano," about a day's march east of Puerto Principe, they would be delivered to him. This communication was sent by mounted courier, and was delivered at the outposts of Puerto Principe, seventy miles distant, in less than twenty-four hours. Messengers were sent out to bring in the organizations that as before stated had been sent away during the siege, and preparations made for the march to "El Platano" without waiting for a reply to the letter to the Spanish commander. Insurgent commands from remote parts of the Oriente had been coming in, so that the force that took up its march on the morning of the 31st reached the respectable total of four thousand men.

It was the height of the rainy season, and for months we had been accustomed to being drenched at any time day or night, so that the good night's sleep in the buildings of

Guaimaro had been very much in the line of a treat. It must be remembered that there was not a tent in this whole force, and all were expected to take the weather as it came. The march was painfully slow, the roads being in shocking condition, and much delay was caused by the slow progress of the prisoners carrying their wounded comrades in improvised litters. The rain poured in torrents, day and night, and it was almost impossible to build fires for cooking. At our first camp a Cuban officer, talking to the sorely wounded Spanish commandant just as I happened to pass, said to him, I thought with wretched taste, "That American is the man who gave you your wound, as he personally sighted every shot at the church on the last day." The wounded officer, a very handsome and dignified man with snow-white hair and beard, looked at me in a reproving and wondering way, and I slunk out of sight, my peace of mind pretty badly disturbed. After four days of gruelling work we reached our destination, and had only a short time to wait for the train of ambulances escorted by a detachment of insurgent cavalry from among those constantly watching every outlet from Puerto Principe. Several surgeons and a detail of men of the hospital service accompanied the train, and were much interested in the rather formidable array of insurgents camped where they could be well seen along a couple of miles of the road. The Spanish and Cuban officers treated each other with the most punctilious courtesy. The wounded were delivered to their countrymen, and started on the journey to Puerto Principe, travelling more comfortably than they had during the past four days. The brave old commandant survived his wounds only a few days more. The remaining prisoners were held for some months at a camp far back in the woods, but were eventually released, the problem of feeding our own people being one that taxed the ingenuity of all. Our force now marched to the *potrero*, "Auracana," near La Yaya, and I had the pleasure of receiving my commission as major, dating from the fall of Guaimaro, and of seeing it signed by both our chieftains.

The fall of Guaimaro gave the Spanish commander of this district grave fears for the safety of the little garrison of Cascorra that had successfully resisted our attacks in September, and he determined to relieve it and abandon the town, and so came out with a force of more than four thousand men. Gomez and Garcia resisted desperately with a like number, and the next week saw some of the hardest fighting that ever took place in Cuba. For four days it was almost one continuous battle, but limitations of space compel passing over this campaign other than to say that the Spaniards finally reached their goal, after losing several times the number of men that they had come to rescue. In this fighting General Garcia had his magnificent saddle-horse, of which he was very fond, killed under him.

Gomez now marched to the westward to take charge of operations in the province of Santa Clara. Huntington went with him and was shortly afterward killed in battle. All of the remainder of us artillery officers remained with Garcia, who kept all the guns.

The moral effect of the Guaimaro victory on the Cubans was very great. For the first time they had made assaults on men in trenches and protected by barb-wire entanglements. They were schooling themselves for the far bloodier work at Jiguani and Las Tunas, to be related in the next and closing chapter of these Cuban reminiscences.

IV

A DEFEAT AND A VICTORY

JIGUANI

NEARLY five months had passed since the victory of Guaimaro, and in this time the forces of Garcia had roamed at will through the provinces of Oriente and Camaguey. Large convoys escorted by formidable bodies of Spanish troops moved slowly along the main roads, carrying supplies to the isolated garrisons of the interior, and were harassed and fought from the time of starting until their return. Occasionally a column unhampered by transport would sally out on operations, and move ponderously for a week or so from town to town; but it was never for a moment out of sight of the Cubans, who fought it or not as seemed most expedient. Now and then a band of guerillas, well mounted and thoroughly familiar with the country, would dash by night out of one of the larger garrisons and raid through the country, cutting up such small bodies of insurgents as they might encounter, and making a specialty of hunting out our hospitals and murdering the helpless wounded found in them. These detestable wretches were more mobile than the insurgents themselves, their horses being better fed, and usually managed to return to their home stations. When they were run down, however, it was a fight to the death, quarter being neither asked nor given. On one occasion Major Pablo Menocal, a brother of the chief of staff, while scouting with eighty insurgent cavalry in the Holguin district, encountered a band of sixty guerillas on a raid. He formed line before being discovered and made a furious mounted charge. The guerillas fought desperately, but were driven back into a barb-wire fence and annihilated. Not one escaped, and there were no wounded when it was over. In this encounter both sides had gone back to the days of the Crusades, as not a shot was fired, the long machete doing it all. But Menocal's victory cost him heavily in killed and wounded.

During this period no attacks had been made on Spanish towns, however, but early in March the order had gone forth for a part of the troops in the province of Oriente to concentrate near the town of Jiguani, in the Bayamo district of that province. The days of hardship and hunger had come with a vengeance. The thousands of Cuban families living in the "bush," off the lines of operations of the enemy's columns, were eking out a miserable existence. All the able-bodied men being in the war, the women and children could barely raise enough vegetables to keep off starvation. Clothing could not be obtained at any price, and it was no uncommon sight to see women who had been gently reared whose raiment consisted of a patchwork of gunny sacks, while children of both sexes went as naked as they were born. And day and night they lived in terror of the raids of the merciless guerillas. The insurgent forces were barefooted and clothed in rags and tatters, and were always hungry. In this desolated and starving country the question of feeding the more than four thousand men about to be concentrated for the coming campaign was one that taxed the resources of our leaders to the utmost. The remnants of the great herds of cattle that a few months before had been grazing on the plains of Camaguey were gathered up and driven over the long road to the east of the Cauto. Pack-trains scoured the country, taking from the miserable people the last sweet-potato, ear of corn, or banana that could be found. The prefects, officers of the civil government, were ordered to bend every energy to the task, and did their work thoroughly. In a short time all the units ordered to take part in the coming operations were on the move, and, it being in the dry season, the concentration was rapidly effected, and by the 10th four thousand two hundred of us, well armed but ragged and hungry, were in camp. On the first night after our arrival in the camp we Americans indulged ourselves in a picturesque poker game, some one having found a deck of cards. Gathered about a rubber blanket stretched on the ground, the necessary light being furnished by a few candles stuck onto bayonets, and revolver cartridges being the chips, we played far into the night, an audience of Cubans watching every move. I suppose we might have been in better business, but our recreations were certainly few enough.

No time was to be lost, so the whole force marched toward Jiguani and surrounded the town. By this time we Americans were seasoned campaigners, and had been under fire so many times that going into battle awakened no emotions in our breasts, and we went about the necessary preparations with scant thoughts as to what might happen to us individually. We had seen so much of death and misery that we were in a way hardened, and I believe had become the victims of a sort of fatalism, thinking that the war would last for years and that our chances of seeing home again were pretty small. It did not seem important when the end came or how.

We now had with us a gun that had not been used in the sieges described in the two previous chapters, a twelve-pounder Driggs-Schroeder naval landing gun, one of the inventors of which was the present Admiral Schroeder of the United States navy. This gun came near to the field-piece type, having a long barrel and high velocity. It, of course, could not be packed, but was drawn by mules. Like the guns that we already had, it used fixed ammunition, but unlike them, dispensed with the nuisance of the friction primer, the pull of the lanyard causing a bolt to descend through the breech block and fire the cartridge. This weapon had been purchased with funds raised by Cuban residents of Key West, known among Spanish-speaking people as Cayo Hueso, and so came to be known by that name. We always spoke of it as "Cayo Hueso," just as we would have applied the name to an animate being.

The town of Jiguani was much larger than any we had heretofore attacked, being a local commercial centre of importance. The garrison was about eight hundred strong, consisting mostly of infantry, but with a detachment of artillery and a troop of guerillas. The strongest work, and the one that was really the key to the whole situation, was a very substantial two-story masonry fort known as

El Castillo, the Castle. This was situated on the end of a ridge, about eighty feet above the streets of the town, and was surrounded by formidable trenches and wire entanglements, both of which extended for some distance along the ridge to the northward. Very near the fort, in fact almost under its walls, was a small earthen redoubt. In the upper story of the Castle was an eight-centimetre Krupp gun and on the roof was the heliograph station, used in communicating with the town of Bayamo. Around the town was the usual circle of blockhouses, about a dozen of them, connected by barb-wire fences and surrounded by trenches and entanglements, while in the town itself were several well-fortified barracks and other buildings.

Besides Cayo Hueso we had a Hotchkiss twelve-pounder and a two-pounder, the former being our old friend of Cascorra and Guaimaro, and the latter the gun that had riddled the church on the last day at Guaimaro. The ridge, on one end of which stood the Castle, extended for a considerable distance in a north-westerly direction, and eight hundred yards along it from that work we selected the position for our battery, or rather for the most of it, as it was realized that against these masonry walls one might as well use a bean-shooter as the smaller Hotchkiss. On the night of the 12th a strong parapet with overhead cover and embrasures for two guns was constructed at the principal position, and on the south side of the town, in easy range of several of the blockhouses, a smaller one for the two-pounder. I took command of the main battery and assigned the smaller one to Cox, who had Janney

with him, while Jones, Latrobe, Joyce, and Pennie were
with me.

When dawn came, on a beautiful but very hot day,
the Castle loomed big before us, while down to our right
about five hundred yards was a blockhouse, and beyond
that at a like distance another. The town was in easy
range below us to the right front. The more than four
thousand insurgent infantry and cavalry were all about
the place, the strongest lines being near us on the north
side. Down in the town we could hear the calls of sentries,
the crowing of roosters, and the barking of dogs. If the
garrison had discovered our gun positions they made no
sign. Our guns were loaded and pointed and we sat
about waiting for orders. These came just after sunrise,
and old Cayo Hueso with a crash sent a shell that made a
beautiful burst on the identical spot at which it had been
aimed on the side of the fort. We realized that now we
had something of a gun. In a couple of seconds the
Hotchkiss twelve-pounder let fly and scored a hit, and
then we heard away beyond the Castle the bark of the
little gun stirring up the blockhouses. We sent in two
more shells, both of them bursting against the stone walls
without penetrating. The projectiles from the Driggs-
Schroeder would have breached the wall in a hurry but for
the fact that their fuses were so sensitive that they burst
before the full effects of their blows could be felt. At this
time we saw a cloud of smoke puff from a port-hole in the
upper story of the Castle, and soon heard a rumble as of
a train crossing a bridge, followed by the swish of a shell
as it rushed past us so close that the blast of air was very

perceptible. It missed the left end of the parapet about two feet, and slashed through the tree growth behind us with a noise like a runaway team, cutting off branches and tearing up things generally. A regiment of our infantry had been halted a couple of hundred yards behind us at the foot of the slope, the drop of which just about coincided with the angle of fall of the shell. The result was that the projectile landed among them and burst with a very impressive crash. There was no panic, but the men were quickly ordered out of the dangerous locality, but not until another shell just clearing our parapet had burst among them. We had, in the meantime, sent in a couple more, and the fight was fairly on. We were on the point of concentrating the fire of both guns on the port-hole with the hope of disabling the Krupp, when our attention was called to flashes of light from the top of the fort, the heliograph undoubtedly sending news of the attack to Bayamo, to which station General Linares was known to be en route from Manzanillo with a strong column. The heliograph must be disabled first, and I took a careful sight with Cayo Hueso. The shell cleared the top of the fort, and there was borne to our ears the sound of its explosion in the fields beyond the town. The second shot hit the top of the fort in a perfect line and the smoke of the explosion completely obscured the instrument and the men working it. We thought the job was done, but with superb nerve the operators stuck to their post and the smoke of the explosion had barely drifted away when we again saw the little flashes. The next shell was a centre shot, striking the roof right at the instrument, exploding and making a clean sweep of everything. But the two gallant fellows had not died in vain, for Bayamo had the news. In the meantime the Krupp was sending in its compliments as fast as it could be loaded and fired. The shooting was uncomfortably good, but we had to ignore it for the time. One shell made a square hit on the parapet but exploded without penetrating, disarranging the scenery quite a bit, however. Others would barely clear us and burst in the woods behind after cutting down a few trees, while some fell a few feet short, bursting on the stony ground and showering us with pieces of iron and rock splinters. We fired a few more shells against a particular part of the wall where we hoped by a number of hits to breach it and make a big gap, but in vain. Our shells burst too easily, and we longed for solid shot. The fuses could not be removed, being in the bases of the shells. About now the same thing happened to the twelve-pounder Hotchkiss that had befallen one of those guns at Guaimaro. A defective cartridge was fired, there was a stream of flame from the vent, and a shell stuck hard and fast half-way to the muzzle. It may be said in passing that three months were required to remove it. So now it was Driggs-Schroeder *versus* Krupp on even terms. It was a pretty fight, and with a large and appreciative audience, as owing to the fact that both gun positions were well elevated above the surrounding country everybody in the town and probably half of those in the Cuban lines could see the result of every shot. The enemy's gun did not seem to be so accurate as ours, but its shooting was by no means wild, every shell coming in close, and an occasional one making a hit on the parapet. At a burst of smoke from the Castle the one of us on lookout would call out "Down," and every one, no matter what he might be doing, would throw himself flat on the ground. In a couple of seconds the shell would strike and burst, and then we would leap to our feet and try to give them a couple before they could fire again. The discovery was made that by watching carefully we could discern the enemy's shells up in the air when about half-way to us, and several times when we saw that they had a line on the parapet we succeeded in avoiding them by quick jumping to either the right or left. Before the day was over we had become quite expert in judging the shells and getting out of the way of them. The gun that they were being fired from was a Krupp of one of the older models and of low velocity compared with ours, or this could not have been done. A man would have had to get a mighty early start to dodge a shell from Cayo Hueso, even if he could see it.

For a time we paid no attention to the Krupp other than to avoid being hit by its shells, and confined ourselves to trying to breach the wall below it by hammering a particular spot, knowing that if we succeeded the gun and its detachment would be involved in the catastrophe. But the Spaniards' shooting was becoming better and better, and it was only a question of time until they would land a shell on our sole remaining big gun and take from us the last chance of victory. The Krupp must be put out of action. Very careful sight was taken at the port-hole, which was about four feet in diameter, and the shell struck the lower sill, the smoke of the explosion completely obscuring the embrasure. We hoped that the gun had been disabled, but vainly. But the thing that opened our eyes to possibilities was the fact that this shot loosened some of the masonry where it struck, we having seen some of the fragments fall to the ground. In a minute or so came another shot just as the lanyard of our piece was about to be pulled. The customary dive to cover or vigorous side-stepping took a couple of seconds, and then we sent one straight home. Instead of the usual burst on the outside of the wall a torrent of smoke poured from the embrasure, and the sound of the explosion of our shell was muffled. This shot disabled the Krupp for several hours, and as was subsequently learned killed or wounded all but one of the twelve men serving it. This hit was greeted by a tremendous outburst of cheering from all the Cubans who could see it from the lines about the town. The gun having been disposed of, we determined to go about tearing down the fort in a systematic manner. There was one little matter that required our attention first, however. Although we had heard considerable infantry firing on the south side of the town, there had not been a great deal directed against us with the exception that the blockhouse below us to our right front had kept up a persistent and annoying peppering of our position. We were partially protected from this fire by the lay of the land, but determined to endure the nuisance no longer. Three shots did the business, and sent the survivors of the garrison on a run toward the town, we speeding them up with a shell after they had got a good start. We were so much above them that their trenches had been but little protection, as we could fire right down into them.

The next shot was fired at the lower sill of the embrasure of the Castle, and went as true as if it had been fired at pistol range. Half a wagon-load of masonry fell to the ground and some of it rolled down the hill slope. This brought another outburst of cheering. From that time we fired very slowly and carefully, planting the shots alternately two feet to the left of and below the ever-widening gap, until soon practically the whole corner of the fort had been shot away, and we could see a great pile of débris on the ground. The structure was by this time abandoned, and so weakened that it was deemed inadvisable to waste on it any more of our precious ammunition. So we gave our attention to some of the blockhouses and the fortified buildings in the town, more as an object lesson to their defenders than for any other purpose. During all of this time there were occasional bursts of infantry fire against us, and in one of them General Garcia's chief engineer officer who was returning to head-quarters from a visit to us was killed.

It was known that it was the general's plan to make a night assault, but several of us now went to him and pleaded hard and earnestly in an endeavor to induce him to storm the ridge at once, pointing out that the Castle was abandoned and that the men in the trenches could be so distracted by the shells that we could send in on them at the rate of four a minute that they could be overcome by mere weight of numbers. It was argued that to a certainty nearly the whole length of the ridge would be occupied in force as soon as darkness came on, a thing that could not be done in daylight, as our battery would be on an extension of the left flank of a line so formed and would rake it from end to end. The general discussed the matter freely, but was unyielding, being convinced that the darkness would be of more advantage to him than to the enemy as the assaulting line could make considerable headway before being discovered. Furthermore, his orders had been already promulgated and any change in them now might lead to confusion and misunderstanding. It was a terrible and costly mistake, but mighty few men have waged war without making more grievous errors of judgment.

By ten o'clock the day was dragging and it seemed that there would be but little more for us to do than at the appointed time fire the signal for the assault. We could hear Cox's two-pounder barking away and there was some infantry fire of a desultory nature. The heat was terrific, and we were suffering greatly from thirst, water not being obtainable. Latrobe, who had remained in the position all day though very ill from pernicious malaria, was pretty well done for, but stuck it out. A few yards to the left of the parapet was a tree the shade of which was very inviting, and I went over and sat down under it, leaning against the trunk. In a short time I felt something bite the back of my neck and discovered that a lot of little black ants were skurrying up and down, and so shifted my position away from the tree a foot or two. Not two seconds later a bullet hit the trunk at a point where it would have gone through my body. I suppose I should be a friend of ants, but am not.

And so the hours dragged on until about three o'clock, when, no one being on lookout, we heard the boom of the old Krupp, and a shell passed close over us. Leaping to our feet, we saw a cloud of smoke over the small redoubt near the Castle. The Spaniards had removed the injured gun from the fort after the shot entering the embrasure had disabled it, repaired the damage and mounted it in the small earthwork. Hot, thirsty, and hungry as we were, we sprang to Cayo Hueso to begin anew the artillery duel. The enemy's new gun position was infinitely better than his first, as the piece would be shoved up so that only its muzzle appeared over the low parapet of the redoubt, the recoil after firing carrying it down to safety. Time and again we tried to dismount the gun, but to no avail. It was loaded before being placed in the firing position, so that it was exposed for only the couple of seconds necessary to take aim. If we fired on the appearance of its muzzle, which could usually be detected by means of glasses, the gun had been fired and had recoiled to cover before our projectile could reach it. Every one of our shots struck the redoubt at the exact spot or landed in it on a perfect line, and a score of times, as we saw the Krupp's position fairly buried under a shower of earth, we cheered wildly and congratulated ourselves on having put it out of business. But as certain as fate in a few moments the black muzzle would reappear for an instant and be followed by a puff of smoke. Our gun, already being loaded and aimed, would be fired, and we would run into the open in order to be able to the more easily jump out of the way of the shell. As our parapet had by this time been badly battered, and all the enemy's shots were aimed at it in the hope of dismounting our gun, the open was much the safer place. There was one thing that impressed itself on our minds, and that was that side-stepping shells from a breech-loading rifle at eight hundred yards range was no business for rheumatics. Joyce finally got tired of these jumps to the open and announced that he was going to stand his ground. So when the next warning yell came he sat down with his back to the parapet. The shell landed squarely on the top, and burst about two feet above his head. Joyce was fairly covered with a few shovels-full of earth, and a couple of fragments fell in his lap. He arose very deliberately and began to brush his clothes, remarking in a bored way that it was no way to treat a man who had gone to the trouble to dress neatly for this occasion. But the next time he accompanied the rest of us. In front of our parapet about ten feet, and just enough to the left of Cayo Hueso's line of fire not to be injured by its blast, stood a young palm tree about twenty feet high. Shells had barely missed it many times, and we had speculated on the probability of it surviving the battle, but now its turn came, it being struck about three feet above the ground and cut down. The shell exploded from the force of the blow and threw fragments all over Jones and myself, we having jumped to the left when we saw where it was going to strike. This bootless duel kept up until nearly dark, each gun trying in vain to dismount the other. The Spanish gun was quite safe owing to its ability to kick down a slope to cover, but how old Cayo Hueso went through that day without being wrecked is a most unaccountable thing. Certainly fifty shells struck or passed within fifteen feet of it.

In due time orders were received to aim the gun at the ruins of the Castle while it was still sufficiently light, and to fire at exactly ten o'clock. This shot, like the last one at Guaimaro, was to be the signal for the assault. We of the artillery had almost reached the limit of endurance from heat, thirst, and hunger, and dragged ourselves down to camp for a scanty meal, but not for sleep. For there was to be no sleep for human beings at Jiguani that night except for the poor fellows whose bodies in a few short hours were to litter the streets of the town and the slopes of that fatal ridge.

About half-past nine, it now being very dark, we returned to the scene of our grilling day's work and awaited the appointed hour. Without exception we had forebodings of disaster, and well we might, for the commanding officer of this post was the one who had made such a game fight against us at Cascorra six months before. The assault was to be made by about two thousand men. On our right twelve hundred under various leaders were to capture the blockhouses and trenches on the north side and enter the town from that direction. The assault on the ridge and Castle was under the general direction of General Enrique Collazo, who had at his disposal eight hundred men. Of these, six hundred and fifty under Augustin Cebreco were to go up the side of the ridge on our left, while one hundred and fifty under Lieutenant-Colonel Charles Hernandez were to assault the Castle direct up the south end of the ridge, directly opposite the side that we had been battering. This officer, one of the bravest and most capable in the insurgent forces, is well known to many Americans, having been subsequently Director of Roads and Posts during the period of intervention. General Collazo in person accompanied Hernandez's detachment. What we had feared happened. As soon as darkness came on half of the garrison had quietly moved up from the town and occupied the southern half of the ridge in a close line.

As for the last half-hour before the assault at Guaimaro, the silence after the uproar of the day was oppressive. At last our watches marked ten o'clock. I stepped over to Cayo Hueso and pulled the lanyard, and before the crash had died out of our ears a shell bursting against the walls of the Castle lighted up the ruins for an instant. We climbed up on the parapet and strained our ears for the first sound. For a moment the silence was absolute, and then down to our left where Cebreco's men were waiting we could hear a noise like that made by a drove of cattle breaking through brush. Then we made out a few commands and immediately afterward heard a great roar of yells and cries of *"Adelante, Adelante, Arriba, Arriba,"* as they broke into the open and started up. In an instant the whole south half of the ridge was lit up as if by a thousand fire-flies, and a moment later we could make out Cebreco's front by the flashes of the rifles of his men, as firing rapidly and yelling like madmen they pressed up the slope. But it was more than they could endure, and soon they threw themselves on the ground and kept up a fire fight with the Spaniards on the summit, two hundred yards above them. While this uproar was going on the twelve hundred men on our right carried all the blockhouses on their front and reached the shelter of the buildings of the town. In the face of a murderous fire Hernandez rushed his men up the south end of the ridge to within a stone's throw of the trenches around the Castle and for seven terrible hours held on to the position gained. We artillerymen sat on our parapet listening in awed silence to the hellish uproar and wondering whether it would ever end. It must be remembered that the nearly three thousand Spaniards and Cubans using breech-loaders, the most of them magazine rifles, could do as much firing in a specified time as ten times their number armed with the muzzleloaders of our Civil War days. We thought that through the din we could make out the drumming of machine-guns, but I have never learned whether the Spaniards were supplied with them on that occasion or not. But this could not last forever. Cebreco's men began to give up some of the more advanced positions they had reached and to retire down the slope at the foot of which they were re-formed. The fighting in the town after the Cubans penetrated it and began to attack the barracks added to the pandemonium of sound, and we saw flames shooting up from houses that had been fired either accidentally or intentionally.

Although Cebreco had been repulsed the day was by no means lost, as the insurgents had the upper hand in the town and Hernandez was hanging on like grim death to the ground he had gained. And now came the disaster, and from a most unsuspected source. A messenger from the scouts watching the Bayamo road raced into camp with the news that Linares's big column was close at hand and would arrive shortly after daybreak. To be caught as we were with all our forces scattered about the town and with many of them inside it, would spell inevitable defeat. General Garcia was in an agony of suspense as to what he should do, but finally sent officers to call in all the troops and to concentrate them at daylight at a certain near-by point. Cebreco's men and the two thousand that had not taken part in the assault were easily got at, and began their march through the inky darkness. The withdrawal of the men who had penetrated the town was naturally a problem of great difficulty, as they had scattered to loot or were engaged in isolated fights. The first messenger sent to Hernandez was killed in trying to reach him. After waiting for hours, and wondering why he did not come in, the general sent another, who at five o'clock in the morning gave Hernandez his orders, and that courageous officer withdrew with the handful that remained to him. Before daylight it was all over, and we brought the guns back to the general rendezvous.

The sun rose over a sorrowful scene. Our wounded were everywhere, the few surgeons doing what they could to alleviate their sufferings. Our gray-haired and much-loved chieftain sat apart with bowed head, his grief being made the more poignant by the receipt of information to the effect that Linares's column was still miles away, a force of guerillas scouting on his front having in the darkness been mistaken for the main body, so that his withdrawal had been unnecessary. In general, the Cuban scouting service was excellent. In nearly two years I heard of but two false reports being brought in, and this was one of them.

Our losses were heavy. Of one hundred and fifty men, Hernandez had twenty-four killed and of course many more wounded, although the proportion of killed to wounded was unusually large because of the fact that some of the wounded lying for hours under fire were hit several times. His losses reached nearly seventy per cent, but for hours that must have seemed endless he had held his men to their work just outside the impenetrable barb-wire entanglements and had withdrawn only under orders. Cebreco lost twenty per cent in killed and wounded. The losses in these two commands, combined with those of the twelve hundred who had entered the town, brought the total up to about four hundred, just a few short of the losses of Lawton's division of more than six thousand Americans at El Caney.

VICTORIA DE LAS TUNAS

Nearly six months had passed since our futile attack on the town of Jiguani. Garcia's forces, more hungry and more ragged then ever and considerably reduced by battle casualties, continued to range the *Departamento del Oriente*, harassing Spanish convoys and columns sent out on operations and maintaining a sleepless vigilance about all the garrisoned towns. The enemy had long ceased to leave the protection of his forts and blockhouses in columns of less than three or four thousand men, except that the guerillas from time to time ventured out on brief raids.

The march of nearly four thousand of us to the Bay of
Banes to meet the third expedition of the filibuster
Laurada, the fight between the Cubans and the Spanish gun-boat *Jorge Juan* anchored close to shore, the
encounters with General Luque's powerful column sent
to take the expedition referred to, the blowing up by
means of a mine of a small Spanish gun-boat on the
Cauto River, resulting in the death of every one of her
crew of thirty-four, the all but successful attempt on
a transport at the entrance to the Bay of Banes, our
disastrous attack on the town of Sama, and many other
stirring events cannot be told here. Suffice it to say,
however, that this expedition of the *Laurada*, the larg-
est that reached the island during the insurrection,
brought us a new weapon, the newly invented Sims-
Dudley dynamite gun, one Hotchkiss twelve-pounder,
one Colt's automatic gun, three thousand five hundred
rifles with nearly three million cartridges, a considerable
supply of artillery ammunition, some medical stores, and
such sundries as dynamite and machetes.

After the Bay of Banes expedition the various organizations of Garcia's force had scattered to their respective
districts and had engaged in minor operations against
the enemy whenever he ventured outside the towns. In
August orders were issued for a concentration in order to
attack the town of Victoria de las Tunas, in the northern
part of the province of Oriente and very near the Camaguey line. This place was far stronger than any we had
yet attempted to take, but had the fatal weakness that the
town, which lay on a perfectly level plain, was dominated

on the south side by a low ridge within easy artillery range. Doubtless the Spaniards would have been glad to include this ridge in their line of defence, but this would have made it so long that with the garrison available it could not have been strongly held at any one point. The garrison consisted of about eight hundred infantry, a detachment of artillery with two Krupp field-pieces, and a troop of forty-seven guerillas. This force was distributed among twenty-two defensive positions. The outer line consisted of nineteen *fortines* or blockhouses of the usual type and a large brick building which had been a cavalry barrack, and was known as the *Cuartel de la Caballeria*. This structure, the first to be attacked, lay directly south of the centre of the town. Inside the outer line of the defences, and at the north-west corner of the town, was the *Cuartel de la Infanteria*, or infantry barracks, a massive masonry building about two hundred feet long and having extending southward from its west end an L about sixty feet in length. At the north-east corner of the town was the Telegraph Fort, a two-story brick structure surrounded by a brick wall five feet high, this wall enclosing something less than an acre of ground. Many buildings were loop-holed, and everywhere were trenches and barb-wire entanglements.

The insurgent organizations affected by this concentration order aggregated about five thousand eight hundred men. Of these about two thousand were held some distance south of the town to watch the road to Bayamo, a like number under Rabi being to the eastward to watch Holguin, from which point relief was most likely to come. In case a relieving column should issue from either of these places the appropriate force was to make a delaying fight until the other could join it. The troops that were to make the attack on the garrison consisted of eighteen hundred men under the direct command of our chieftain.

We had six guns, as follows: One Sims-Dudley dynamite gun, our old friend Cayo Hueso, two Hotchkiss twelve-pounders, and two two-pounders of the same make. On this occasion a dynamite gun was for the first time to be used in war. The projectile of this weapon consisted of a cylindrical brass case about two inches in diameter and eighteen inches long, containing a bursting charge of five pounds of nitro-gelatine, the whole shell weighing ten pounds. A small charge of smokeless powder was used to compress the air by means of which the projectile was expelled from the gun. The powder charge, of course, could not act directly on this explosive, or the gun would have been blown to atoms at the first shot. The initial velocity of the piece was low, only about six hundred feet per second, so that it had to be fired at a considerable elevation for all but very short ranges. The projectile was easily deflected by wind, so that at the longer ranges it was difficult to do good shooting. The shell could easily be seen in the air, resembling a swallow in flight. Against earthworks and massive buildings the gun was not of much use other than for its terrifying effect, but it blew blockhouses and the weaker class of buildings to rubbish in a few shots.

On August 27 the Cubans began closing in about the town. The Spaniards were on the alert, and on a couple of occasions sent shells from their battery at groups of men who exposed themselves. On the night of that day our artillery parapets were constructed. On the low ridge south of the town, five hundred yards from the *Cuartel de la Caballeria* and about equally distant from the *Concepcion fortin* to the east of it, was our main position, a parapet about sixty feet long. No head cover was made, as we had learned from experience that it could not long survive the blast of our own guns. The parapet was made with the greatest care, as it was known that it would have to withstand a very severe artillery fire. In this position were placed the dynamite gun, the Driggs-Schroeder rifle, and the two Hotchkiss twelve-pounders. Half a mile to our right was constructed another battery, with two two-pounder Hotchkiss guns to bear on some of the lighter blockhouses. This battery was commanded by Jones, who had with him Pennie and a number of Cubans. The larger battery was under my personal command, and I also did the sighting of the Driggs-Schroeder. Janney and Devine, with a number of Cubans, had the two Hotchkiss twelve-pounders. Four young Cubans who had come down to the island on the Roloff expedition had been assigned to the artillery with the rank of lieutenant. These were Portuondo, Poey, Marti, and Sedano. The former had charge of the dynamite gun. Joyce had returned to the United States on leave, and so was not with us, while Latrobe, having been appointed to the staff of General Collazo, was in the force to the eastward, and so missed the fight.

We all went to our respective positions early in the night and remained there watching the construction of the cover behind which we were the next day to fight. When daylight came on the morning of the 28th the mists rose slowly from the level plain on which the town was built and disclosed a scene of absorbing interest. Five hundred yards to our front and about thirty feet below us lay the *Cuartel de la Caballeria* with its trenches and maze of barb-wire entanglements. Seven hundred yards beyond it loomed the masonry walls of the far stronger *Cuartel de la Infanteria*. Twelve hundred yards to our right front was the Telegraph Fort, with the main part of the town directly in line. Blockhouses were everywhere. There was absolute silence, and not a sign of life was to be seen. General Garcia had established his head-quarters on the reverse slope of the ridge about sixty yards to the right rear of our position. Colonels Menocal and Garcia remained the greater part of the day in the battery. At last the former gave the word to open on the *Cuartel de la Caballeria*. The guns had been already loaded and pointed, and to the dynamite gun was given the honor of leading the ball. There was no little uneasiness as to what would happen when this uncanny weapon was fired, and there was not much of a tendency to stand too close to it. When the lanyard was pulled the gun gave what sounded like a loud cough, and jumped a little. We were in some doubt as to whether it had gone off or not, but looking toward the *Cuartel de la Caballeria* saw a most astounding spectacle. A section of the brick wall was blown in, making a hole large enough to have admitted a good-sized truck, while the sound of a dull explosion was borne to our ears. A cloud of dust and fragments of the

wall rose fifty feet in air and descended in a shower on
the roof. We raised a great cheer, which was taken up
and re-echoed by our people all about the town. For the
moment we stood so spellbound and exultant over the
results of this shot that we all but forgot the other guns,
but only for the instant. The dust was still settling down
over the scene of the explosion when every man rushed
to his place, and the other three guns crashed out,
making a wall of smoke in front of our position. Then
we heard the cracks of Jones's two-pounders to our right.
In no time the battle was fairly on. From the various
forts and blockhouses came a crackling sound that soon
swelled almost to a roar, and in less than a minute a
big puff of smoke rose from a gun-pit about two hundred
yards beyond the *Cuartel de la Caballeria* and a little
to its right, and almost instantly a shrapnel burst in
front of our parapet, showering it with fragments and
bullets. Then came a puff of smoke and a boom from
another pit near the first one, and a second shell barely
cleared our heads, bursting a few yards to the rear. For
the time we paid no attention to the enemy's guns, but
continued to fire on the cavalry barracks. While the
shells from our rifled breech-loaders made very respectable holes in the walls, those from the dynamite gun created
havoc, every shot blowing quantities of bricks and roofing
tiles high in the air. Very wisely, the garrison had vacated
the building after the first shot, and now from the trenches
around it maintained on us a hot and persistent fire. The
barrack having been wrecked in short order, there was
nothing to be gained by a further bombardment of its

ruins, and we aimed at the trenches with the double purpose of throwing shells into them and of breaking up the
wire entanglements immediately in front. Our elevation
above them made it comparatively easy for us to burst
shells right in the trenches, and as we were using so many
guns, and at so short a range, the Spaniards could not keep
up firing and save themselves by squatting down on the
flash of a gun. The result was that we fairly smothered
the fire of the hundred men in those trenches, and turned
our attention elsewhere. All of this time we were being
pelted by shells as fast as two Krupp breech-loaders
could be served. Shells were bursting all about us, and
occasionally one would wreck a portion of the parapet. I
hope it will not be taken as unseemly boasting, but as
stating an absolute fact, when I say that far from feeling
any uneasiness we were as cool as cucumbers, and considered that we were having the time of our lives. But
it had taken participation in a good many stiff fights to
bring us to such a state of mind. Above the noise of our
fight we could not now hear the reports of Jones's guns,
but could see the puffs of smoke from them as they engaged the Telepraph Fort and the blockhouses in its
vicinity. Shortly after our fight had begun it had developed that the weeds on our front were interfering with
the sighting of the guns. I considered cutting them out
of the way a soldier's and not an officer's job, and called on
several of the rank and file, but they were so slow in re-
sponding that Janney ran out into the open and with his
machete did the work, utterly oblivious of the bullets and
shells that were coming in thick and fast. At this time

something went wrong with the breech mechanism of one of the Hotchkiss twelve-pounders, and for the time being we were reduced to three guns in the main battery. The enemy's guns must now be attended to, or we would soon have no parapet left, and there was much uneasiness lest a shell should strike the dynamite gun while it was loaded and blow up the whole battery and everybody in it. So we switched our fire from the trenches around the cavalry barracks to the gun-pits, but as soon as the shells began to strike around them both pieces were dragged out of action and hidden behind near-by buildings. To our right front, and distant only five hundred yards, was the Concepcion blockhouse, the garrison of which had with a strange fatuousness remained inside the structure instead of taking to the trenches, and were firing rapidly from the port-holes of the lower story. But their time came quickly. The dynamite gun was dragged from behind the parapet in order that it could be brought to bear, and careful aim taken. When it gave its characteristic cough we saw the projectile sail gracefully through the air and strike the blockhouse squarely in the centre. The shell penetrated and burst inside, killing every one of the sixteen defenders. The structure was all but demolished, portions of the roof being blown a hundred feet in air.

One of the few Americans serving with the Cubans, and not attached to the artillery, was Joseph Napoleon Chapleau, who had the rank of lieutenant-colonel. As his name would indicate, Chapleau was of French descent, and he had all the characteristics of his race. He was volatile and dashing, and had made a reputation for dare-devil exploits. The Americans whose service under Garcia antedated mine knew him well, but I had not met him until the Bay of Banes campaign. On this occasion he was with some infantry just to our right. When he saw the disaster to the Concepcion blockhouse he took his cue and waited for no orders. With about fifty men he rushed it under a hot fire from the trenches around the cavalry barracks. There was not room for all his men in the trenches, and so Chapleau and some of them fought on the outside, exchanging shots with those who now opened on them from several positions. Chapleau himself, using a rifle and encouraging the men with him, received a wound that cut a blood-vessel in his neck. He was brought back under fire and attended by a surgeon attached to General Garcia's head-quarters. The general with his staff was only a short distance to the right rear of our battery, and as soon as it was learned that Chapleau had been brought in wounded I stepped over to inquire as to his condition. There I saw the general and his staff, standing uncovered and with bowed heads, while the blood gushed in torrents from the wounded man's throat, drenching the surgeon who was attempting in vain to stop its flow. Chapleau, perfectly conscious, was muttering, "It is finished," "It is finished," "It is all over," his voice growing gradually weaker until his head sank down on his breast, and another brave man had died a soldier's death. The scene just described is such a one as we have all seen on the stage in melodramas and military plays, and have always thought overdone and unreal. But within a stone's throw was a battery in action, and as Chapleau sank into the last sleep with the silent and uncovered men about him, the last sounds he heard were the booming of its guns and the crackle of the Mausers and the whistling of their bullets while the wisps of smoke blowing back from the battery gave a setting that could not be had on any stage.

The men who had taken the Concepcion blockhouse held on to it until the end, although under heavy fire from time to time. The fast work had heated our guns until I believe eggs could have been fried on their barrels, and it was necessary to suspend fire for awhile, this being feasible as we thought we had scared the Krupp guns out of the fight. Our parapet was badly shattered and at one end nearly demolished, but was still serviceable. The only thing that had saved us was that the enemy had used shrapnel as well as common shell, and these former, often bursting by means of time fuses in front of the parapet, had done it but little damage. While we were resting, allowing the guns to cool and taking stock of the wreckage, to our great surprise the Krupps reopened on us from a new position somewhat in rear of the old gun-pits, and we went for them in a hurry. Portuondo landed a shell from the dynamite gun squarely under one of them. The explosion killed every man serving the piece and completely wrecked it, shattering the carriage and one wheel. After the surrender we examined this gun with the greatest interest. One peculiar fact was that the minute fragments of the thin brass case that contained the bursting charge had been blown into the steel barrel so hard that they remained there and made it look as if it had been inlaid with gold. The other gun "dusted" for cover before we could hit it, and a little later fired several shots from the streets, but never more than one from the same place. Finally it was removed to a pit near the Telegraph Fort, and from time to time fired on us until it met its fate from old Cayo Hueso. We now began to take shots at the various forts and blockhouses, giving every one two or three in order to get the ranges of all, and then deliberately destroyed several of the latter. It was now discovered that the dynamite gun could not be depended on for work at over nine hundred yards range, as its velocity was not sufficient to make it accurate. Several shots from it fired at the Telegraph Fort fell on the roof of the hospital, which was in direct line, and, as we afterward learned, created a panic among the sick and wounded. At this juncture some one called attention to what seemed to be a white flag flying from the roof of one of the buildings of the town. By a mere coincidence the Spanish infantry fire died down at the same time. Captain Cardenas of the staff mounted his horse, and holding aloft a white flag rode into the town, passing within a few rods of the wrecked *Cuartel de la Caballeria.* Cardenas was allowed to enter unopposed, and upon inquiring as to the meaning of the flag found that no one had seen it until he pointed it out. It was discovered that a Chinese shopkeeper, hoping that the emblem of his country might save him from our shells, had hoisted this work of art, which was a black dragon on a white ground. The trouble with his flag was that it was very old, and the dragon had washed out to such a degree that it could be detected only by minute inspection. The Spanish commander had it hauled down at once. The officers crowded about Cardenas and inquired as to the nature of the terrible bombs that were being thrown against their defences, and were told that they were from a dynamite gun. It seems that they had never heard of the weapon. The Spanish commander took advantage of this interview with Cardenas to ask for permission for all the women and children to leave the town. This was granted, and all firing was suspended until the sad procession of a hundred or more, weeping and wailing and wringing their hands, had passed over the ridge just to the right of our battery, at which they cast frightened glances. They were the families of Spanish residents and of the guerillas. It was a sight to unnerve the best of us.

We now fired slowly and carefully at the two strongest positions, the *Cuartel de la Infanteria* and the Telegraph Fort. The walls of the former were too strong for our shells, which burst on the outside, though we managed to do damage by landing several on the roof. The latter was exceedingly hard to hit except on its upper portion because of the hospital being in direct line. The remaining Krupp now opened on us from excellent cover and a well-screened position near the Telegraph Fort, and did good shooting, the gun detachment evidently being cooler than they had been while fighting at the shorter ranges. To dismount this gun had to be the work of the Driggs-Schroeder, as it was beyond the range of the dynamite gun and better shooting would be required than could be done with the Hotchkiss twelve-pounder. I aimed a number of shots very carefully, and though every burst seemed to be right on the spot, it would be only a moment until another flash would presage the coming of a shell. It will be recalled that at Jiguani we had taken pride in our ability to get out of the way of the shells from the Krupp used there, but these guns were of much higher velocity. At the ranges at which they had been fought earlier in the day the shell would follow the flash so quickly that one scarcely had time to move, but now at twelve hundred yards one could dive to cover if he lost no time. Immediately after sighting Cayo Hueso I had been climbing part-way up on the parapet to the windward of the smoke to observe the effects of my own shots. Whenever in this position I saw the flash of the enemy's gun I would yell "Down!" and would drop into one of the short ditches with the others. Finally I took a foolish notion that this getting down with such haste looked undignified, and that I would do no more of it. So when the next flash came I gave the warning cry and stood my ground. A couple of seconds later I was literally hurled backward through the air for fifteen or twenty feet, landing on my head and shoulders and being half buried under earth and poles, and at almost the same instant heard the explosion of the shell. I heard Menocal cry out, "My God, he is cut in two!" and a second or so later was half drowned under a deluge of filthy water. Colonel Garcia had picked up a bucket containing the water in which the sponge used in swabbing out one of the guns from time to time had been dipped, and had poured it over me. About a year ago I inquired of him as to the object of this well-meant attention, and was informed that it had been the only thing handy, and that water is always good for people. This having been the color and something like the consistency of printers' ink, I certainly was not a very inspiring object when helped to my feet, and was not fit to appear in polite society without a change of raiment and a bath. The shell had pierced the parapet about two feet from me, and had burst some twenty feet beyond. But my revenge was coming, and in about two shots more the offending gun was dismounted and the enemy left without artillery.

It was well on in the afternoon of a wild and stirring day when Menocal told me that the trenches around the cavalry barracks were to be assaulted and that the guns would support the attack until the last moment. Owing to the close and accurate work required, the dynamite gun could not be used, but Janney took one of the Hotchkiss twelve-pounders and I the Driggs-Schroeder. The assault was to be made by the Victoria Regiment, and was to be led by Colonel Carlos Garcia of the staff. This organization, about three hundred strong, had lain all day in a shallow draw two hundred yards in front of us and three hundred from the position to be attacked. For hours the shells of the artillery duel had swished only a few feet over their heads. For a few moments we shelled the trenches as rapidly as the guns could be served. I heard some one cry out, "There they go!" and saw two lines of men emerge from their cover and rush toward the front, yelling like madmen and firing with great rapidity. The next moment was certainly the most intense in the lives of any of us serving the guns. The slightest mistake might result in landing a shell among our own people. I know that, inured as I was to scenes of war, I fairly shook with excitement, and kept saying to myself, "Keep cool, keep cool." In a very short time the charge reached the maze of entanglements. Our shells, plunging at the rate of three a minute from each gun into the trenches, were demoralizing the defenders to such an extent that they could do but little firing, but from a trench on its right the attacking regiment was brought under a hot flank fire at seven hundred yards range, and suffered severely. A number of the officers having been shot down, and it seeming impossible to get through the entanglements, some confusion arose. The men began to bunch up and lie down. Of course our shells, barely clearing their heads and bursting thirty yards in front of them, did not add to their equanimity. It looked as if the gallant attack must fail, and that it was only a question of drawing out those who could be saved from the wreck, when Menocal and two other officers of the staff mounted their horses and at a dead run rode into the charge, actually coming within thirty or forty yards of the trenches before their horses all went down killed and Menocal had his leg shattered. But the other two officers, with Colonel Garcia and those of the regiment, rose to their feet and, with cries of *"Al machete,"* rushed into the barb wire. The men followed their lead, and with their machetes began to hack frantically at the wires, and in a few moments had cut their way through. We had continued our artillery fire until this time, but now were glad to cease. The Spaniards took advantage of the opportunity to escape while the Cubans were getting through the entanglements, and under cover of the ruins of the building reached the town, and were distributed among the other defences. They had left behind a very considerable number of killed and wounded.

All of us Americans, in common with many of our Cuban comrades, were suffering from a very severe form of malaria, and took it as a matter of course that about every other day we were to go through the racking experience of a burning fever with its accompanying delirium and the depressing chill in which it seemed that every man was trying to shake his teeth out. At this juncture I felt mine coming, and knew that in a short time I must be unconscious and delirious, and so turned the battery over to Janney, and led by my faithful orderly, fifteen-year-old Sergeant Cecilio Betancourt, stumbled back to the head-quarters camp, distant half a mile. During my ravings, while imagining I was another person, I could hear a long-continued roar of infantry fire punctuated by cannon shots. Finally came the welcome unconsciousness, and when I awoke late at night there were no people near except Sergeant Betancourt and my striker, Juan Gonzalez. About ten o'clock I felt able to mount my horse, and riding back to the artillery position found that all the guns were gone. A few men who happened to be in the vicinity informed me that they had been taken into the town. We rode down past the ruins of the *Cuartel de la Caballeria*, making inquiries from persons encountered en route, and I finally rejoined my command. The roar heard during my delirium was occasioned by the Spanish sortie, made in an attempt to retake the works lost and probably with the intention, if successful, of sweeping over the artillery position. The attack had been repulsed after severe fighting. There was more or less desultory firing going on all of the time, the Cubans having loop-holed a number of the houses to facilitate their operations against those of the Spanish works that had not yet been taken. The whole force of insurgents, with the exception of those men stationed to escape on the north, were now in the town in the shelter of the houses. The capture of the cavalry barracks and the Concepcion blockhouse had opened the chain of defences on the south side, and the insurgents in making their entry had taken by assault a number of the blockhouses adjacent to these two works on either side. So there had arisen a peculiar situation, in that the remaining defences, which included two of the strongest works, were to be attacked from the interior of the town instead of from its outside.

There would be no use for the guns until morning, so, hungry, tired, and sick, we sank down on pavements or on brick floors to get what rest we could. The only one of us artillery officers hit during the day was Lieutenant Francisco Sedano, killed late in the afternoon.

With the breaking of day on the 29th we began prospecting for positions from which to attack the remaining forts. The strongest work was the *Cuartel de la Infanteria.* Its masonry walls were three feet thick, loop-holed, and defended by two hundred men. The main business street of the town could not be crossed by us, being swept by the fire of this work at one end and by that of the Telegraph Fort at the other, so that in our operations we were confined to the south half of the town. No building could be found from which a fire could be delivered that would strike the walls of the big barracks at right angles, so we were obliged to content ourselves with a warehouse distant from it one hundred and fifty yards, but so situated that our shells would strike the walls at an angle of thirty degrees, a most serious disadvantage, as much of the force of their blows would be lost. The ammunition of the Driggs-Schroeder was nearly exhausted, and as it was thought best not to try to use all the guns, embrasures were made for two, the dynamite gun and one of the Hotchkiss twelve-pounders. The latter had to be made very large, as the barrel of the piece was not long enough for the muzzle to clear the wall, which would have been shattered by the blast. The guns had to be dismounted to get them through the doorway, but by ten o'clock were in position. The protection was the best we had ever fought behind, we being perfectly safe from infantry fire except for such bullets as might come through the port-holes. But we had a sneaking fear lest the enemy had another Krupp up his sleeve. If he had, it would have been over with us in short order, as the walls of the warehouse could have been breached very quickly. The breaking through of the port-holes for our two guns had been the signal for a hot fire from the line of loop-holes in the great barrack which loomed up across two vacant lots. We kept under cover and allowed this spurt to die out and then gave it to them. I had had a small observation port-hole cut for myself, and saw the two projectiles strike. The Hotchkiss shell glanced from the wall and then burst. That from the dynamite gun made a terrific explosion, but the result was about the same as would be caused by throwing an egg against a house. There was a fine spatter and nothing else. Not a stone was displaced by either shot. But the moral effect of the explosions of the nitro-gelatine bombs was in time to do the work. The defenders of the building poured such a fire against our embrasures that the greatest care had to be used in serving the guns. Immediately on being discharged each piece would be dragged out of danger, loaded, and carefully run into position again. A moment's respite in the fire would give the few seconds necessary to take aim. On the smooth concrete floor the Hotchkiss cut the most astounding antics. In spite of brake ropes it would recoil clear to the opposite wall, and once turned over and bent the sight, which we had got into the bad habit of not removing for each shot. And so it went on all of a long, tiresome, and dreary day. From illness and hunger and as a result of the exhausting work of the preceding day, we were in a half-dazed condition, and could keep on our feet with difficulty. Yesterday had been my day with the fever, and to-day some of my comrades took their turn, and sank on the floor to let it work its devilish will. For the several reasons given our fire was exceedingly slow. During the day we got in twenty-eight shots from the dynamite gun and about forty from the Hotchkiss. The most of our fire had been concentrated on certain spots in the hope of weakening the wall, but to no avail. Several of the stone columns in front of the building were shattered, and toward the last some shells from the dynamite gun, landed on the roof by most careful aiming, had terrified the defenders by showering them with tiling and broken timbers. Devine, becoming disgusted with the work of the artillery, borrowed a Mauser and spent an hour or two at a loop-hole of his own, sharp-shooting at those of the enemy. More or less infantry fire between the Spaniards and Cubans at other positions had taken place during the day, but at no time reached any great volume.

At last night came again to give us some rest and sleep, and we stretched ourselves on the hard floor. About ten o'clock it seemed that the Spaniards in the barrack had been struck by some sort of a panic, probably believing that the Cubans were about to assault, and opened a terrific fire. This was taken up by the Telegraph Fort and the uncaptured blockhouses. This stirred up the Cubans, and they began to reply, and for an hour or two both sides kept up a most shocking waste of ammunition. We of the artillery listened to the uproar for awhile, and then went to sleep in the midst of it.

When daylight came again the fight had lasted forty-eight hours, but the end was near at hand. Very early in the morning a soldier had escaped from the *cuartel* and brought to Colonel Menocal the information that he was an emissary from his comrades, who had come to the conclusion that they had reached the limit of human endurance. They were in sore straits from hunger, thirst, and fatigue, and their nerve had been completely shattered by the explosions of the nitro-gelatine bombs. The commander and the other officers would fight to the end, but if he would take possession at daybreak they would throw down their arms. It was evident that they were not made of the stuff of the defenders of Cascorra or of Baler in the Philippines. But they knew the situation to be absolutely hopeless, and did not propose to be sacrificed to save the honor of their officers.

The sun had not yet risen when a few officers, including Janney and myself, left the warehouse and walked into the open. We felt a bit ticklish as we approached the grim line of loop-holes, but no flash came from them, and at a run we went over the mound of earth protecting the great gateway. The door swung open and the haggard and wasted men, barely able to stand, threw down their arms, while their officers looked on in helpless astonishment. But they accepted the inevitable, and made no resistance.

I was so hungry that I had pretty nearly lost all regard for the proprieties, and made a quick run for the kitchen, a Spanish soldier showing me where the officers' provisions were kept. The first thing I found was some sausages in cans, and cutting one of these open by one blow of my machete, began to get at the contents in the most primitive way imaginable. I saw two Spanish officers looking at me with disgust plainly evident on their features, but feeling sure that I would never meet them socially, went on appeasing my hunger.

During the night the insurgents had penetrated the north part of the town by running a trench six feet deep across the main street, swept by the fire of the two strongest works, and swarming into the houses had opened fire on the two blockhouses occupied by the local detachment of guerillas. The defenders of these two positions saw the fall of the *Cuartel de la Infanteria*, and knew that it was only a question of time until the deadly dynamite gun from the shelter of near-by houses would blow their flimsy blockhouses to bits. They were in a terrible position, as they could not expect the quarter given the Spanish regulars. Their captain came out to ask what terms would be given them. The laconic reply was, "The same that you have given the helpless wounded in our hospitals." It was merely a choice of the form of death, so they marched out, threw down their arms, and to their credit met their fate with courage. They were cut down with the machete. It was a shocking spectacle, but it was retributive justice if there is such a thing, for these men had never known what mercy was. Other blockhouses, garrisoned by regulars, now gave up one by one, and at eight o'clock only the Telegraph Fort held out. Its brick walls would quickly yield to our artillery, and Menocal and I went to select a gun position. This was found in the residence of the surgeon of the garrison, a brick building directly across the street.

And now occurred a lamentable tragedy. Lieutenant-Colonel Angel Guardia, only twenty-four years of age, had obtained some liquor from one of the looted stores, and had taken several stiff drinks. Tired and famished as he was, the stuff had gone straight to his brain and converted him into a madman. He walked boldly out into the street within fifty feet of the walls of the fort, began flourishing his machete and cursing the Spaniards, telling them that they had murdered his father in the Ten Years' War and that he wanted nothing better than to get at them. The unfortunate man's comrades called to him and begged him to come back. The Spanish officers pleaded with him to return, stating that they did not wish to kill him. But he was lost to all reason. Finally a sharp command rang out from behind the brick wall, fire spurted from the loop-holes, and the poor fellow fell riddled with bullets. He was the last man killed at Las Tunas. It speaks well for General Garcia's sense of justice that he did not hold the commander of the Telegraph Fort to account for this incident.

We of the artillery, gathered in the parlor of the residence of the surgeon, breached the wall from the inside and looked through at our expected target, distant only sixty feet. Men had been sent to bring up a gun, and while we were waiting Captain "Barney" Bueno of the staff sat down to the piano and played the "Bayames," "Yankee Doodle," and the "Washington Post March." A lot of our men were sprawled about the floor looking at the pictures in some French periodicals. Outside there was still some exchange of rifle shots. The Spanish commander knew that we had him in a trap, and rather than have his men uselessly slaughtered, hauled down his flag, and at nine o'clock the fight was over, having lasted without cessation for fifty-one hours. To say that we were glad of the end but mildly expresses our feelings.

It was a good piece of work, the best the Cubans ever did. They had gone at the thing right, pressed every advantage, hung on like grim death, and made no serious mistakes. We had captured two Krupp guns, both disabled, with some ammunition for them, fifteen hundred rifles, there having been stored in the town a number in excess of the needs of the garrison, more than a million cartridges, some real food, and, most precious of all, seven hundred and fifty pounds of quinine. The day was spent in resting and sleeping and the night in feasting and rejoicing. Salvador Cisneros, the aged president of the provisional republic, with his cabinet, had arrived from Camaguey during the siege, and we artillery officers had the old patriot to dinner as our special guest. Our cooks outdid themselves in getting up a fine meal from some of the captured food supplies.

For a couple of hours in the afternoon we roamed about the town admiring the havoc wrought by our shells. The streets in places were littered with timber, brick, and tiling, while shell fragments were everywhere. Our guns standing in the street were surrounded by Spanish officers, who took the most interest in the dynamite gun. They were a fine, game lot of fellows, and were generous enough to express a high opinion of the service of our artillery. It is a pleasure to state that they and their men were well treated. It was impossible for the Cubans to feed them, and the Spanish authorities would recognize no parole given to the insurgents, so they were marched to near-by garrisons, turned in under the flag of truce, and in a short time were in the field against us.

General Garcia showed his appreciation of his artillery officers by promoting all of them one grade, so that I became a lieutenant-colonel, the highest rank I held in the insurgent service. Our first sergeant was a negro as black as night. He was a brave and faithful fellow and had long ago deserved promotion in the organization in which he had served, but our chief had feared that we Americans would resent such action. But Las Tunas settled it with us, and we went to the general in a body and said we would be glad to have him as a fellow-officer. He was glad to comply, and it was my pleasant task to surprise the gallant soldier by handing him his commission as second lieutenant.

After so many years I cannot give the losses suffered by both sides. They were very considerable, but not excessive, so much of the fighting having been under cover. Naturally the Spaniards got the worst of it, owing to the effects of artillery fire on some of their flimsy defences. They had about two hundred killed and wounded.

The end was still nearly a year in the future, when American intervention put a finish to this destructive war. How it would have terminated had it not been for intervention is a question which it is about as futile to discuss as it is to waste words over the old controversy as to whether our own forefathers would have won their fight for independence without the assistance of the French. Had the Spaniards succeeded in carrying out all over the island the policy of concentration of the Cuban population which they were able to enforce in certain districts, it is quite possible that in the course of time the war would have ended owing to the extermination of the people. After the cattle had been destroyed we in the field were dependent for subsistence on what could be raised by the thousands of women and children cultivating small patches of ground far back in the woods, where the Spanish troops seldom went. But Spain, too, was fast being worn out by the drain on her resources, and there were at home mutterings of revolution. In Havana and Matanzas provinces the insurgents in the field were pretty well used up and were being chased from pillar to post. In Pinar del Rio and Santa Clara it was about give and take, while we of the eastern two provinces of the island had the decided upper hand, and if we wanted a fight had to look for it.

Owing to the not very efficient assistance rendered our army by the insurgents during the Santiago campaign, there has grown up among our people an idea that they never did any fighting to amount to anything and that their efforts were bent entirely to the destruction of property. There were two things that the insurgents did especially well, one being their scouting and the other the keeping of records. After the close of the war a commission of which Maximo Gomez was president revised the rolls of the army, and after long and patient investigation made its report. This shows that from first to last 53,744 individuals served in the insurgent forces as officers or men. Once incorporated in this force, so far as a native-born Cuban was concerned, there was no getting out except by death, desertion, or absolute disability. The few foreigners in their service could quit whenever they wished. The result of this holding every man to service was that the great majority of them were in the field until

the end. It is estimated that at the time of the intervention there were still about 35,000 actually under arms. Of
the total number serving in the war, 3,437 died of disease
and 5,180 were killed in action or died of wounds. As
to these latter, their names, the organizations to which
they belonged, the engagements in which they were killed
or mortally wounded and the dates thereof, are to-day in
the files of the national archives at Havana, and cannot
be disputed. The killed and died of wounds of the land
forces of the United States, as taken from official records,
in four of our wars were as follows: War of 1812, 1,877;
Mexican War, 1,721; Spanish War and Philippine insurrection, in round numbers, 1,300—a total of 4,898. It is
difficult from data that I have consulted to segregate the
losses in the last two wars named, for the reason that a
number of organizations suffered losses in both wars and
I have never seen any table which separates, for instance,
losses suffered in fighting the Spaniards in the Philippines
and in the same organizations fighting the insurgents a
few months later. For the Spanish War, however, the
battle fatalities were approximately 300 and for the Philippine insurrection 1,000. So we arrive at the astonishing
fact that not quite fifty-four thousand Cubans in three
years of war had more battle fatalities than the several
hundred thousand Americans who fought in the four wars
named. Could anything more be said on that subject?
There are no data to show the battle losses in the American
Revolution, but no one who is reasonably familiar with
the history of that struggle believes that anything like
five thousand men were killed in action or died of wounds

in that war. It is not that there were any great battles in the Cuban insurrection, for there were not; but for that matter neither were there in the other wars named. There were no engagements in the Cuban insurrection of the magnitude of Bemis Heights or the Brandywine, and no siege to compare with Yorktown, but there was almost no limit to the number of encounters that in numbers engaged and in casualties exceeded many of the engagements of that war, the names of which are familiar to every American school-boy. For swift marching and almost continuous fighting there was nothing in the American Revolution that approached Maximo Gomez's great march of more than six hundred miles from east of the Cauto River to the very environs of Havana, striking column after column of Spanish troops sent to intercept him. There was more fighting on that one march than in our whole War of 1812. Throughout the whole struggle it was the vast number of engagements in which from five hundred to four thousand men were engaged on either side that finally made up that fearful percentage of casualties, almost unprecedented in modern wars.

There were many faults on both sides, so far as the conduct of the war was concerned. The Cubans did not take full advantage of the great superiority that their mobility gave them, and having won a success they seldom followed it up properly. They took poor care of their arms, wasted ammunition in battle, and too often were not dependable under fire. One of their chief faults was that one never knew just what they were going to do. At times they would go to pieces with no reason, and at others stand up to their work manfully and fight splendidly. The Spanish soldier was brave, patient, and by no means the inhuman brute that he has been made out to be, but he had little heart in the war and was always getting yellow fever and other undesirable things. The Spanish strategy was all wrong. They tied up in the garrisoning of unimportant towns and *trochas* tens of thousands of men who had better have been left in Spain. If they had held only a few places on the coast as bases of operations, and had covered the country with fifty thousand mounted troops, they would have kept us on the jump. But their ponderous columns of infantry, hampered by transport, wore themselves out in aimless marches along the main roads, to find finally that the Cubans were all about them, shooting into the column front, flank, and rear, only to desist when they thought they had had enough of it.

I believe that fair-minded Americans who will familiarize themselves with the history of Cuba's two great struggles for independence and consider the tremendous sacrifices made by the people of the island will want to see the young republic endure. I am sure that is the attitude of the few of their countrymen now surviving who shared with the patriots the dangers, the hunger, and other privations of the final struggle.

A pleasant sequel of my own service came a few years ago when I was the guest of honor at a banquet given in Havana by my old comrades of the revolution. The present Cuban minister to the United States, General Carlos Garcia, was toastmaster, and at the table were eighty-one former insurgent officers, one of them being the present president of the republic. Sixty-five had been old comrades of the *Departamento del Oriente*. It was hard to realize that those well-groomed men in evening dress were the worn and wasted men who had led the Cubans at Cascorra, at La Machuca, and many another good fight, and had stormed the ridge at Jiguani and led their men through the wire entanglements at Victoria de las Tunas; or were the same comrades, always kindly and considerate, who in the grim days of hunger always saw that the American *mambis* got their share when food strayed into camp. That one evening of reminiscence and good-fellowship was pay enough for it all.

PHILIPPINE EXPERIENCES

I

THE MAKING OF A REGIMENT

TEMPORARILY broken in health, I had returned to the United States from Cuba early in 1898, and was at my old home in Kansas, enjoying the companionship of family and friends, and doing my best to obliterate the memory of lean days in the "bush" by a generous patronage of everything in the nature of real food. The *Maine* had already been blown up, and the country was full of the rumblings of the approaching war with Spain. To the last I doubted whether it would really come to a clash, having in mind several cases within my own recollection when we had apparently come to the verge of war, but in which the matters in dispute had been settled without recourse to arms. But the clamor of the yellow section of the press and the deliverances of politicians playing to the galleries so inflamed public sentiment that the hand of the administration was forced, and we were in for a sharp and short little war, with its sequel in the form of a more protracted and far bloodier struggle in the Philippine Islands.

Although my health had been quite restored by the time of the outbreak of hostilities, I had but very little hope or expectation of participating in the coming war, as I was without friends or acquaintances among those high in official life in Washington, and took it for granted that in filling the quota of my own State the governor thereof would utilize as far as possible the existing organizations of the national guard, of which I was not a member. The governor of Kansas, John W. Leedy, was one of those who had come into power as the result of recent victories of the Populist party. He was a man of many admirable and sterling qualities, but immovably stubborn, once he had made up his mind on any proposition. He had two pet aversions, the regular army and the national guard, rather unfortunate prejudices for one upon whom was to be thrown the responsibility of organizing several regiments for possible active service. On a visit to Topeka several weeks before the declaration of war, I had met Governor Leedy, and had had a very pleasant interview with him. He was much interested in my accounts of fighting between Spaniards and insurgents in Cuba and in descriptions of conditions on the war-wasted island. When the President issued to the governors of the various States his call for volunteers, Kansas was asked to furnish three regiments of infantry of about one thousand men each. Under a subsequent call there was organized a two-battalion colored regiment, and three hundred recruits were provided for each of the three existing regiments. Immediately upon the issue of the first call, Governor Leedy sent me a telegram requesting that I come to Topeka at once. Upon reporting, I was informed that he had determined to ignore the national guard organization of the State, building three new regiments from the ground up. Members of the national guard could enter these organizations as individuals. I was to be named as colonel of one of the three regiments. I protested against the expediency of a policy which I thought might keep out of the service a number of officers and men who had had at least the rudiments of military training, and further stated that while I had seen much campaigning and no little fighting, my service had been in a force in which drill or other training was a practically unknown quantity. I felt that the instruction of a regiment made up largely of absolutely raw material should be under the direction of one who knew at least something of infantry drill. But the governor told me bluntly that he had not sent for me to hear my views, as he had some of his own. If I did not take the regiment he would give it to Mr. So and So. I knew that I could not be a worse colonel than the man named, and accepted. With all due respect to my excellent friend, the former governor, I think he was taking some pretty big chances in his rather off-hand way of selecting officers. Mr. Edward C. Little, a well-known lawyer of the State, formerly United States consul-general to Egypt, and at the time private secretary to the governor, was chosen lieutenant-colonel. He had had no previous military experience. As the regiment, although one of three battalions, was to have but two majors, the lieutenant-colonel was to command a battalion, and, of course, the regiment in case of the absence or disability of the colonel. The majors were Frank H. Whitman, a second lieutenant of the Second United States Infantry, who had graduated from the Military Academy two years previously, and Wilder S. Metcalf, colonel of one of the now disbanded national guard regiments. John A. Rafter

was surgeon, with the rank of major, while Henry D.
Smith and Charles S. Huffman were assistant surgeons,
with the rank of captain. John G. Schliemann was chaplain. All of the above-named served through the campaign in the Philippines with the regiment. William H.
De Ford and L. C. Smith were adjutant and quartermaster, respectively, with the rank of first lieutenant. Both
resigned before the regiment left for the Philippines.

The field and staff officers included in the above were
sent separately to twelve different towns to recruit the
various companies. There was no dearth of applicants
for enlistment, the recruiting officers being fairly overwhelmed with them. If a town had a national guard
company its members had precedence in enlistment, so far
as they could meet the physical and other requirements,
but had to come in as privates, regardless of whatever
rank they may have held in their old companies. After
them came applicants in general, and the companies were
soon filled to the authorized strength. The regiment as
it existed before the second call brought some three hundred recruits, was about one thousand strong, and included
in its roster about three hundred former national guards-
men and sixty former soldiers of the regular army, the
balance being men without any military training whatever.
Company officers were chosen by the indefensible system
of having the men elect them. However, the results on
the whole were more satisfactory than would have been
anticipated. In a town where a national guard company
existed the officers thereof were usually chosen for the
corresponding grades in the new company, with the result

that the captain in selecting non-commissioned officers largely chose those of his old organization, so far as these had enlisted. Three of the officers were veterans of the Civil War, and two were former enlisted men of the regular army, while a considerable number had seen service in the national guard. The remainder were without any previous military experience, but some of them by virtue of hard work and natural aptitude became highly efficient. Taking the officers of the regiment through and through, some of them after a few months' service were as capable in the performance of their duties as the average regular officer of corresponding grades, others were of rather mediocre quality, and a very few were not worth the powder it would take to blow them up. Three of them were killed in action and ten others wounded. I never knew of one of them showing the slightest "yellow streak" under fire, though some of them brought occasional discredit on their uniform by personal misconduct. In due time I found out that the best way of getting rid of an officer who was attempting to establish a reputation as the regimental "cut up" was to prepare a carefully written set of charges covering such of his antics as had come to light, and at the same time his resignation from the service, the latter lacking only his signature. An invitation to call at my tent and read both papers usually resulted in making the latter document complete and ready for transmission to the War Department. It should not be inferred, however, that all resignations were forced, as several officers left the regiment in that manner with perfectly clear records.

The rank and file of the regiment consisted in the main

of an especially fine body of young men. Naturally there were among them some with physical or moral defects, but a process of elimination by one method or another had rid us of the most of these before we took our place on the fighting line, nine months later.

While the various companies were being raised, Governor Leedy had telegraphed an inquiry to the War Department as to whether the Kansas regiments would be supplied with uniforms before leaving the State or after reaching the concentration camps. The reply was to the effect that as soon as organized they would be sent to Fort Leavenworth for immediate equipment. Warm weather had already set in in Kansas, and winter clothing had been packed away in moth balls. It would have been most uncomfortable to wear it at that season, and it was not desired to have the men placed under the necessity of returning their civilian clothing to their homes by express. So instructions were issued for all of the men not provided with national-guard uniforms to leave their homes with clothing that they would be willing to throw away in a couple of weeks. The result was that about seven hundred men of my regiment reached Topeka clad in a fearful and wonderful aggregation of seersucker coats, linen dusters, and "ice-cream" trousers, and for weeks they shivered in these garments on the fog-drenched and wind-swept sand lots of San Francisco. It was a shocking and cruel blunder, costly in the lives and health of not a few of them. And the fault did not lie with any one in Kansas. It is not pleasant to write these things, but the Spanish War is now as much a part of history as is the Civil

War and one is under no obligation to assist in covering up anything connected with it. With the War Department conducted as in recent years it would be impossible for such a thing to occur.

The companies of the regiment to be were sent to Topeka as soon as recruited, and, in common with those destined to form the other two regiments, went into camp on the State Fair grounds, State tentage and other equipment being used. Kansas had had nineteen regiments in the Civil War, and in numbering those raised for the Spanish War the same sequence was followed, my regiment becoming the Twentieth Kansas. The muster into the service of the United States, an impressive ceremony, took place on the 13th of May. The only officers and men provided with uniforms being those who had come from the national guard, I was still in "cits," and consequently on the day of muster-in played a part in a rather ludicrous incident. I was staying at a Topeka hotel, and on going out to the camp to participate in the ceremony, was halted at its boundary by a sentry in the national-guard uniform, who informed me that visitors were not allowed within the limits of the camp. I replied somewhat icily that I was the colonel of the regiment. The sentry was a very tall man, and altitude has never been one of my charms; so the man bent his head until his mouth was within a couple of inches of one of my ears, and, as a most engaging grin overspread his features, whispered, "Try the next sentry. He's easy." And he was so stubborn and immovable that the officer of the guard had to be called before I could join my command. The man's face, when he saw what a break he had made, was a study. The recollection of incidents of this kind is one of the many things that make life worth living.

On a visit to Fort Leavenworth a short time before the declaration of war, I had met Colonel Hamilton S. Hawkins, United States Army, who a short time later was to render such gallant and distinguished service as a brigade commander at the battle of Santiago, and had told him something about conditions as they had existed in Cuba a few months before. Colonel Hawkins had written a letter to the War Department suggesting that it would be worth while to send for me in order to obtain such information as I might be able to give relative to the strength, etc., of the insurgents in that part of Cuba in which I had so recently served, and the distribution and approximate strength of the Spanish garrisons in the same region, as well as other data that might prove useful for our army, about to campaign in a country of which we really knew but very little. The result was that a day or two after the muster-in of the Twentieth Kansas, I received a telegraphic order to proceed at once to Tampa, and report upon my arrival to the commanding officer of the troops being concentrated there. Arriving at my destination, I reported to General Shafter, and was turned over by him to Lieutenant-Colonel Arthur L. Wagner, intelligence officer attached to his head-quarters. This officer questioned me thoroughly on all points, and made copious notes, and after several days had succeeded in pumping me pretty dry. I doubt if any of the information obtained from me was ever of any value, except that as to general conditions, as I was not familiar with the country in the immediate vicinity of the city of Santiago, the scene of the only campaign. Had it been otherwise, I am of the opinion that the data as to roads, rivers, and the practicable crossing-places thereof, as well as other information on local conditions, which had been given in such detail, would not have been utilized. General Shafter seemed to regard me with suspicion, while General Miles, who had in the meantime arrived, was very courteous, but neither officer seemed to care to talk with me as to conditions on the island, and I had too much self-respect to give unasked-for information. This was the attitude of the higher officers generally, a number of whom I met, but it was different with those of lower rank, bright and capable men, enthusiastic over the fact that they were going to their first war. One could scarcely answer their questions fast enough. Years afterward, when I was stationed in San Francisco, in command of the Department of California, and General Shafter, then on the retired list, was living in the city, I came to know him quite well, and we were good friends. But I never mustered up sufficient courage to ask why I had made such a poor impression on him at Tampa. He was a blunt man, and might have told me. In the meantime I had learned that my own regiment had been ordered to San Francisco, and as it was not then known that land forces would be sent to the Philippine Islands, I supposed that to be its finish, so far as any participation in the war was concerned. I therefore indulged myself in a hope that I might be sent to Cuba on detached service with the Fifth Army

Corps, and be able to render some service on account of my knowledge of the country. But General Miles, who was then commander-in-chief of the army, took a different view of it, and very properly stated that, as a colonel, my place was with my regiment, and directed me to join. I am, of course, now heartily glad that he did so. For the reasons stated above, I could have been of little or no use in the Santiago campaign.

Proceeding direct to San Francisco, I found my regiment in tents at Camp Merritt, in the western suburbs of the city. The department commander, General Wesley Merritt, had his head-quarters in the city, while General Elwell S. Otis was in command of what was known as the Independent Division of the Eighth Army Corps, the force of about ten thousand men, mostly volunteers from the Western States, at Camp Merritt, and lived at the camp. The Twentieth Kansas had been assigned to the brigade commanded by General Charles King, the well-known soldier and writer, the other two regiments in the brigade being the First Tennessee and the Fifty-first Iowa. The Independent Division at Camp Merritt was really a "feeder" to the troops now being sent to the Philippines to take part in the land campaign against Manila, each regiment, as soon as its equipment and training made it serviceable, being sent out on one of the expeditions that from time to time left the port.

My first duty after joining was to pay my respects to the brigade, division, and department commanders in succession. As General Merritt was soon to leave for Manila, and as from the nature of things I was not brought in close contact with him, my acquaintanceship with that officer was limited to one or two brief interviews. We young officers, knowing of General Merritt's achievements in the Civil War, in which he had commanded a division before reaching the age of thirty, stood in considerable awe of him, though there was nothing in his manner to inspire fear, as he was very kindly and courteous to all of us who met him. General Otis was of a somewhat different type. While always civil, he was a very reserved man, and an indefatigable worker, who took upon himself the decision of all sorts of minor matters, ordinarily left by a general officer to the members of his staff. One would about as soon think of cracking a joke in his presence as of trying to pull his beard. It should not be inferred that he was of the pompous type, for he was anything but that, being a most simple and unaffected man, though without the saving grace of humor. We were most fortunate in our brigade commander, General King, who was, as he still is, a captain on the retired list of the regular army, having been compelled to leave active service some years before because of a very severe wound received in the Indian wars. He had returned to active service with the rank of brigadier-general of volunteers. Though his retirement dated back to 1879, he had kept closely in touch with military matters and was thoroughly up to date. General King's temperament was peculiarly suited to his task of commanding a brigade of raw volunteer troops, and directing their training. His keen eye took in every defect and noted every improvement. In the former case the needed correction or admonition was made in a way that left no sting, he never being either brutal or sarcastic. His readiness to encourage or to praise stirred all to put forth their best efforts.

The location of Camp Merritt was in some respects most unfortunate, especially for those who, like so many members of the Twentieth Kansas, had not yet been supplied with warm uniforms. Chilling fogs and cold winds make San Francisco's summer climate anything but comfortable except for those who have been properly prepared for it, and the camp was located at the extreme western limit of the city, within a mile or so of the beach, where the winds had full sweep. I have seen the fog so dense that one could with difficulty see from one flank to the other of a company in line. Everywhere was sand, sand, sand, deep and fine, blowing into tents, getting into the food, and making itself generally an unmitigated nuisance. Several car lines furnished easy access to the heart of the city, and the camp was naturally at all times overrun with swarms of visitors, not only from San Francisco, but from all over California, while venders of fruit, candies, and pastries, who could not be kept off the public streets running through the camp, made officers responsible for the health of their men long for an open season as regards these particular pests. San Francisco was then, as it is now, a gay and beautiful city, there being nothing just like it in the whole country. The people are proverbially hospitable, and laid themselves out in those days to give the soldiers in their midst a good time. The most of the men of the Twentieth Kansas were from the farm or from small towns, and the life and gayety of the city seemed quite to overwhelm them, so much so, in fact, that there was from the start too much of an idea that they were out on a magnificent lark, instead of for the serious purpose of training for war. It would have been vastly better from the stand-point of the health and general well-being of the men, as well as from that of their training, if the camp had been somewhere along the coast line of the Southern Pacific, anywhere from ten to thirty miles south of San Francisco. There would have been found ideal conditions as to climate, while the appreciable distance from the attractions of a great city would have been especially desirable, as well as relieved us somewhat from the crowds of sight-seers. In that region there would have been available for extended order drills and field manœuvres thousands of acres of diversified country, instead of our being confined for such work to the limited area of the Presidio reservation, a mile or two from the camp, where there was great difficulty in deploying and exercising in battle tactics a force larger than one regiment, and where we always had to work over practically the same ground. With all its disadvantages, one thing, however, could be said for Camp Merritt, and that was that the water supply was ample and convenient, the mains of the city system running through the entire camp.

The three hundred recruits raised for the regiment under the second call had arrived at about the same time I did, and brought its strength up to nearly 1,400, officers and men, a force equal to many of the brigades that fought in the Civil War.

I found on arrival that considerable progress had been

made in the elementary training of the regiment, principally in guard duty, the manual of arms, and company
drills in close order.   A few battalion, but no regimental,
drills had been attempted.   In this preliminary training
of the regiment the services of Major Metcalf were invaluable, his energy, tact, and comprehensive knowledge of
the drill regulations making him indispensable.   For myself the struggle was a hard one, as to me the drill regulations were Greek.   From previous experience in war I
knew mighty well that I could march and fight a regiment if the opportunity arose, but realized that we could
not hope to be given a chance for field service until we
could go through the complicated movements of regimental
drill in close order and take part in reviews and parades
without tying ourselves into a hard knot.   Parades and
reviews are non-essentials in war, but are in a measure
valuable in the preliminary training of troops, while some
of the simpler movements of regimental close-order drill
are often quite necessary before actual deployment in extended order for fighting.

It was not long after my arrival that those of the men
of the regiment who had not uniforms were able to discard the fearful and wonderful assortment of old summer
clothing that they had brought from Kansas, and appear in
something that was at least warmer.   At the breaking out
of the Spanish War there had been in the country but a
small quantity of the blue cloth from which all military
uniforms were then made, the demand for it under normal conditions being very limited, so that large quantities
of cloth of proper weight and texture, but not of the desired

color, were obtained and dyed, and then made into uniforms. The spectacle the troops made after the dye began to fade, which it did in a few weeks, would have been laughable if it had not been so maddening to those most concerned. But the new clothing was warm, and answered a good purpose until it could be replaced by better.

In due time came the Fourth of July, and of course the whole Independent Division had to turn out for a parade through the streets. Owing to the prevailing uncertainty as to whether we were going to the Philippines or whether we were to remain for an indefinite time in San Francisco, none of the officers of the regiment required to be mounted had purchased horses, but hired from livery-stables those needed at drills. I had, after a few hair-raising experiences, got one brute so that he would not turn a somersault or execute a waltz every time a band struck up or a body of troops came to "order arms," and expected to use him at this formation. But he had suddenly become lame, and the stable sent out to me on that never-to-be-forgotten morning a handsome black animal with arched neck and ugly eye. The regiment had formed prepared to march in column through the streets the several miles to the foot of Market Street, where the parade was to start. I mounted with some difficulty, and the band broke forth into a lively air as the regiment stepped out. That horse quivered in every limb for an instant and then bolted. I might as well have tried to hold a cyclone. In front of the tent that was my home was a large fly, and under, this the animal went, and I was ignominiously scraped off in the presence of some thirteen hundred grinning and delighted patriots. Right there I became an ardent admirer of the soft and bottomless sand that passed for ground at Camp Merritt, and considered myself lucky also that I had not been impaled on my sabre. In his struggles the horse tore down the tent fly and was with some difficulty got out from under it. All the way down to the starting-point of the parade he cavorted, danced, and threatened to bolt, but the real trouble began after the parade had formed and the thousands of men, filling the wide street from curb to curb, and with the blare of many bands, swept up Market Street. The hoodlum men and big boys had unrestrained license. They were well supplied with firecrackers, and the helpless officers on their horses were from their stand-point fair game. The police were useless, and might as well have been so many cigar-store Indians. The clubbing of these miscreants would have been a positive pleasure to any right-minded man. The whole thing was a disgrace to the city. My horse, probably the worst in the lot, became wild with terror after half a dozen "cannon" crackers had been exploded under him, and charged and reared from one side of the street to the other, often endangering the lives of people on the sidewalks. One big ruffian, having made a bad throw, lit another large cracker, and under the very nose of a policeman ran out into the street and tried to throw it under my horse. Right then and there murder came into my heart, and I made a hard and conscientious effort to kill him. Of course, I was carrying my sabre, and at the proper instant cut at him with all my strength. Only a quick jump backward saved him from death or a severe injury, as the point of the blade passed within six inches of his throat. I deeply regretted my failure, and would have been willing to take my chances with any American jury as to the outcome. I have seen too many good men go down to death to have had any more compunctions about killing a hoodlum of that type than over despatching a savage dog. Before the parade had ended my left arm had become so exhausted from efforts to control the mad brute that I was riding that I was compelled to sheathe my sabre in order to take the reins in my right hand. Finally the ordeal was over. I have been in but few battles in which I would not rather take my chances than to repeat the performance.

Time passed pleasantly enough for the next few weeks. The days were filled up with drills and other duties, but our evenings were free, and the theatres and restaurants of the city gave ample opportunity for relaxation; besides many of us had had opportunities of meeting socially very agreeable people. There are no other people in the country just like the San Franciscans. They are in a class all by themselves, and can certainly do more things to make pleasant the stay of the stranger within their gates than the people of any other American community. Manila had not yet fallen, and expedition after expedition sailed from the port, taking the various regiments from Camp Merritt as their training and completeness of equipment justified. There was much chafing and disappointment in the Twentieth Kansas as the regiment was time and again left behind, but the large percentage of untrained men in it was a handicap not to be overcome in a few short weeks. General Merritt sailed for the Philippines, shortly to be followed by General Otis, the former being succeeded as department commander by General H. C. Merriam, while General Marcus P. Miller succeeded General Otis as commander of the Independent Division. I had been pretty much impressed by the somewhat austere demeanor of General Otis, and when I went to pay my respects to his successor, approached his tent with some misgivings, supposing that all division commanders were necessarily alike. When I entered, saluted rather stiffly, and announced the object of my visit, General Miller looked up, and, as a kindly smile overspread his features, said, "Well, well. So you are a colonel, are you? Sit right down on this box and tell me how anybody came to make a young chap like you a colonel?" He talked to me a long time in a fatherly sort of way, and told me to come and see him any time that I felt blue or discouraged. He was one of the kindest and most considerate of men, and a mighty good soldier, too.

One thing about the chill summer climate of San Francisco is that people soon become accustomed to it, and learn to enjoy it, and this with the fact that the regiment had been supplied with suitable clothing made life in camp much more agreeable. Under the watchful eye of General King the regiment made satisfactory progress in its training, and soon began to have regimental drills. When I gave a command I flattered myself that I had a voice that would reach from one end of the regiment to the other, but at first could not always tell whether the move had been properly executed or not. One day General King mentioned to me the fact that my regiment did not seem to be as spry as some others in turning out the guard to do the required honors to officers entitled to them, and requested that I give the matter attention. It should be explained for the benefit of readers not familiar with military matters, that turning out the guard for an officer consists in the sentry at the guard-house, or structure which does duty as such, calling out as the officer approaches, "Turn out the guard—general officer," or whatever other it may be for. The members of the guard at the guard-house, which means all not at the time on sentry duty, fall into ranks under arms, ready to be inspected. On returning to the regimental camp after this conversation with the brigade commander, it occurred to me to ascertain if the sentry then on duty at the guard tent, which was just inside the entrance to the camp, knew what to do and how to do it in that respect if the occasion should arise. In response to an inquiry as to what he would do if the brigade commander should approach his post, he said he would turn out the guard. This was quite satisfactory, but further questioning developed the fact that he was not sure whether he knew that officer by sight. I briefly described General King, and further said that he had two rows of gilt buttons on his blouse and always rode a big, bald-faced sorrel, and then went into my tent, little dreaming of what was to follow. I had scarcely had time to remove my sabre when I heard the deep voice of this same sentry bawl out, "Turn out the guard—general officer." I stepped out of the tent to greet the new arrival, and was inwardly congratulating myself on having primed this particular sentry in time, when to my horror I saw Captain James G. Blaine, Jr., the adjutant-general of the brigade, mounted on General King's bald-faced sorrel. The guard was forming in commendable haste, and Captain Blaine seemed so overcome by the unexpected honors thrust upon him that he forgot to call out, "Never mind the guard," the only way to untangle the mess. After dismissing the guard, I strode over to the unfortunate sentry in righteous wrath, and said, "What in thunder did you do that for?" The man replied in tones of sorrow, "Well, I knew that must be the horse, but I forgot to look for the buttons."

The hospitable ladies of San Francisco were continually sending out to the various camps contributions of cakes, pies, and other articles of food not included in the ration. This was very commendable on their part, but I would have done almost anything to be able to put a stop to their benefactions without mortally offending them, as one of the essential things connected with the training of troops is to get them used to the army ration and have them satisfied with it. This ration is, and was then, ample and nutritious, but men were not going to eat it if all of their storage capacity was taken up with sponge-cake. One officer tried to remedy the matter, so far as his own company was concerned, by himself eating its quota, but gave up when there seemed no end to the supplies of this nature. Flowers were often sent to us, and these did no harm except on one occasion. I was going the rounds of the camp to see if the sentries were on the alert, when to my horror I espied one of them, Private John M. Steele, calmly walking his post with his blouse decorated by a bouquet that would not have shamed a débutante at her coming-out ball. At the same time I saw General King coming from the opposite direction, and at such a distance that we would certainly meet opposite the flower-decked sentry. Regulating my voice so that the sentry would hear me and the general would not, I called out frantically, "Steele, take that damned thing off. Take it off, I say," repeating this command with appropriate trimmings several times. The rattled Steele jumped about, apparently uncertain whether I wanted him to take off his blouse or his trousers, and finally wound up by coming to "present arms" to General King and myself alternately. The general passed on with a look more of sorrow than of anger, and in a few moments the floral decorations were scattered on the sidewalk.

In time most of the regiments at Camp Merritt had sailed for the Philippines, and our brigade was moved to a much more desirable camp site on the Presidio reservation. On August 5 General King himself sailed for Honolulu, to proceed later to the Philippines, and I, ranking by a few days the commanders of the other two regiments, succeeded to the command of the brigade, but at the same time retaining command of my own regiment. At the Presidio we had target practice and many battle exercises with blank ammunition, and the men began to get a mild foretaste of what a battle is like as the advancing companies rushed forward, throwing themselves prone at every halt, their front thick with smoke, while the roar of the old Springfields drowned all commands, and could scarcely be pierced by the shrill notes of the bugles. Finally came the news that the Spanish War was over. It seemed that all our work had been for naught, and except that we entertained a vague hope that we might have a short tour of garrison duty in either Hawaii or the Philippines, looked as if we might as well be mustered out. Under the circumstances it was no easy matter to keep up interest in the daily round of drills and instruction. But it was all to be for the best, for when the regiment finally saw service in a different war than the one for which it had been enrolled, the long, dreary months of training counted, and it knew its business. Another advantage derived from the long delay was that before sailing we had rid the regiment of a considerable number of men who were physically not up to the mark or who were in various ways unsuited to the service. The resignations of the regimental adjutant and regimental quartermaster, both of whom felt compelled to leave the service for personal reasons, left two important vacancies which were filled by the designation for those positions of Lieutenants Charles B. Walker and Walter P. Hull, both of whom proved highly efficient. One captain was mustered out, and a second lieutenant resigned. These vacancies, after the necessary promotions had been made to fill them, resulted in the promotion from the ranks of four of the most capable non-commissioned officers, while the resignation of another second lieutenant just before sailing brought up another man from the ranks. One of the first sergeants promoted was Clad Hamilton, now a well-known lawyer of Topeka and member of the State senate. Without previous military experience, he had enlisted as a private, made himself so proficient by study and hard work that in a few weeks he was first sergeant, and was finally mustered out of the regiment a captain. Edward J. Hardy, another of the first sergeants promoted at this time, developed into a dare-devil sort of scout, and also came home a captain. The promotion of the regimental sergeant-major, Frederick R. Dodge, made a vacancy in his position that was filled by the promotion to it of Corporal Cassius E. Warner, who was destined to be mustered out with the regiment as its adjutant. A man who can go out as a corporal and come home regimental adjutant can look back to his military career with no small satisfaction. During the fighting in the campaign up the railroad from Manila I always kept Warner, who was still sergeant-major, at my side, and used him as a highly intelligent orderly, one who could remember a message given him and transmit it correctly. We went through it all unscathed until Santo Tomas, when we were hit within two seconds of each other, and in exactly the same place. It was a queer, almost uncanny, coincidence.

October came, and found us still at the Presidio going through the daily grind of drills. Hope of going to the Philippines or anywhere else had practically been abandoned, and we were expecting the order to return to Kansas for muster-out, when we were electrified by the order to sail for Manila on the transport *Indiana* on the 27th of the month. During our stay in San Francisco I had met Miss Eda Blankart, of the near-by city of Oakland, and we were married on the 25th of the month. This is by all odds the smartest thing I ever did in my life.

At last came the great day, and the *Indiana*, bearing the head-quarters and the second and third battalions of the Twentieth Kansas, and cheered by a great throng, pulled away from the wharf and started on the eight thousand miles' journey to Manila. Nobody supposed that we should ever see any fighting, as it was thought that our duties would consist in helping to sit on and hold down the "little brown brother" for a few months; so that the transport carried as passengers the wives of Major Whitman, Captain Buchan, Chaplain Schliemann, and Lieutenant Haussermann. Mrs. Funston was not ready to sail, and followed on the *Newport*, which left on November 8, carrying among other troops the first battalion of the regiment. The voyage of the *Indiana* was without incident, but was broken by a pleasant stay of four days in Honolulu. Kansas has a law, enacted during the Civil War, to the effect that members of military organizations raised by the State may participate in State elections, even though they be at the time outside its boundaries. Ballots had been received before sailing, and election day finding us at Honolulu, the Hawaiians had their first object-lesson in civil government under the American flag, the voting booths being erected on the wharf alongside the transport. A rather amusing incident was the attempt of one captain to compel his whole company to vote the Populist ticket.

As darkness was settling down on the night of November 30 we passed Corregidor Island, at the entrance to

Manila Bay, and at midnight the engines of the *Indiana*, that had never ceased their throbbing since we had left Honolulu, three weeks before, were still, and we were anchored off the big city. Going ashore the next day, I paid my respects to General E. S. Otis, commander of the Pacific Division and Eighth Army Corps, and was informed that my regiment would not disembark for some days, as there was doubt as to what command it would be assigned to. In about a week we were assigned to the First Brigade of the Second Division, and ordered to disembark. The head-quarters of the regiment and the second battalion were quartered in a large building in the Binondo district, and the other two battalions in other buildings in the Tondo district, the first battalion having in the meantime arrived on the *Newport*. Our brigade commander was General Harrison Gray Otis, the well-known editor and owner of the Los Angeles *Times*. He was not a regular officer, having come in for the Spanish War with volunteer rank. He had served through the Civil War in the same regiment with President McKinley, and had made an excellent record. He should not be confused with the corps commander, General E. S. Otis. I believe they were not related. Our division commander, Major-General Arthur MacArthur, had been in the regular army ever since the close of the Civil War, in which as an officer, while but little more than a boy, he had especially distinguished himself. He had commanded a regiment in that war when he was twenty years of age, and had been awarded the Medal of Honor for gallantry at the storming of Missionary Ridge. At this time he was a lieutenant-colonel in the regular army, his commission as a major-general being in the volunteer forces.

General MacArthur's division, consisting of the brigades of Hale and Otis, furnished the details for a strong line of outposts covering the city on the north and north-east. All of the regiments of this division were quartered in the buildings of the city, with the exception of the First Nebraska, which was in camp at Santa Mesa, on the extreme right of the division's line. The First Division, Eighth Corps, Major-General T. M. Anderson commanding, covered the south side of the city, its right resting on Manila Bay and its left on the Pasig River, directly opposite the right of the Second Division, which swept in a curve to the west and north-west for about five miles, its left resting on the marshes and sloughs that cut up the shore line immediately north of the city. The extreme left of this line was assigned to the Twentieth Kansas, the line to be guarded by it extending from the salt marshes on the left to the line of the Manila-Dagupan Railway on its right, where it connected with a battalion of the Third United States Artillery, eight hundred strong, serving as infantry, under the command of Major W. A. Kobbé. The regiment kept about seventy men on outpost duty day and night, these covering a front of about six hundred yards. Close in front of them were the sentries of the insurgent Filipinos, who faced the American line through its entire length. The Twentieth Kansas outpost line was intersected at right angles by a wagon road and the tramway connecting Manila with the suburb of Caloocan. The wagon road was lined on both sides with nipa houses, each surrounded by trees and garden, so that the view to the front was much obstructed. Appropriate orders had been issued to the effect that regimental commanders should at all times have their respective commands in readiness to move out at short notice in case of trouble to support the outposts of their regiments. We had not been many days in Manila when we realized that there was something a great deal more interesting than garrison duty ahead of us, it being the almost unanimous opinion of officers who had been on the ground for some time that unless we got out of the islands in a short time a clash with the numerous, truculent, and well-armed forces of the so-called Filipino Republic was inevitable. The only question seemed to be as to when it would start and how. The most stringent orders had been issued to the American troops to the effect that they should bear insults and threats in silence, and under no circumstances take things into their own hands. It was the evident intention to lay the onus of starting the trouble on our opponents, a plan which worked out all right, as the Filipinos began soon to take our forbearance for fear, and brought on themselves a swift and terrible retribution.

The various regimental commanders of the division were detailed in turn as division officer of the day, their duties being to inspect carefully the entire line of outposts and report any lack of watchfulness on their part. These rides, which came to every one of us in six days, were most interesting, and I always looked forward to them with the greatest anticipation. One could not help being impressed with the formidable lines of intrenchments that sheltered the Filipinos at nearly all points opposite our line. Incidents showing their aggressive spirit and desire to start trouble were not lacking. One morning while I was officer of the day a Filipino soldier strolled over to one of the sentries on the outpost of the First South Dakota and asked the man for a cigarette. As the Filipino was unarmed, the American was somewhat off his guard, and, as he started to search his pockets for the desired smoke, was terribly cut across the face by a bolo which the ruffian suddenly drew from under his clothing. Though blinded by his own blood, the plucky soldier managed to settle the score then and there, fairly blowing the man's head off with a short-range shot with his big Springfield. I came along on my tour of inspection a short time later and saw the man lying where he had fallen. He looked as if he had been struck by a shell. There was one thing to be said for those old Springfields that the volunteer troops were armed with, and that was that if a bullet from one of them hit a man he never mistook it for a mosquito bite. On one occasion a large force of Filipino soldiers engaged in drill advanced on the outpost of the First Montana. The sentries of the latter fell back on their supports, and the trouble came within an ace of starting right there, instead of several weeks later. These are but sample incidents. It was a condition that could not last long. Unarmed Filipino soldiers were allowed to come through our lines to visit the city, and occasionally Americans were allowed to go through their lines. It occurred to some of us that turn about was fair play, and as a number of the "enemy," as we already considered them, had passed through the outposts of the Twentieth Kansas, one day early in January, Lieutenant-Colonel Little, Major Metcalf, Captains Bishop and Boltwood and myself mounted our Filipino ponies and set out up the road toward Caloocan. Riding through our own line, we presented ourselves to the Filipino post a hundred yards beyond and requested that we be taken before the officer of the day. This functionary was found about half a mile up the road, and in reaching him we passed over the ground that we were to charge over on that never-to-be-forgotten 5th of February. We gave our swords and revolvers into the keeping of the Filipino officer and proceeded on our way a short distance beyond the town of Caloocan, passing within a stone's throw of the church that we were to take by assault on February 10th. The knowledge of the ground that we were so soon to fight over obtained on this trip, as well as information as to the location and strength of the insurgent trenches, proved of no little value.

Major and Mrs. Whitman, Major Metcalf, and Mrs. Funston and myself had started up house-keeping in a very passable house in the Binondo district. Our orderlies slept in the same building, and the horses were in a stable in the court-yard. On the night of February 4 we had just retired, and I was not yet asleep when Major Metcalf pounded vigorously on the door and called out, "Come out here, Colonel. The ball has begun." I scarcely realized at first what he meant, but hastily slipped on a few clothes and came out into the hallway. Metcalf conducted me to a window, and asked, "Did you ever hear that racket before?" And sure enough, from a little north of east, floating over the house-tops of the great city, came the distant rattle of the Mausers. There was no mistaking it, and we realized that a war had begun. As the preliminary rattle swelled into a great roar, there were excited voices in the streets, rapid closing of doors and windows, the sound of people running through the streets, and then the city became almost as quiet as death. In the meantime our orderlies had been awakened and were saddling our horses in frantic haste. We dressed hastily, said hurried good-bys, and in a few moments were galloping through the silent streets to the regimental headquarters. The men of the various companies were already dressing and falling in. It was plain to be seen that their condition was one of suppressed excitement. But as they heard the ominous sound borne to their ears, I will warrant there was not one of them who grudged the dreary months of drill at San Francisco. It all seemed well worth while then. Getting onto the roof of the building I could make out that the fighting was entirely along what we knew as the "north line," that is, the front of the Second Division. The First Division did not become involved until daybreak. We were just ready to march out when the telegraph instrument in the building clicked out the order from the brigade commander to proceed at once with two battalions of the regiment to support our own outpost line, the other battalions to be for the time being left in the city as reserve. So we swung down the Calle Lemeri, the second and third battalions, in column of fours. As we made our way to the northward through the darkened streets we could hear firing directly on our own front, and knew that our own outpost must be contending against great odds. The commander of the outpost, Captain Adna G. Clarke, now a captain in the regular army, and the officer on duty with him, Lieutenant A. H. Krause, had taken prompt steps as soon as they had heard the firing break out on the front of the First Nebraska, miles to their right, and were alert and ready for business with the full strength of the outpost, some seventy men, when the Filipino fire, gradually extending to the westward, struck them. Sheltering their small detachment as well as the conditions would permit, they replied with vigor, directing their fire toward the flashes of the enemy's rifles. Of course, this sort of fire fight in the darkness is not very productive of casualties, and by the time the main portion of the regiment had arrived only one man had been hit. In the meantime the nearly a thousand of us were coming along at a fast walk. Already the spiteful bullets from the enemy's Mausers were enlivening the air overhead with their peculiar popping noise, or striking the roofs or sides of the nipa shacks. The men of the regiment were strangely silent as they trudged along listening to the sounds made by these messengers of death. It was a new world for all but a few of them. As we were coming up in rear of our own outpost, of course no advance-guard was necessary, and a small group of us officers were riding just a few yards ahead of the column. Just as we reached the tramway car barns there was a tremendous boom half a mile or more to our front, and a couple of seconds later something struck the ground a few rods ahead of us, bounded into the air, passed overhead with a loud "swish," traversed the length of two companies, and then, with a sound like a young cyclone, demolished two or three nipa houses. It was a bit amusing the way the front half of the regiment all but prostrated itself as the big round shot passed overhead, though such action was the most natural thing in the world. During the night and the next day this gun fired thirty-eight shots at us, causing no casualties, though there were a number of narrow escapes. It was captured a few days later standing by the railroad round-house at Caloocan, and proved to be a bronze, muzzle-loading siege-gun of the type of sixty years ago. Its projectiles were spherical cast-iron shell, not loaded, so that in effect they were solid shot. Only a bend in the street, which caused the shot to be a few feet to one side of the column when it struck the second time, saved the regiment from a terrible disaster, as had it ploughed its way through the six rear companies of the two battalions in column it could scarcely have killed or disabled fewer than a hundred men. By all the rules of the game, being now under artillery fire, we should have formed line in order to minimize the effect of a projectile striking the regiment, but the maze of fences and houses, not to speak of a slough, or *estero*, a short distance ahead, which would have to be crossed at the bridge, made such action impossible. There was nothing to do but to double time and as quickly as possible get to the comparatively open country where we could deploy. The command was given and forward we went at a good, swinging trot. Another boom, and a second big shot came tumbling and bounding along, but was a few feet to the right of the street, and so did not give us so close a call as the first one. By the time the third one came we had cleared the nipa houses and crossed the bridge, and were deploying in the fields on either side of the road. All of this time the rattle of rifle fire was not diminishing, and now the bullets from the Mausers were not only passing overhead, but striking all about. The detail on outpost, that had now been fighting for an hour or more, was relieved by several companies, while the others were sheltered as well as possible, and held in reserve for the time being. For an hour or so the companies that we had deployed on the firing line did some firing, mostly in the form of occasional volleys, but as there was not much but the noise on our front as a target, it seemed rather unprofitable business, and the men were ordered to lie down as closely as they could behind the rice dikes and take it easy, getting what sleep they could. Of course enough men were kept on lookout to give warning of any attempt to rush us. There was scarcely any diminution in the fire of the enemy, it being so incessant that the darkness on our front seemed to emit an almost continuous roar. But it was badly directed, as the Filipinos were evidently crouching down in their trenches and using their Mausers as rapidly as they could, but simply splattering the whole country with bullets, the great majority of them going far over our heads. The big cannon, in an excellent gun-pit a thousand yards up the road, let fly from time to time, and the shot, like overgrown croquet-balls, would come tumbling and bounding along, smashing down the bamboos and occasionally wrecking a house behind us. The men soon got over whatever uneasiness they may have felt regarding these projectiles, and began to call out derisively, "Low ball" or "High ball," according to the merit of each shot. We had a few men wounded during the night. It will be wondered why our casualties were not quite severe under so heavy a fire, badly directed though it was. But a line of men lying close to the ground behind rice dikes gives mighty little chance to bullets fired at random through the darkness half a mile away. The Filipinos would have done well to have saved the possibly a million cartridges that they fired at the Second Division on this night, for we were no more deeply into it than the other regiments along the front to our right.

The longed-for daylight came at last, and with it some lessening in the fire of the enemy. Two field-pieces of the Utah Artillery Battalion had arrived during the night, having been dragged by hand, none of the batteries having yet been supplied with horses, and as soon as they could do so to advantage, opened fire up the road, giving their principal attention to the big gun, the approximate position of which could be made out from the smoke which a few seconds after each discharge could be seen drifting over the tops of the bamboos. The exact location of the gun could not be made out. Major Richard H. Young, commanding the Utah Artillery, and I were standing talking a few feet to the rear of the two guns while they were in action when we heard again the boom of the bronze siege-gun, and an instant later we saw a dark object coming down the road, just a few feet above the ground. The shot cut off a banana-stalk not more than four feet from the right wheel of one of the guns, struck the ground a few rods down the road behind us, tore up a lot of earth, and the last we saw of it was rolling and bounding along, looking like a small iron kettle that had suddenly come to life. It would have been interesting to see what that field-piece would have looked like after the thing was over if this shot had passed a few feet nearer the centre of the road.

Company M of the Twentieth Kansas, under the direction of its commander, Captain William H. Bishop, was just to the right of the road, fairly well protected by a rather high dike, and was firing volleys slowly, when Private Charles Pratt, the first man of the regiment to die in action, sank down without a sound, shot through the brain. For some time his body lay there, a grewsome spectacle for those who had occasion to pass near the company and were not yet used to such sights.

General Otis, our brigade commander, visited the regiment several times during the forenoon, but spent most of his time farther to the right. We were hoping for an order to advance and bring the thing to a close, so far as it concerned ourselves, but fearing to disarrange the plans of our higher commanders, I thought there was nothing to do but bide our time and make the best of it. A short time after noon came the order to advance as far as the Lico road, which ran parallel with our front, about six hundred yards in advance. In the meantime the first battalion of the regiment had come out from the city, and two of its companies were placed on the firing line. The battalion was under the command of Captain Frederick E. Buchan, Lieutenant-Colonel Little having a couple of weeks previously been so unfortunate as to be severely wounded by the accidental discharge of his own revolver. At the order the line rose to its feet and, without firing, advanced rapidly, the movement not being detected by the enemy, owing to the heavy growth of trees and bamboo between the lines. But we had scarcely got into our new position within three or four hundred yards of the enemy's trenches, and begun to construct hasty intrenchments, when a terrific fire was opened on us. The two Utah guns were brought up and, without cover, in the middle of the road, fired several shots. But such a fire was concentrated on them at this short range that the men were ordered to leave them for the time and take cover. The five companies that constituted our firing line were working their Springfields for all they were worth, and their front was blanketed with a pall of white smoke that resembled a fierce prairie fire, for we had not yet received smokeless powder for these weapons. It was an impossible situation. The enemy in his excellent trenches was pouring into us a fire that we could not hope to overcome by merely firing back at him. There was no time to ask for instructions from the brigade commander. It was one of the times when subordinates must take the bits in their teeth. I stepped over to Captain Bishop, and, more to hear what he would say than because I had any doubts on the subject, asked him if the men were equal to it. He replied, "You bet they are!" I turned to Chief

Trumpeter Barshfield, at my side, and directed him to blow "Cease firing." Then the order was passed down the line to fix bayonets, and the ominous clatter could be heard along the whole front. Then to our feet, and forward on a fast walk, firing as we went. The advance was much interfered with by fences, but the men, now yelling like fiends and fairly smothering the yellow tops of the earthworks with their fire, pressed forward. Company F, Captain Charles I. Martin, got the worst of it, and had six men hit. I particularly recollect a sergeant in L company, an old regular, who was having the time of his life, addressing imprecations impartially to the enemy and the men of his section, and at the same time plying his rifle with vigor. When we were within seventy yards the "Charge" was blown, and the yelling and excited men dashed forward on the run, and in a few seconds we were over the works. The enemy did not wait for the bayonet, but broke and ran as we made the final dash, many of them being shot down in their flight before they could reach cover. We found in the trench some thirty killed, while others were scattered here and there as they had been brought down in flight. There were also some badly wounded, but very few of those, as men fighting up to their necks in trenches do not expose their legs and the lower parts of their bodies. One of the imbecile and childish things that the insurgent leaders had done was to organize in the mountains of northern Luzon several companies of Igorrote spearmen. These poor naked savages had been drilled in some sort of fashion, but were provided only with their spears and shields, and then, apparently under the impression that their very appearance would frighten the Americans into retreat, had been distributed here and there through the insurgent trenches. A few of them were in the works carried by us, and three or four lay dead. One poor fellow was on his back, his spear lying across his legs and his shield over his breast. A ragged hole showed where one of the heavy bullets had gone through the shield and then through his body. That spear is one of the few relics that I brought from the war, and that did not go up in the San Francisco fire. While the men were cheering over their first victory, and, I regret to say, getting the companies pretty well tangled up, fire was opened on us from what was known as Blockhouse No. One, about two hundred yards to our right front. This was a part of the old Spanish line of defences against the insurgents. The men were so mixed up that it was hopeless to get a company or platoon intact, so I gathered about a dozen of the officers and men nearest me, and we carried it with a rush, killing or capturing every man in it. "Assembly" was blown as soon as possible, and the companies formed. While this was going on, we witnessed to our right, about half a mile, an inspiring spectacle, the Third Artillery storming the Chinese cemetery. The well-trained regulars swept up the hill as if they were merely doing a "stunt" at manœuvres, but we could see that they were having a fight of it. I had at once sent to the brigade commander a verbal message to the effect that I had advanced beyond the Lico road, and giving the reasons for doing so. Shortly after the regiment had assembled orders were received to fall back to the road and bivouac along it for the night in a line facing the enemy. As we were marching back we narrowly escaped a disaster. The cruiser *Charleston*, in the bay opposite our left, had thrown during the day a number of shells at the enemy's works, and had now been relieved by the *Concord*. This vessel, not knowing that the enemy's works had been carried, the distance being great and the country close, opened fire. For a while it looked bad for us, as one shell barely missed cutting through a company in column. We had to run for it, and put the regiment to double time. The men were cool, and there was no tendency to break ranks. In my opinion the commander of the *Concord* was in no way to blame, as we were not supposed to be so far in advance, and would not have been except for the reasons stated.

We reached our position, formed line, and prepared to spend the night. Firewood and water were abundant, and the men were soon munching bacon and hardtack and drinking "soldier-coffee." They were a happy lot, having gone not without credit through their first engagement, and spent a good deal of the time, when they should have been sleeping, in exchanging experiences. They seemed to worry themselves but little over the serious business ahead, and were inclined to let each day take care of itself.

II

CALOOCAN AND ITS TRENCHES

Shortly after daylight on February 5 [1899], orders were received for the Twentieth Kansas to advance from the Lico road and occupy a line somewhat beyond the trenches captured on the preceding afternoon. It was not known whether these had been reoccupied by the enemy or not, but after a part of the regiment had been deployed scouts were sent to work their way carefully to the front in order to report on the situation. These men stated that the enemy had not returned, so that there would be no necessity to fight in order to regain the ground given up. The regiment moved into its new position without incident, and was soon intrenching. As the lagoons from the bay did not come in so close at this point, we had more room, and it was found practicable to extend our left so far that with its right resting on the railroad the regiment could have every one of its three battalions on the line. Immediately on our right we joined with the Third Artillery, which, it must be remembered, was serving as infantry, which in its turn connected with the First Montana, occupying the high ground near La Loma church. Six guns of the Utah Light Artillery Battalion under Major Richard W. Young and two guns of the Sixth Artillery under Lieutenant Adrian Fleming were posted at advantageous points along the line. During the day we could hear some firing far to our right, but there was little done on our own front, though the occasional crack of a rifle in the woods and the "zip" of a bullet furnished the necessary incentive to make the men cautious about exposing themselves. The left of the regiment fronted on dense woods, where nothing could be observed, but its right was partially in the open, while the other two organizations of the brigade were entirely so.

During the day an officer rode over to my regiment, stated that he was Major Bell of the division staff, and desired that I should furnish him with a non-commissioned officer and a few other men in order that he might ascertain something as to the location of the insurgent trenches covering the town of Caloocan, on our front. At this I bristled up somewhat and announced that if there was any scouting to be done in advance of my regiment I could do it myself or have it done. Upon being assured by Major Bell that he was acting under orders of the division commander, I yielded the point, but I fear not with very good grace. Thus, rather inauspiciously, began my acquaintance with my excellent friend, the present Major-General J. F. Bell, who was destined, because of his exceptional services in the suppression of the Philippine insurrection, to rise within a few years to the highest rank now attainable in our army. I suppose that General Bell has by this time entirely forgotten the incident described. Later in the campaign that officer had at his disposal for scouting purposes a picked body of men, and did some most astonishing things in the way of penetrating the enemy's lines and bringing back information as to the location of his trenches. The non-commissioned officer that I directed to report to Major Bell on this occasion was Corporal Arthur M. Ferguson, a man whose soldierly qualities and daring were eventually to win him the Medal of Honor and a commission in the volunteer service and afterward in the regular army. We shall hear more of him later in connection with the passage of the Rio Grande at Calumpit. Of course, whatever information Major Bell obtained on this reconnoissance was transmitted to the division commander. I was desirous of learning something on my own hook, and later in the day took a few men and crawled with them into the dense woods in front of the left of the regiment, working gradually around to the right until we were within a few hundred yards of the trenches just south of the Caloocan church. The country here was comparatively open, and we could see that the Filipinos were working with feverish haste in improving their defences. Being so close, the temptation to stir them up with a fusillade was very great, but it would never do, as we might be cut off before we could fall back on our lines.

I had established regimental head-quarters about two hundred yards to the rear of our trenches, just to the right of the Caloocan wagon road, which cut the regiment's line at right angles about one-third of the distance from its right to its left. As night came on the men were instructed to lie down and get what sleep they could behind the low shelter that they had constructed, a number from each company being detailed to remain on lookout in order to give warning of any attempt to rush our line.

It was not thought best to have men on outpost in the woods on our front, as in case of a sudden attack they would mask the fire of the regiment, or possibly be sacrificed before they could retire to its line. So far as firing was concerned, we had a quiet day of it, but nightfall brought trouble. The regimental staff officers with myself and a few orderlies had just spread out our blankets and were preparing to lie down, when a lively rattle of fire opened up in the direction of the enemy's lines, and bullets began striking about us and whistling overhead. I was of the opinion that it was a mere spurt and would die down, but nevertheless rose and walked over to the trench, where I was joined by Major Metcalf. The firing increased in volume, and apparently was not coming from the enemy's trenches, which were eight hundred yards on our front, but rather from a point about half-way to them. None of our men were asleep yet, and some of them began to reply without orders.

There was some delay in finding a trumpeter to blow "Cease firing," and in the meantime one of our men was hit, and gave a shriek that was heard almost the length of the regiment. In an instant the men were beyond control. As the firing on our front increased they thought a charge was coming, and, kneeling behind the low shelter, worked their old Springfields for all they were worth. It was a form of panic, but not half so bad as bolting to the rear. The men were in as close a line as they could be and work their rifles, and they crammed cartridges into them and fired as rapidly as possible. The roar was deafening, while the rapid spurts of flame along the whole line made in the darkness a show of fireworks that was not to be despised. The dense blanket of smoke, added to the gloom, made it impossible to see anything. We soon had every trumpeter in the regiment blowing "Cease firing," but in some cases blows and kicks had to be resorted to in order to bring the men to their senses. As our fire died down enough for one to be able to make himself heard, the officers began to open the vials of their wrath on their respective companies, while I, having to "cuss" twelve companies instead of one, was quite overcome by my efforts. But the insurgent fire had absolutely ceased, the enemy having stirred up more of a hornets' nest than he had bargained for.

What had occurred was that several hundred of them had advanced from their trenches to a point where there was good natural cover, whence they had started a fire fight, which they were doubtless glad to cease. It was in no sense an attempt to take our line by a rush, but that was what the men had feared. The regiment expended about twenty-five thousand rounds of ammunition in this piece of foolishness, but it was the last performance of that kind, involving any considerable number of men, that we had during the campaign. One of the insurgents wounded in this affair was the Filipino major, Hilario Tal Placido, who, captured more than a year later in Nueva Ecija province while I was in command there, became an "*Americanista*," and accompanied me on the expedition that brought in his old chief, Emilio Aguinaldo. Hilario, after I had come to know him, assured me that this experience cured him of any further desire to assist in unnecessarily stirring up the Americans just to see what they would do, and that he felt lucky in getting out of it with nothing worse than a big bullet through one of his lungs.

The next day while visiting La Loma church I took occasion to express to General MacArthur, who had his head-quarters there, my regret that the regiment had got into such a panic, but was assured by him that it was nothing to feel badly about, as it is a very common experience of troops until they have been under fire a few times. As a matter of fact, very few regiments in the Philippines escaped going through the same thing during the process of getting used to being under fire.

During the afternoon of the day following this incident, it being very quiet, I rather unwisely sent word to Mrs. Funston, in Manila, telling her that if she wished she could come out to the lines for a short visit, as it would give her an opportunity to see something of troops in the field, and we could have a brief chat. But in the meantime Captain Christy, who was officer of the day and was patrolling in front of the regiment with a few men, became involved in a sharp fight at about two hundred yards range with some hundred and fifty of the enemy, who had advanced from their trenches and were behind a dike, probably the same one from which they had fired on us during the night. I went out into the woods to investigate, and found that the redoubtable Christy had bitten off considerably more than he could masticate. He had only a few men, but they were fairly well sheltered and were having a hard fight, being so deeply involved that it was going to be a problem to get them out. I crouched down with the men for a few moments in order to decide what to do, and finally, by having them cease fire suddenly and then spring to their feet and make a dash by the right flank to some "dead" ground, stopped the fight. Going back to my head-quarters, behind the regiment's line, I found that Mrs. Funston had arrived, escorted by my orderly and Major Metcalf's. She had ridden in a *carromato*, a Filipino vehicle distantly related to the one-horse buggy, it being driven by one of the soldiers while the other rode along on horseback and acted as escort. The party had arrived during the skirmish in the woods, and as quite a few bullets were flying overhead, Mrs. Funston was sheltered for a time behind a portion of the Filipino earthwork that we had assaulted and carried two days before. Realizing that another fight was liable to break out at any moment, she went back to the city after a brief stay.

The hope that the Filipinos who had been stirred up by Captain Christy would desist, now that they were being let alone, proved an illusory one, as they kept up a slow fire on that portion of our trench nearest to them. Deeming it necessary once for all to break up this form of amusement, and fearing that it might continue throughout the night, I sent a staff officer to explain the situation to the brigade commander and requested leave to administer the necessary castigation. The desired permission was granted, but I was cautioned not to attempt any pursuit after the force annoying us had been dislodged, as it was feared that such action might bring on a general engagement, thus interfering with the plans of the division commander. Three companies were considered more than sufficient to do the work, and their commanders were directed to hold them in readiness. It was not known how far into the woods the enemy's right flank extended, and an attempt to turn his left would have exposed us to fire from the trenches near Caloocan, so that a frontal attack was decided upon as giving the greatest chance to inflict heavy loss.

Major Metcalf was to assist me in leading the attack. At the word of command the three companies rose to their feet and fixed bayonets. Leaping over the trench, the start was quickly made. Our right was directly opposite the enemy's left, but it developed that our left considerably overlapped his right. For the first hundred yards the woods screened our movements, but when we broke into the open at a distance of three hundred yards from the dike we could see that it was fairly alive with the straw hats of the Filipinos, and they opened on us as rapidly as they could fire. Our men, perfectly steady, did not reply until ordered to a few seconds later, and when they did they fairly combed the top of that dike with bullets. We were advancing at a walk and it was point-blank range, and our fire so disconcerted the enemy that though they plied their rifles with great vigor, they were not exposing themselves enough to get any sort of good aim. They were armed entirely with Mausers so that they had no smoke to interfere with them, while our Springfields produced the usual prairie-fire effect. What little wind there was, however, served to drive the smoke behind instead of ahead of us, so that we were not so much troubled by it as ordinarily.

The men were under perfect control, and while somewhat excited, were attending to their knitting. There had been scarcely a word spoken except for the occasional commands given by officers and non-commissioned officers, but when we were within eighty yards I had the "Charge" blown. Only the men near the trumpeter could hear it, but as they raised a yell and went forward on a run the others followed suit. It does not take long to cover eighty yards if you are in a hurry, and in no time we were among them. Of course, as soon as our men began to run, they ceased firing, though it was recommenced to a certain extent when we closed. As we reached the position and went over the dike all of the Filipinos who had not been killed or disabled rose to their feet and tried to get away. If we had molested them no further, and had let them go, it is probable that the fight would have ended at once, but our men were among them and a good many fought to save their lives. It did not seem to occur to them that they would be spared if they threw down their arms, but they had been used to fighting Spaniards, who had given them the same kind of quarter that they had given the insurgents of Cuba. A confused mêlée followed. It was the only time in my life that I saw the bayonet actually used.

Within twenty feet of me, a plucky little Filipino, one of the few of them who had his bayonet fixed, made a vicious jab at one of our sergeants, and a second later was run through the body. And he was not the only one to get the cold steel. During the mix-up I saw a Filipino raise his rifle and at a distance of only a few yards take a shot at one of our men. Just as the bullet struck the soldier in the thigh he saw the man who had shot him lowering his rifle. At first he seemed dazed, dropping his own weapon, but without stopping to pick it up sailed into that Filipino barehanded, twisted his rifle out of his hands and beat his brains out with it. The enemy had a very fine silken flag with the emblem of the Katipunan embroidered on it. A number of them tried to get away with it, and it became the centre of a short and sharp struggle in which fire-arms could not be used. In fact, it resembled as much as anything some of the confused scrambles that are seen on the foot-ball field. When we finally got the flag it had been riddled by bullets and was drenched in blood. It is now in the State House at Topeka. All of the Filipinos who could do so were getting toward the rear as rapidly as possible. Those who could cover the sixty yards to the dense underbrush were safe, as our orders did not permit us to follow them.

The whole affair had lasted less time than it takes to tell it. The companies were assembled as soon as possible, preparatory to returning to our own lines, as a counter-attack which might be made on us by the Filipinos in the Caloocan trenches, distant only a few hundred yards, might have brought on the general engagement that I had orders to avoid. The Filipinos suffered severely in this combat, but we did not take the time necessary to make a complete count of their dead and disabled, though along the left of their trench, where the hardest fighting had taken place, I counted thirty dead. There were not a great many wounded left on the ground, as all who were able to rise had escaped to the rear. Among the dead we were surprised to find a very large and coal-black negro. As this was many months before any of our colored troops had been brought to the islands, the man could not have been a deserter from them, but was probably some vagabond seaman who had run away from a merchant-vessel in Manila Bay. The storm of bullets that we had poured into the enemy as we advanced, disconcerting and "rattling" him, as well as the fact that the Filipinos were absolutely no match for our much larger men in the hand-to-hand struggle, had saved us from heavy loss. First Lieutenant Alfred C. Alford, commanding Company B, an excellent officer, who had been one of my schoolmates at the University of Kansas, was killed just as we carried the position. Sergeant Jay Sheldon, of Company I, was so badly wounded that he died the next day, while five other enlisted men were wounded, all severely. After we had returned to our line I went over to the dressing-station to see our wounded. I tried to cheer up and encourage Sergeant Sheldon, though the surgeon had told me that his condition was very grave. He was a plucky fellow, and, though suffering greatly, made the remark, "Well, it was worth getting hit to have been in so fine a fight." We had left the enemy's wounded where they had fallen, knowing that their friends would come for them during the night, now close at hand.

After the affair just described practically nothing of note occurred along the front of the Twentieth Kansas until the afternoon of the 10th, though we could occasionally hear firing far to the right along the front of Hale's brigade. After consideration of the situation General MacArthur determined to rectify the line occupied by the division to the extent of advancing our brigade, the First. From left to right the three regiments of the brigade were distributed as follows: Twentieth Kansas, First Montana, and Third Artillery, the last-named organization connecting with Hale's brigade on the ridge near La Loma church. The contemplated movement really constituted a partial wheel to the right, pivoting on the right of the Third Artillery, so that that regiment had to make a very slight advance, the First Montana considerably more, while my own regiment had to push forward through the woods for more than half a mile, incidentally taking the town of Caloocan and the trenches covering it. Major Whitman had become ill a day or two previously and had returned to Manila, so that his battalion was commanded by Captain Edmund Boltwood, a gallant old veteran of the Civil War, in which he had served as an officer.

After the orders for the attack had been issued I had a heart-to-heart talk with Major Kobbé, of the Third Artillery, and confided to him that I expected my regiment to lose heavily, as it would have to carry the strong trenches covering Caloocan on the south, as well as the massive church and adjacent wall. That officer agreed that I had a hard job cut out, and coincided with my view that the best way to avoid heavy loss in the advance would be to cover the Filipinos with fire as we attacked, and to make no attempt to save ammunition. The experience obtained in our attacks of the 5th and 7th had convinced me that by sweeping the ground that we were advancing over with a storm of bullets we could so demoralize the enemy that his fire would be badly directed. Appropriate orders were issued to battalion and company commanders, and we formed for the attack, being, so far, completely screened from the enemy by the woods on our front. The preliminary bombardment of the Filipino position by several vessels of the fleet and all our field artillery took half an hour, and fairly filled the air with its roar. Owing to intervening tree growth the trenches could not be seen from the fleet, but their positions were approximately known, being marked by the church, which was in sight. The eight-inch and six-inch shells, following each other in quick succession, were continuously exploding in the woods to our front. They must have been a severe trial for the insurgents, as they had no adequate protection from them.

Of course, however, the fire of the fleet had to cease before the beginning of the infantry attack, so that they had some time in which to recover their composure. At last the pandemonium of sound ceased, and we dashed forward into the woods. Although the insurgents could not yet see us, they knew from the movements of the other two regiments in the open ground that the advance had begun, and how they did fill those woods with bullets! We had all twelve companies on the firing line, our support marching in rear being a battalion of the First Idaho, brought over for the occasion from the First Division, and the whole regiment as the bugles rang out the command to commence firing became wreathed in smoke, while the noise was so great that it was out of the question to make one's self heard. The attack was made at a walk, the men firing to the front as rapidly as they could, regardless of the fact that at first no target could be seen. Many bullets were stopped by tree trunks, but thousands more, striking about the Filipino trenches or passing close over them, so demoralized the defenders that their fire, while of great volume, was very wild. I had started to ride my horse through the fight, but finally concluded to dismount, as fences confined me largely to the road, down which was coming the heaviest fire. So I followed the attack on foot, immediately behind Company C. We passed over the scene of the severe little fight of the 7th, and saw the Filipino dead still lying where they had fallen, though their wounded had been removed. In this company was a unique character, Sergeant John C. Murphy, who died only a couple of years ago as a retired officer of the regular army. Throughout the whole advance Murphy serenely smoked a large brier-wood pipe, which he only removed from his mouth when it became necessary to address some pointed remarks to the men of his section. He saw one of his men crouch quietly down behind a low shelter as if he contemplated remaining there as the company passed on. Murphy walked back to the man, deliberately removed his pipe, as if he were afraid of biting the stem in two, and then with unhoneyed words fairly kicked him up onto the firing line, where the man made up for lost time by plying his rifle with great vigor.

The five companies on the right of the regiment had now broken into the open in full view of the church and the trenches near it. These trenches and the top of the wall near the church were alive with straw hats bobbing up and down, while from both came a severe but badly aimed fire. It was a pretty exciting moment. For half a minute one company showed some signs of disorder, the men beginning to halt and lie down, but Major Metcalf and the officers and sergeants of the company strode up and down the line and quickly got them going again. I ordered the "Charge" blown, and all who could hear it sprang forward, the men to the right or left taking the cue and advancing with them, the whole regiment breaking into yells as we closed. In no time we were over the trenches, the survivors among the defenders bolting to the rear, the wall near the church being abandoned at the same time. Some of them were shot down as they ran, but our men were so "winded" that their shooting was not so good as it might have been. Major Metcalf saw one man bring down a fleeing Filipino by hurling his rifle at him with both hands, muzzle first. The bayonet passed entirely through the man's skull. The bottom of the trench was a shocking spectacle, being simply covered with dead and wounded men, the most of whom had been brought down in the brief fire fight at close range that had preceded the final rush. The town had been fired in many places by the Filipinos as they retired. The nipa houses burned like tinder, and through the smoke and flames we took up the pursuit.

There was a moment's delay after the church was reached, the field and staff officers remounted their horses that had been brought up in the rear of the line, and the irregular and waving line of a thousand yelling men pushed through the burning town in pursuit. We were soon in the open country, but the fleet-footed Filipinos had several hundred yards the start of us, and we did not bring down many of them, the excitement of the chase and the exhaustion of the men not being conducive to good shooting. Occasionally a group would turn and fire on us for a few seconds, but the most of their efforts were bent on placing the Tuliajan River between themselves and our line. We chased them to the summit of the ridge overlooking that stream, about half a mile beyond Caloocan, and then halted, being far beyond where we had been directed to establish our new line.

The dusk was now gathering, but across the river near Malinta we could see long lines of the enemy, some of whom opened on us with a rather sharp but quite ineffective fire, the distance being about twelve hundred yards. We did not at first reply, but finally Captain Orwig of his own initiative began volley-firing with his company. I rode over to his position and pitched into him rather savagely in the hearing of his men, telling him that we could not hit anybody with our old Springfields at that distance, and that the fire of the enemy could do us no harm. Hardly had I delivered myself of this sage opinion when my horse whirled suddenly and began to sink down. Dismounting immediately, it was discovered that the animal had been shot clear through the neck, one of the surgeons later removing the bullet from under the skin on the right-hand side. In view of my heated remarks only a moment before, this incident caused a derisive chuckle throughout the whole company. The horse, a fine little bay of the better type of Filipino pony, sure-footed, and indifferent to the noise of firing, completely recovered in time, and I rode him through all of the campaign up the railroad.

After dark the regiment fell back to a point about four hundred yards north of the Caloocan church where it was to intrench and remain until the general advance, six weeks later. Considering the heavy fire that we had been under, especially while the right flank of the regiment was engaging the trenches near the church, our losses had been small, consisting of two enlisted men killed and Captain Christy and eight enlisted men wounded. This did not include several slight wounds and contusions from spent bullets. The next morning we counted sixty-four insurgent dead, mostly in the trenches near the church or in their vicinity. Their wounded who had been left on the ground we gathered up and sent in to the hospital with our own. About one hundred rifles and several thousand rounds of ammunition were captured and destroyed, as we had no way of sending them back to the city. We also found standing near the railway repair-shops the big bronze siege-gun that had fired at us during the fighting of the night of the 4th and the next day. It had not been used in the present engagement, possibly because its ammunition had been exhausted. It must by no means be inferred that all the fighting on this day had fallen to the Twentieth Kansas, as the other two regiments of the brigade were just as severely engaged, but in the open country; while a detachment under Major Bell had assisted in the operation by crawling up a ravine and attacking the enemy in the left flank.

The regiment's new line was an undesirable one for several reasons, all of them beyond the control of anybody other than the insurgents. Its left was on the narrow causeway which connected Caloocan with the considerable town of Malabon, this causeway being parallel with the regiment, or rather being on an extension of its left flank. This condition subjected us constantly to a long-range enfilading fire which in the long run cost us numerous casualties, but which was in a measure provided against by the construction of sand-bag traverses six feet high in the shelter occupied by the battalion on the left. On the front of this same battalion the woods and bamboos came very close, and the ground was cut up by shallow ravines, the insurgents thus being enabled to construct trenches almost under our noses. The town of Malabon could not be taken except under the most disadvantageous conditions until our line had been advanced beyond the Tuliajan River, as the only method possible would have been a charge up the narrow causeway, flanked on both sides by swamps, and would have been a costly enterprise, especially as a bridge on it had been removed.

A week or so later I volunteered to try to rush the causeway by night with a small detachment in the hope that we could effect a lodgment in the town and hold on until the arrival of reinforcements. But General Mac-Arthur did not think much of the project, and I have no doubt that his judgment was correct. At the time we had not a sufficient number of troops to hold the town even if we had succeeded in taking it. The centre of the regiment occupied an old Spanish trench which we improved, while the right, extending across the railroad, made some very satisfactory cover for itself. All day of the 11th was spent in intrenching, the work being done under an almost incessant long-range fire from Malabon. The left flank battalion was protected by a loop-holed sand-bag parapet six feet high, and was provided with traverses at short intervals. Just to the front of the centre of our right the field artillery constructed a redoubt open to the rear in which were installed several field-pieces. Lieutenant Seaman, of the Utah Artillery Battalion, was wounded while supervising the work, and was succeeded by Lieutenant Fleming, Sixth Artillery, who, under the general direction of Major Young, the chief of artillery, had charge of the battery thereafter. The Twentieth Kansas had four men wounded during the day, while two men of the Thirteenth Minnesota who in order to see some fighting had run away from their own regiment, which was still on duty in the city, were also hit, which came about being what they deserved.

General MacArthur established himself in the temporarily abandoned residence of Mr. Higgins, general manager of the Manila-Dagupan railway, this building being located in a very exposed position just west of the railroad track and less than a hundred yards behind the trench of my regiment. The brigade commander, General H. G. Otis, was camped in the open in the rear of the centre of his command. As head-quarters for my own regiment, I took the Caloocan church, and rather think that I had the better of my superiors.

On the previous evening, just after bringing the regiment back from the ridge overlooking the Tuliajan, I had entered the building for the first time, and had had a small adventure that was to rise up and plague me months later. I had found there, rummaging about among the few articles that had been left in the building, an iron-visaged American woman, somewhat past middle-age. I had seen her on several occasions, and knew her to be one of those self-appointed, so-called nurses, but really meddlesome busybodies, who are so apt to be found in the wake of armies in the field. This person had two names, or at least went by two different ones. Women of her type should not for a moment be confused with the members of that splendid and efficient body who go to make up the Army Nurse Corps, who remained on duty in the hospitals where they belonged, and who never made nuisances of themselves. I watched the woman for a few moments, and seeing her roll into a bundle a few articles of really no intrinsic value, told a sergeant to inform her quietly that she would not be permitted to take anything from the building. She replied to the effect that she would do as she pleased, and that it was nobody's business what she took. This courteous message having been delivered to me, I walked over to her, made her drop the bundle, and received a most artistic tongue-lashing in return. I closed the scene by telling her that if she did not at once leave the building I would send her under guard to Manila, even if I had to tie her up. She flounced out of the building in high dudgeon, vowing she would have me dismissed from the service. As a matter of fact, the things that she had attempted to take were of no intrinsic value, being merely an old and much-worn priest's robe and some sheet music, there being nothing else left in the church; but our orders to prevent looting, and especially to protect the churches, were so strict that I did not feel justified in permitting her to remove anything.

The rapidly moving incidents of the campaign made me all but forget this affair, but on my return to the United States, this woman, having preceded me to San Francisco, made and furnished to the newspapers an affidavit to the effect that she had entered the Caloocan church immediately after the battle and had seen me kick open a glass case containing a statue of the Virgin, from which I had stripped a gold-embroidered robe worth more than a thousand dollars, sending it to my wife in Manila. I made indignant denial, but a day later a man named Fitzgerald came out with another affidavit stating that he had been a witness to the occurrence. That, of course, settled it. This man was a fireman who had deserted from one of the transports, weeks after the taking of Caloocan, and had followed the army as a hanger-on during the campaign that had ended in the taking of Malolos, nearly two months later. One day shortly after the taking of Malolos I had caught him coming out of an abandoned residence with his arms full of clothing, and had sent him before the provost-marshal, who had punished him severely.

The allegations of this sweet-scented pair of perjurers all but ruined me. It almost destroyed my faith in the fair-mindedness of my countrymen, that except among my friends my denials went for absolutely nothing. The whole pack, from high dignitaries of the church down, were after me in full cry, and the only thing that saved me at all was the vigorous defence of me by my excellent friend, Chaplain McKinnon, of the First California, himself a Catholic priest, who stated that, having come out to see the fight as a spectator, he had entered the church before I did and that there was in it no statue of the Virgin, or for that matter anything else of the slightest value from either a sacred or any other stand-point. The idea that nothing of value would have been left in a building in which services had not been held for nearly a year, and which during all of this time had been an insurgent fort and barrack, never seems to have occurred to my detractors. But to this day not one of the men who took the matter up through the press and in public addresses has had the decency to express regret for his action. There never was a grosser slander against an army than the stories of church-looting in the Philippines. That there may have been isolated instances I am not prepared to deny, but such articles as the soldiers brought home were usually purchased from Chinese or Filipinos who had themselves stolen them from the churches when these were abandoned by their priests, which was long before the outbreak of the insurrection against the authority of the United States; and in most cases the purchasers knew nothing of any sacred character that these articles may have had. So far as the incident recounted has had any effect on myself, I feel that there is one thing mighty certain, and that is that if Uncle Sam should ever in a moment of confidence intrust me with the command of an army in the field, no camp-follower, male or female, will ever get within sight of it.

We now settled down to a by no means humdrum existence, waiting for the arrival of troops from the United States, who were to hold the "north line" of Manila while our division advanced against the insurgent capital. In the Twentieth Kansas was a large number of railroad men, and we soon had the tramway to Manila in operation hauling out to the front ammunition and subsistence supplies. On the wheezy engine at our disposal the men painted such legends as "Kansas and Utah Short Line," "Freddy's Fast Express," and such other bits of soldier humor as occurred to them. The insurgents were heavily intrenched within two hundred yards of the left of our line, having taken advantage of the cover afforded to dig themselves into the ground. We could have chased them out by an attack, but it was contrary to the plans of the division commander to bring on a general engagement before he was prepared to follow it up. So we had to bide our time. In spite of all precautions bullets from the trenches on our front or from Malabon kept taking their toll. If a man moved about by daylight for a bit of exercise he was liable to become the target for a hundred rifles and have to dive for cover. Fortunately a Filipino seldom hit anything that he shot at, so that the greatest danger arose from the long-range dropping fire from Malabon.

There would be days of comparative quiet, and then others in which the enemy would sweep us with a hot fire for half an hour or so. He seemed to have no end of ammunition, and was not lacking in a willingness to expend it. The field-guns in the redoubt sent occasional shells at our opponents, but they seemed so well sheltered that but little harm could be done them. But they had awaiting them a most unwelcome surprise, for in a few days a field-mortar was installed among the other guns. A mortar, it should be said for the benefit of non-military readers, is a very short gun using a small charge of powder. Instead of sending its projectile a long distance on a comparatively flat trajectory it throws it up into the air, and it comes almost straight down, being especially useful against troops behind cover at short range. There was one big yellow trench opposite the left of my regiment that had peppered us persistently, and the mortar gave it attention first. When the odd little gun was fired we saw the projectile mount a couple of hundred feet into the air and then sweep down with a graceful curve. It was a shrapnel with time fuse, and burst about thirty feet above the trench, being an absolutely perfect shot. The Filipinos swarmed out of the work like bees and began to run for cover. Several companies of the regiment had been warned to be in readiness for the occasion, and at short range poured in a fire that littered the ground with them. An occasional mortar shell at those of the trenches that we could see served to keep the enemy out of them during daylight, forcing them to lie behind low and inconspicuous cover. The trenches opposite our right, distant about eight hundred yards, caused us some annoyance, but did not do harm to compare with the others.

Among the vessels lying in the bay was the great

British cruiser, *Powerful*, commanded by Captain the Honorable Hedworth Lambton, who less than a year later with his officers and crew was to win world-wide renown for his work with the naval guns in the defence of Ladysmith. The officers of the cruiser frequently came out to our lines, and were much interested in the novel situation. Commander A. P. Ethelston and I had become great friends, and one day he visited us accompanied by about a dozen junior officers of the *Powerful*, saying that he would like to show them about. I was very uneasy about having them visit the trenches, fearing that so large a party might draw fire, and some of them be hit, especially as they were quite conspicuous on account of the white uniforms worn by them. I, however, felt some delicacy about referring to the possible danger. We walked down from the church to the right of the regiment's line, and then slowly strolled toward its left. We had covered half the distance, and I was beginning to thank my stars that we were going to get through without mishap, when the trouble began. About twenty men in a trench some six hundred yards distant opened on us, and bullets whistled all about, several passing through the group without hitting any one. As soon as the fire began I quickened the pace to a fast walk, and Ethelston, looking around at the young men with him, saw one or two of them flinch to the slightest degree, and spoke out sharply, "Remember, gentlemen, no ducking," and they threw their heads back and went through it without batting an eyelash. But they were all soon to go through a war that must have made our Philippine affair seem like play, and poor

Ethelston himself, only nine months later, was to die a hero's death in the desperate assault of the naval brigade at Gras Pan in South Africa.

The night of February 22d was the date set by the insurgent leaders for a grand *coup*, a demonstration against our north line to hold all our troops in it, while a large number passed our left flank, which it has already been explained did not reach to the bay shore, and entered the city, where they were to be joined by the so-called militia, a lot of riffraff numbering several thousands, armed mostly with bolos. They were then to set fire to the city in numerous places and attack Americans wherever they could be found. Up to a certain point this admirable project was carried out according to programme. Just after nightfall a severe fire was opened along our whole front, the entire brigade at least being attacked, and this continued almost without cessation until daylight. At times it was so severe that we anticipated that it was the prelude to an assault. The regiment had a number of men hit, despite the fact that we kept the men well down and did not allow them to reply except by a few volleys fired under the direction of company commanders. Major Metcalf had a very neat hole punched through his right ear close up to the head by a Mauser bullet. It was as close a call as one could get and not be killed.

On this night occurred a very unique incident. Company L was firing a few volleys, and one of the men having just discharged his piece felt a second blow against his shoulder, it being almost as hard as the kick of the gun.

Upon trying to reload it was found that the breech of the piece could not be opened, and it was laid aside to be examined by daylight, which was done in the presence of a number of us officers. Upon forcing the breech open it was found that the base of the copper shell of the cartridge that had been fired just before the weapon had been disabled had been shot away, while mixed all up in the breech mechanism we found the remains of the steel jacket and the lead filling of a Mauser bullet. There was a very pronounced dent on the muzzle of the piece. What had happened was that while the man had the gun extended in the firing position a bullet had gone down the muzzle. A man will go through a good many wars before he will encounter another such case. This weapon is now in the Army Ordnance Museum in Washington.

While we were having all this furor on our front, about a thousand of the best insurgent troops, taking advantage of low tide, crossed the estuaries between Malabon and the Tondo district of Manila, attacked and drove from the tramway car-barn the small guard of half a dozen men of the Twentieth Kansas, wounding one of them, and then swarmed through the Tondo and Binondo districts, setting scores of fires and attacking detachments of the provost guard. The street fighting came within a few blocks of the business centre, and the portions of the city burned aggregated probably a hundred acres, mostly the poorer class of nipa houses. From Caloocan we anxiously watched the glare of the great conflagration and listened to the continuous rattle of rifle fire miles in the rear of our lines. It was a bad night for those of us who had their families in Manila, but it was out of the question to think of leaving our posts for the purpose of protecting them.

The whole regiment had, of course, been awake and on the alert the entire night, and shortly after five o'clock the next morning, while I was down on the trench line, I saw a big puff of smoke rise from the summit of the hill near Malinta, about four thousand yards to the north. In a second came the telltale rumble, like the sound made by a train crossing a bridge, and at the same time a loud report was borne to our ears. When we first saw the puff of smoke it was thought to be the result of an accidental explosion, but the sound of the coming shell told us what to expect, and in a couple of seconds we saw it come sweeping down in a beautiful curve. It struck fifty yards in front of that portion of the trench occupied by Company E, threw half a wagon-load of earth into the air, and exploded with a noise like the report of a young cannon, while what looked like a general assortment of shelf hardware flew in all directions. The report had brought almost every man in the regiment to his feet, but the way the men of Company E dived to cover when the thing struck was worth going to see. It was subsequently learned that the shot was fired from a Krupp breech-loading rifled coast-defence gun which, after what must have been infinite labor, had been brought from either Cavite or Subig Bay. It was served by Spanish artillerymen who were prisoners among the Filipinos and who were compelled to do the work. It had been aimed at the Higgins house, known to be General MacArthur's head-quarters, and was an excellent shot, being in perfect line and less than a hundred and fifty yards short.

During the first day's fighting, as has been told, we had been fired at a number of times by a good-sized gun of antique type, and one day a shell from a Nordenfeldt field-gun had landed among us while in the Caloocan trenches, though it had not exploded; but we were greatly astonished to receive the attentions of so large a weapon as this one. We were still discussing the matter when another cloud of smoke rose at Malinta. This shot was perfect on elevation, but a few yards to the right. It cleared the trench by only a few feet and exploded when it struck. The thing was becoming interesting, and all eyes were riveted on Malinta. After a few moments came the third, and poorest shot of all, it being far to the right and with too much elevation. It struck about halfway between the trench and the church, and did not explode, but sailed up into the air and, tumbling end over end, passed a hundred feet over the roof of the church and fell to the south of it. A number of the men went out and brought it in. It was an elongated projectile about six inches in diameter and weighed about eighty pounds. The gun from which these shots were fired was dug up in the streets of Malolos after the capture of that place.

In the meantime Captain Edgar Russell, chief signal officer of the division, had been wigwagging from the church tower certain angles, elevations, and other scientific stuff to a couple of naval vessels, the *Monadnock* and *Charleston*, if I am not mistaken, lying off Malabon, and soon puffs of smoke rose from them as they began to take an interest in the proceedings. The distance was great, but the shooting was beautiful, especially when it is considered that the target was not in sight. The shells struck all about the offending gun, blowing big craters in the ground as they exploded, and we heard no more from it. For months we took it for granted that the navy fire had either disabled the gun or made the gunners afraid to serve it, but the Spaniard, Segovia, who was serving as an officer with the insurgents, and who was present at the time, told me more than a year later that the third shot had broken the elevating gear of the gun and that they were trying to remove it when the navy opened, the shells coming so close that everybody ran from the piece.

Soon stories began to drift in to us to the effect that twenty-four men had been killed by a shell at Malinta, and our field artillerymen began to pride themselves that one of their long-range efforts had potted a group of insurgents. But this same Segovia gave me the facts when I came to know him, and his statements were corroborated by Filipinos. According to him, the day after the occurrences just described a number of men of the Nueva Ecija Battalion, from the province of that name, dug out of the ground an unexploded navy shell, which from the description given me must have been of either ten-inch or eight-inch calibre. They were unable to carry it, but managed to stand it on end, point down, and a large crowd gathered about, among them General Llanera and his adjutant, Segovia. Finally most of the group dispersed, their curiosity satisfied, but a considerable number remained, and by much effort, using a hammer and chisel, managed to unscrew the fuse which was in the base of the shell. Of course, all crowded around to look into the aperture, and a corporal who was smoking a cigarette, being jostled, let it drop from his mouth into the shell. When the smoke cleared away half an acre of ground was littered with fragments of human beings, the head of one man being found in a mango tree, a hundred yards away. Strangely enough, several who were in the group recovered from their injuries, one of them having been close enough to see what had caused the accident. It was hopeless to arrive at the number of killed by trying to match the fragments scattered about, but twenty-four men of the battalion who had responded to roll-call that morning were never heard of again. The story has some rather improbable features, but I believe it to be true, as it was common talk in Nueva Ecija, where I afterward served for two years. At any rate, on the day after we had been fired on by the big gun, those of us at Caloocan had seen a big puff of white smoke at Malinta and had heard an explosion. To my mind this incident furnishes a most convincing argument against the use of cigarettes, especially while looking into loaded shells.

But to get back to what was happening to us. During the forenoon of this day, the 23d, a strong demonstration was made against our lines, without actually attempting to drive home the attack. The ridge opposite our right and centre was lined with Filipinos lying down and firing, while those in the trenches on our left were very active. Even Malabon contributed to the gayety of the occasion with its long-range fire. Our field-guns were in action at

intervals during the day, and the regiment did considerable firing. We had a number of casualties, and the
demonstration did not cease until toward noon. In the
meantime the Filipinos who had sneaked into the city
and the bolo-men who had joined them there were meeting
a terrible retribution at the hands of the provost guard,
consisting mostly of the Twenty-third Infantry and the
Thirteenth Minnesota. There was much fighting behind street barricades, which were assaulted by our troops.
After it was over hundreds of dead were found. I saw
one barricade, while on my way into the city that afternoon, behind which the ground was literally covered with
dead men. We had been actually cut off from our base
for hours. In opening up communications, Major J. S.
Mallory of the division staff, who had gone back with a
company of the First Montana, had had a very severe but
successful fight near the scene of the Twentieth's baptism
of fire on the night of the 4th.

The next few days were ones of comparative quiet,
though we had to contend with the continual sniping.
Captain David S. Elliott, one of the three Civil War veterans in the regiment, and a most efficient officer, was
mortally wounded on the 28th, dying the next day. Pathos
was added to his death by the fact that he had two sons
in his company. A day or two after the death of Captain
Elliott a flag of truce appeared in front of the centre of
the regiment, and I went out to meet it. It was a commission from the insurgent government desirous of having
an interview with the military governor, General E. S.
Otis. Before admitting them through our lines I had to

receive the authority of the division commander, and this took some time.   While the flag was flying it was very amusing to see the Filipinos as well as our own men crawl out of their holes and move about with unconcern.   The enemy's trenches fairly swarmed with men.

The truce gave me an opportunity to talk with a Filipino officer commanding the troops opposite our left, and I told him that in my opinion the everlasting sniping that his men and ours were doing at each other served no useful purpose and was making life a burden to all concerned, calling attention to the way everybody was enjoying himself during this brief respite.   I told him that I had no authority to make any agreement with him, but that I could assure him that my men would do no more firing unless his people started it.   He seemed rather favorably impressed with my views, but said that he could make no definite promise.   The results of this interview were most gratifying.   I at once issued orders to the regiment to do no more firing until ordered, but for a while to be careful about exposing themselves, and not to gather in large groups.   From that time for three weeks not a shot was fired along the front of the Twentieth Kansas, though conditions did not change on the front of the other two regiments of the brigade.   Gradually our men became more confident and moved about with the utmost freedom. Some of them even wanted to visit the insurgent lines, but this, of course, was not allowed.   A couple of baseball teams were organized, and played numerous games in full view of the enemy.   The Filipinos showed the same disregard of our presence that we did of theirs, and could be seen taking their ease on top of their trenches instead of down under the ground. In fact, life became much less irksome for all of us. But the oddest thing was brought about by the fact that our band sent in to Manila for its instruments, the men since the outbreak having been fighting in the companies, and every evening we had a concert on our lines. The Filipinos would crowd the tops of their trenches to hear the music, and would vigorously applaud pieces that struck their fancy. Every concert closed with the playing of "The Star-Spangled Banner," at which not only our men but all the Filipinos stood at attention, uncovered. This state of affairs was the cause of much wonderment among visitors to our lines, and well it might be.

But it was too good to last, and one day the discovery was made that the enemy was running a zigzag trench toward our left, the work being done under cover of dense undergrowth. They were already within seventy-five yards of the left flank of the regiment and within fifty of the Malabon causeway. This would never do, as it would enable them to get in our rear by running a short sap under the causeway and the left of our trenches. In this way they might by a sudden rush do us great damage, even if they did not for a time drive us out. Holding aloft a white handkerchief, I walked out in front of the sand-bag parapet that covered the First Battalion and approached the working party, but was warned back by an officer. I called to him that we could not allow the work to proceed, but received no reply, his attitude being distinctly hostile. Going back to the regiment, I had Company F fire a volley into the brush, and the long truce was broken. In a minute came the spiteful popping of the Mausers, and everybody dived into the earth. The trenches that half an hour before had been busy with life looked deserted. It would be interesting, however, if we could know how many casualties were avoided by this informal arrangement. But we were nearly through with the Caloocan trenches, as the arrival of a number of regular regiments from the United States had increased the number of troops at the disposal of the division commander, so that the longed-for campaign against the insurgent capital could begin.

On the afternoon of the 24th of March orders were received making radical changes in the distribution of the troops of the division preparatory to the advance. The First Montana, which had been on the centre of the brigade line, was shifted to its extreme right, where a portion of Hale's Brigade had been, and, having sent back to Manila all its useless impedimenta, the Twentieth Kansas just after dark formed in column of fours and moved away from the position that it had so long occupied, and in which it had had one officer and seven men killed and two officers and fifteen men wounded, marching in rear of the line to La Loma church, where in line of masses it went into bivouac for the night. Hale's Brigade had been moved by the right flank, and now my regiment was sandwiched in between the First Montana on its right and the Third Artillery on its left, this organization not having changed its position. Troops recently arrived from the United States occupied the old trenches on our front, in order to hold them and thus deny access to the city during the advance of the Second Division. The positions in the trenches on the extreme left of the division were occupied by what was known as the Separate Brigade, temporarily attached to General MacArthur's command. This brigade consisted of the Twenty-second United States Infantry and the Second Oregon, the first-named regiment having just recently arrived from the United States. It was commanded by Brigadier-General Loyd Wheaton, a dashing and aggressive soldier who was to win great laurels in the coming campaign. He commanded our own brigade later, and we shall hear much of him in the story of the campaign north of Malolos.

We of the Twentieth Kansas were in a measure disappointed that the changes preparatory to the advance spoiled our chance of settling a few scores with the insurgent trenches that had been on our front for six weeks. The Second Oregon, that was the next day to take them by direct assault, had very severe fighting, losing more men, I believe, than any other organization did in any one fight in the Philippines. To the right of Hale's was still another brigade, that of Brigadier-General Robert H. Hall, which for a day or two was to act in conjunction with the Second Division. The general plan for the coming advance was for the brigades of Hale and Otis to advance rapidly just after daybreak and carry the insurgent lines on their front, Wheaton's brigade for the time to stand fast. After forcing the passage of the Tuliajan River the brigades of Hale and Otis were to execute a wheel to the left as rapidly as possible in order to cut off the main force of the insurgents near Malinta and pin them up against the bay shore north of Malabon. After the attack had progressed to a certain point Wheaton was to carry the trenches on his front, the hope being that the men falling back before him would find their retreat barred at Malinta. Hall's brigade on the extreme right was to engage the attention of the enemy on his front and protect the right of the Second Division.

Not counting the troops to be left in the trenches to cover Manila, this movement was to be participated in by about nine thousand men on a front of eight miles. The enemy opposed to us was of about equal strength, well armed, with an abundant supply of ammunition, and occupying an almost continuous line of trenches and field-works. These facts are submitted for the prayerful consideration of those who affect to think that there was nothing but guerilla fighting in the Philippines. The next day was to see the most extensive combat that United States troops have been engaged in since the Civil War, with the sole exception of the 1st of July, 1898, at Santiago.

III

UP THE RAILROAD TO MALOLOS

THE bugles blowing reveille on the morning of the 25th ushered in the longed-for day when the Second Division was to take up the march for Malolos, the insurgent capital, and we knew that before us was a week or so of almost continuous fighting, for the way was barred by the best troops of the rebel army, commanded by Antonio Luna, far the ablest and most aggressive leader in the service of Aguinaldo. The insurgent troops were better armed than were the volunteers that composed the bulk of the Second Division, having that splendid weapon, the Mauser, while we still used the Springfield, of much shorter range. It might be said here that the advantage had by a weapon of high velocity over one of low is that the former, having a flatter trajectory, is not so much affected by errors in aiming or in estimating distance. The Springfield could reach as far as effective fighting could be done with any small arm, but at a thousand yards its bullets were coming down at a very considerable angle, thus diminishing the dangerous space. But we were through with our black-powder days, as we had now been supplied with cartridges which, while not absolutely smokeless, did not at once shroud us in a cloud of our own making.

The force opposed to us was about equal in strength to our division, and was an enemy not to be despised, as it was made up mostly of former native regiments of the Spanish army. These had gone over to the insurgents intact, keeping their former organization, and largely having their original officers. They had been in service more than a year, and had had considerable training in the matter of drill, but I fear not very much in target practice. They retained their old Spanish uniforms, so that these became really the insurgent uniform. It was not until the later period of guerilla warfare that the Filipinos fought in civilian clothing. While not very capable troops on the offensive, these insurgents showed no little mettle in defending positions, for they often stuck to them until the bottoms of the trenches were literally covered with their dead. Some of our people have affected to despise the courage of the Filipino; but the most of them are among those who did not get mixed up in the fighting until after the greater part of those who fought us during the first four months had been killed or disabled, and their places had been taken by yokels snatched out of their rice fields and compelled to fight. The real test of the *morale* of troops is the ability to bring them time and again to face the music, to suffer almost inevitable defeat, and to have their ranks decimated by appalling losses. Judged by this standard, the Filipino does not by any means stand at the foot of the list.

Deaths from bullets and disease, as well as a considerable list of sick and wounded in the hospitals, had reduced the Twentieth Kansas to a strength of about a thousand men. These, as soon as the bugles rang out, set themselves to making coffee and broiling bacon, and had soon made away with a typical soldier breakfast in the field. Lieutenant-Colonel Little had recovered from his accidental injury received before the outbreak, and was now in command of the First Battalion, while Major Whitman, returned to duty from sick leave some weeks before, had his own battalion, the Second. Our orders were to have two battalions on the firing line and one marching in rear as a regimental reserve.

Night passes into day quickly in the tropics, and the sun had almost risen by the time the men had stowed their mess tins in their haversacks, buckled on their tin cups and cartridge belts, and stood at ease awaiting the first order. This was not long in coming, and we soon formed line, still in close order, marched the few rods to the summit of the ridge, jumped over the trenches occupied by the men of one of the recently arrived regular regiments, and started down the gentle slope. As soon as we had cleared the steeper part of the slope the Second and Third Battalions began deploying, while the First remained stationary, with orders to let us have five hundred yards start, when it was to follow in line of platoons in column. The First Montana, on our right, had already started, as also had Hale's brigade, still to its right, and already the crackle of the Mausers was heard to our right front as these regiments came under fire. The Third Artillery, on our left, waited until we were even with its position and then leaped over its trenches and started for the goal. We were crossing an almost level plain, and nearly all of the two brigades could be seen at one time, as they silently advanced in a long, irregular line toward the woods that sheltered the enemy's outpost line. It was a spectacle enough to inspire any man. It looked like a manœuvre, but it was war. Already the woods fifteen hundred yards on our front were crackling and popping and the bullets were kicking up dust spots on the dry ground.

All our fighting heretofore had been in close country, so that we had not tried the advance by alternate rushes, but this was a good place for it, and although the distance was too great for us to begin firing with effect, we put into practice what we had learned on the drill ground at the Presidio. One platoon, that is half a company, would rush forward for about fifty yards and throw itself prone, while the other platoon would rise and rush past it. Of course this made an irregular and apparently waving line, but we were getting over ground at a good rate.

Hale's brigade, not having so far to go to close with the enemy, had opened fire, as also had the First Montana, and now we were within seven hundred yards of the woods. I turned to Chief-Trumpeter Barshfield walking, or rather trotting, along beside my horse and ordered "Commence firing" blown. The men had been anxious to reply, and went at it with a vengeance, each platoon firing while it was prone, and then rising at the word of command and dashing to the front. My horse, the same little bay that had been shot under me at Caloocan, showed that he remembered something, and for the first time was skittish under fire. Nothing could be seen on our front that looked like an enemy, so that our target was the edge of the woods, where it was known that the line must be. The fire of the enemy not being of much volume, we knew that this must be merely a line of strong outposts, and that the real trouble would be farther in the depths of the woods.

During this advance by rushes a man in Company D received a most peculiar wound. He had just thrown himself prone when he felt a severe blow on his right shoulder, being completely prostrated. The Hospital Corps men who accompanied the firing line applied the first-aid bandage and sent him back to the dressing-station at La Loma church. Here an examination disclosed the wound of entrance in his right shoulder, and also the supposed exit of the bullet in the form of a hole in his right side just where his cartridge belt had been. Sent into the First Reserve hospital in Manila, he was treated under the very natural supposition that he was rid of his bullet, but eleven days after his admission one of the nurses in bathing the man noticed what appeared to be a swelling just above his right knee. Calling the attention of the surgeon to the matter, that individual went after the object with his instruments, and extracted a Mauser bullet. The missile, traversing his body lengthwise close to the surface, had struck the tight and unyielding belt where it would have made its exit, but, being foiled, and having considerable energy left, had continued its journey through the unfortunate man's anatomy until its force was expended just above his knee. It is disturbing to be shot through the body in the orthodox manner, but it is enough to make one positively peevish to have a hole drilled through him lengthwise. Astonishing to relate, the man recovered in a short time.

We continued the advance by rushes until within about two hundred yards of the enemy, when the "Charge" sent the two battalions over the remaining ground in no time, the enemy's weak line bolting into the woods. It was only a line of outposts behind not particularly good cover, and ought not to have remained as long as it did, but when we opened fire should have retired on the main line.

The men of Company G had a bull-dog that they had brought with them from Coffeyville, Kansas, and of which they were exceedingly fond. I had heard much of the antics of this animal in battle, and on this occasion had an opportunity to see him perform. He was perfectly frantic with excitement, apparently thinking that the whole show was something for his especial benefit, and ran up and down the line of his company barking furiously. At the charge he distanced everybody in the race to the enemy's position. This dog was in every engagement that the company was in, and went through it all without mishap, but after his return he indiscreetly bit Coffeyville's police force in the leg and was promptly shot, an ending for the company pet that all but started a riot.

The Filipino line having been weakly held, we naturally found but few of them on the ground. I do not know the number that were along that portion of their line carried by my regiment, but counted seven dead at the place struck by the right of our line. There were also two badly wounded that they had not been able to remove, and these we sent in with our own wounded. At the same place we picked up nine rifles.

Positive orders had been issued before the advance for the First Montana to keep its left on a road which ran at right angles with its direction, while the right of my own regiment was to rest on the same road. But from the start the regiment named had inclined too much to the left, and before we reached the enemy's line nearly two companies were on our side of the road. We were being telescoped, and in order to avoid crowding the Third Artillery on our left we had to take several companies out of the firing line, but not until I had lost my temper and "cussed out" an officer of the offending regiment, who bristled up and told me he took no orders from outsiders, and that he had no instructions to keep his left on the road. Filled with wrath, righteous from my own stand-point, I determined to appeal to higher authority. The brigade commander was somewhere in the rear of the line of his command, but I did not know just where. However, a group of mounted officers only a short distance back on the road I recognized from the distinguishing flag as General MacArthur and his staff. While the regiment was straightening itself out and getting its breath I rode back as fast as my horse could run and sputtered out my tale of woe. The general looked at me in a quizzical sort of way and said, "Well, well, Funston, is that all is the matter? Let's not get excited about little things. It is better to wait for something serious." But he sent an officer to straighten out the tangle. He evidently was considerably amused by my outburst.

Returning to the regiment, which by this time had got itself pulled together, we resumed the advance, now over somewhat rougher ground and through woods that in places were rather dense, but here and there comparatively open. We knew that somewhere on our front was the Tuliajan River, but owing to the wretched maps of the country that the Spaniards had made, the distance was uncertain. Naturally our own people had never been able to map this region, lying as it did in the insurgent lines, nor would it have been possible for patrols to have made the necessary examination.

The whole brigade was, of course, participating in this renewed advance, and we were working our way cautiously forward, examining the country on our front as well as we could under the circumstances. The ground was sloping gently downward, and it was realized that we must be near the river. An occasional rifle shot and a bullet zipping through the tree tops was the only sign of an enemy. We suddenly heard a most terrific crashing in the woods to our left as the Third Artillery engaged in a desperate close-range struggle in which it lost about thirty men killed and wounded, and in an instant the woods on our own front added to the pandemonium. It was exceedingly difficult to decide what to do. To rush the men down to the river, which we could now make out about three hundred yards ahead of the line, might place the regiment in a position where it would be shot to pieces by the well-intrenched enemy on the opposite bank in case it should be too deep to wade. To retire was of course out of the question, so the only thing to do was to close as rapidly as possible and take chances on the depth of the stream. Past experience had shown us that even with the enemy intrenched we could overcome his fire. So the companies on the firing line now rushed down the bank, threw themselves flat, and fought desperately.

In order that I might be able to exercise some influence on the firing line as a whole, and not get mixed up in a local fight where I could see only one or two companies, I remained about two hundred yards behind the line for the time being. Here I was joined by the well-known correspondent, Mr. James Creelman. I had sent Sergeant-Major Warner and Trumpeter Barshfield away to carry orders, and was glad to have company. The noise was so overwhelming that it was difficult to think, for the whole brigade was fighting as hard as it could and the woods were filled with the roar. Creelman and I sat on our horses for awhile, and then unanimously dismounted, the idea seeming to strike both of us at the same time. Companies E and H had struck the worst of it, being opposite the most formidable trench, and Creelman and I were directly behind them. A natural tendency of the Filipino, and for that matter, most people, to shoot high made our position one of the warmest places I have ever been in. Only once, and that at Cascorra in far-away Cuba, had I seen bullets thicker. The two companies were right on the river bank, and as the stream was not more than forty feet wide, and the Filipino trenches were on the opposite bank, the two firing lines were not more than fifty feet apart. The river looked deep, but as yet our people had not overcome the enemy's fire sufficiently to allow the matter to be tested.

Captain Adna G. Clarke, now a captain in the regular army, was in command of Company H, and I could see him standing erect in order to better direct the fire of his men, who were lying down. In a short time I saw him crumple up and go down with a wound from which I believe he has not fully recovered to this day. Majors Metcalf and Whitman were close up to the river bank, their two battalions being most hotly engaged. Finally I could stand it no longer, and in the hope that a place could be found where there was a practicable crossing, rode toward the left of the regiment, which had not been so severely engaged, but managed to get my horse stuck in a boggy ravine, and so gave that up and, dismounting, started on a run to join the two companies that were so deeply involved, in the hope that by swimming, if necessary, we could bring the thing to a finish. Passing a little clump of bamboos, I heard a groan coming from them, and saw four of our poor fellows scattered on a space no larger than an ordinary bedroom.

As soon as I reached the firing line I motioned, for no commands could be heard, for some of the men to get into the water and try to cross. Captain William J. Watson, commanding Company E, and two or three men plunged in and struggled across, the water being nearly to their shoulders, and were followed by a number of others, the men holding their rifles over their heads. As the first of these men came up the bank the Filipinos bolted, knowing it was all over, and but few of them could be brought down in flight, as the north bank was higher than the one our men were on, and the men could not see them. However, I saw Lieutenant Colin H. Ball do some good short-range work with his revolver, he being one of those who had crossed.

In the meantime my horse had extricated himself from the mud, and had come trotting toward the excitement. A soldier caught him and brought him to me, and by the time I had mounted, the fighting on our front was over. A better crossing was found about a hundred yards down-stream, and I had no difficulty in getting the pony through. The men of the regiment, now that the fighting had ceased, waded the stream at the same place, and were allowed to throw themselves on the ground to rest until further orders should be received.

Only a very small portion of the regiment had been seriously engaged, as the enemy's trenches were not continuous, although there had been resistance all along the line, but in many cases the fire had come from men lying down a hundred yards or so from the river bank. After our men had got close to the river they had not suffered much, as the Filipinos did not like to rise up enough to do even fairly good shooting, but Companies E and H had been pretty well shot up in getting to close quarters.

Our loss was Privates Craig, Anibal, and Plummer killed, and Captain Clarke and twelve enlisted men wounded. Craig was the youngest of three brothers in the same company, one of them being a first lieutenant and the other a sergeant, these last two being now officers in the regular army. In and near the trench that had given us the most trouble we found twenty-nine of the enemy's dead. As usual, the most of his wounded had succeeded in escaping, though we found seven. Scattered about on the ground were about thirty rifles that we broke up and threw into the river.

In the meantime the Third Artillery, on our left, had fought its way across the stream, overcoming more serious difficulties than those that had confronted us, as in addition to trenches they had to take an elaborate and obstinately defended field-work.

The First Montana had had a fight about as stiff as our own, and had crossed the river to our right. Still farther away we could hear a scattering fire as Hale's brigade was making its way, overcoming great difficulties in the way of dense brush and badly cut up country. Still farther to the right Hall's brigade was having its fight, but the sounds of battle, if they reached our ears, were confused with that of other firing in the same direction. Much nearer in, on our right, at the place where the Novaliches wagon road crosses the Tuliajan, was an almost incessant small-arms fire punctuated with cannon shots and the tap, tap, tap of a Colt automatic gun. At this place a very strong field-work and flanking trenches, constructed for the purpose of protecting the crossing, were stoutly resisting a detachment of the Fourth Cavalry and some artillery. A field-piece and the automatic gun were run up to the bank of the river and served in the open at a distance of a few rods, and it was not until the shells began to pierce the well-made parapet that the defenders fled. The Colt gun was under the command of Ensign Cleland Davis of the navy, he having a detachment of three marines to serve it. Ensign Davis had joined us in the Caloocan trenches, and had had occasional opportunities to try out his weapon. He accompanied us through the whole campaign to Malolos, and we often heard the rhythmical popping of the little gun, which could be distinguished through quite a heavy infantry fire. Davis always got into close quarters with his little weapon whenever there was opportunity, and made it count. The navy's detachment was very popular with the army, and they seemed to enjoy their part of the campaign immensely.

According to the plans of the battle, Wheaton's brigade, which, it will be remembered, was on the extreme left of the line, occupying the old Caloocan trenches, was to wait until the brigades of Otis and Hale had pierced the centre of the line and then move out straight to the front, the supposition being that Hale's brigade by making a rapid left turn would cut off the retreat of the enemy. We were straightening ourselves out after the rather confused crossing of the river, and were sending out patrols to the front, when we heard toward our left rear a crackle of rifle fire, which in a moment swelled into a most appalling amount of sound, and we knew that the fiery Wheaton was going after them hammer and tongs. His brigade was more than two thousand strong, and was resisted by a somewhat larger number of the enemy occupying successive lines of trenches.

If any one thinks that more than four thousand men using breech-loaders as rapidly as they can load and fire cannot wake the echoes, I wish he could have heard the astonishing roar that smote our ears on this occasion. There was no rattle, just a roar that drowned individual shots, and through which the crashes of the field-pieces could barely be distinguished.

This brigade soon reached the south bank of the river, but did not cross, as it was now known that our turning movement was meeting with difficulties, and it was not desired to push the insurgents any farther up the railroad at present. The country on the front of Hale's brigade was to us a veritable unknown land. To have explored it before the outbreak might have precipitated matters with the insurgents, and any attempt to examine it after the war began could only have resulted in the loss of the detachments sent out for the purpose. It turned out to be a dense tangle of forest and undergrowth, cut up with ravines. It was out of the question for troops in extended order to make any rapid progress through it, and the day had turned out to be very hot. The situation made it necessary for us to remain where we were until the next morning, and we proceeded to make ourselves comfortable, no difficult matter with water and firewood in abundance.

The brigade commander had joined us at this point just after the crossing of the river, and camped near us. It was in the midst of the dry season, and the men did not even use their shelter-halves, commonly known as pup tents, so that all that was necessary was to stretch ourselves out under the stars and sleep as well as the hard ground would let us. It was, in fact, campaigning under almost ideal conditions.

During the night we were aroused by about a dozen shots from one of our outposts, and a man came in to report that a small band of the enemy trying to sneak up on it had been driven off. The officer of the day went out to investigate, and after some searching found a very old and innocent-looking carabao bull in the last stages of dissolution, with half a dozen bullet holes in him. The men of this outpost had to stand considerable chaffing from their comrades the next day. But they were at least entitled to credit for good shooting.

The next morning, the 26th, an adjustment of the line made it necessary for us to move half a mile up the river, and a little before noon the march was resumed, this time in a westerly direction along a wagon road leading from the Novaliches ford across the Tuliajan toward the town of Malinta. We were still in rather close woods. The Third Artillery had the advance, and we followed. We could hear heavy firing toward Malinta, and knew that Wheaton's brigade was shoving the enemy out of the trenches near there. It was evident from the amount of firing that the fighting was severe. As we approached open country, the great level plain that stretches northward for two or three miles from Malinta, we could hear firing on our own front, and soon saw that the Third Artillery was deploying in open country and firing into the flank of a large body of the enemy, more than two thousand strong, flying before Wheaton's brigade. One portion seemed to have kept its formation, and was replying to the Third Artillery with a brisk fire. Two field-pieces under Major Young, that were with the advance, were already in action, and it looked as if we were going to have a fine fight. General MacArthur and his staff were sitting on their horses near the guns, and I rode up in advance of my regiment and asked for instructions, being directed to deploy on the right of the Third Artillery and close in as rapidly as possible. The artillerymen were fairly skipping over the ground in an endeavor to come to close quarters, and with their Krags were delivering an effective fire, having a splendid target, the flank of a large body of broken infantry.

I put my regiment to double time, moved to the right of the road, and crowded the men for all they were worth. It was rather a poor piece of business, for by the time they began to deploy they were so "winded" as to be almost useless. Finally we got a few companies in line and commenced firing, at the same time going forward by rushes. But the distance, nearly fifteen hundred yards, was too great for our Springfields, and I doubt if we hit a man. The men fell out by dozens, completely exhausted. I rode among them and I am afraid did not exactly bless them, but it was no use. Soon the fleeing Filipinos were out of range of even the Krags of the Third Artillery, and the affair was over. The Twentieth Kansas had had only one man hit, Private Fairchild, killed.

If we had only had a regiment of cavalry well in hand at the time we came into the open, there would have been a different story. A man might go through several little wars before he would again see such an opportunity for a cavalry charge. The country was perfectly open and as level as a floor. There was no escape possible in the time that it would have taken cavalry to reach the enemy. I do not believe that a hundred of them could have escaped, possibly not one. Whatever doubt there may be as to the possibility of cavalry charging infantry in line, there is none as to what it can do if it gets in on the flank of a disordered and retreating force. But we had but little cavalry, and that not properly mounted.

We again formed column and resumed the march to Malinta, which place we found occupied by Wheaton's brigade after severe fighting. I saw General Wheaton and was informed by him that Colonel Egbert of the Twenty-second Infantry had been killed a short time before. The place where that gallant old veteran died is now marked by a monument which can be seen a few hundred yards to the east of the railroad track just south of Malinta. Our part of the fighting was over for the day, and we were allowed to take it easy.

Hale's brigade had pushed through the woods toward the town of Meycauayan, where the insurgents made a strong stand in trenches previously constructed. At a distance we watched the beautiful fight taking place in the open country, and with our field-glasses could make out quite well what was going on. In this combat General Hale was slightly wounded, and Captain Krayenbuhl of his staff was killed. Enough high bullets from the fight dropped among us to give us something of a personal interest in the matter, and a man of the Third Artillery near us was wounded by this long-range, dropping fire. There are some disadvantages about being even spectators of a fight when the modern high-power rifles are being used, for, if they are given too much elevation, as the Filipinos were very prone to do, the bullets sometimes do not come to earth short of a couple of miles.

After the fight was over, and Hale's brigade had occupied the town with the fearful and wonderful name, or rather the place where it had been before the Filipinos in their retreat burned it, our brigade resumed its march for a couple of miles, and bivouacked in line in the open fields. Near the Twentieth Kansas were a number of stacks of rice straw, and everybody in the regiment had a soft bed that night. As there were other troops ahead of us, we were not required to place outposts, so that all had a much-needed rest.

The big town of Malabon had been burned as soon as Wheaton's brigade had begun its advance past it, Malinta had gone up in smoke on the morning of this day, and Meycauayan, in spite of its name, had met a like fate in the evening. It was evident that the Filipino leaders were carrying out with a vengeance an idiotic policy of destroying the property of their own people under the impression that such action would hurt our feelings or make us peevish. A few days later, a copy of the order to destroy all towns before delivering them to the Americans, signed by Luna himself, was found. This action did not even inconvenience us, as in such weather all preferred bivouacking in the open to taking chances with vermin and dirt in the native houses. But it seemed a terrible pity to see these towns, some of them well built, go up one after the other. We did all we could to save them, but usually could accomplish nothing, as they burned like kindling-wood. The enemy also destroyed as many as possible of the bridges, both on the railroad and the wagon roads, and destroyed the telegraph line, and took out consider-able sections of the railroad track. These acts of destruc-tion were, of course, justifiable from the stand-point of military necessity, and caused us no little annoyance and delay.

The morning of the 27th we arose refreshed from our beds of straw, had our bacon, hardtack, and coffee, and began a rather strenuous and noisy day. The work of Hall's brigade, so far as it bore on the Malolos campaign, was over, and it operated in and near the Mariquina val-ley. Wheaton's brigade, which really belonged to the First Division operating south of Manila, was to follow us up and act as a reserve, and guard our line of communica-tion with Manila, while the Second Division was to re-sume the march on the insurgent capital. Hale's brigade was to march on the right of the railroad, while ours,. Otis's, was to keep on the left. The Third Artillery was again to have the advance in our brigade, followed at a distance of five hundred yards by the Twentieth Kansas, and behind us came the First Montana, the two last-named regiments marching in column in the road.

As we pushed slowly north, the advance of my regi-ment five hundred yards in rear of the Third Artillery, a lively popping broke out a mile up the road, and we knew that the advance guard of the brigade was again getting into touch with the enemy. For a time two or three of the companies of the Third Artillery had been in column on the road in the heart of the town. We noticed that most of the men seemed to be in little groups along the side of the road, apparently very busy about something, but had no idea what was keeping them so occupied. As the firing on the front increased Major Kobbé ordered all his men to the front to reinforce the advance guard. The men fell in and marched up the road toward the sound of firing, casting longing glances toward the place they had just left. My regiment marched up to this point, and we at once saw the cause of the tender solicitude on the part of the gallant artillerymen. All along the road were little fires, and over each one was broiling a chicken. The men had had less than an hour in which to catch and dress them and get them started to broiling, so that they were not yet done, and as a half-cooked chicken is a little worse than none, they were compelled to leave them to the mercies of the Jayhawkers. It is an ill wind that blows no good, and as we halted to await the progress of events, the men were allowed to fall out. They did so with great alacrity. Only the leading battalion got any benefit from this windfall, as every chicken had been pre-empted before the men of the other two could arrive, they having been halted a little farther down the road. One artilleryman had lingered and was carefully watching one bird. I asked him why he did not join, suggesting that his company commander might call him to account for straggling. "No sir. He won't. It's his chicken. I'm his striker. But I'll have to let it go. It won't be done in time." I replied that it would be a shame to waste so fine a bird, and that

I would see that it was well appreciated. So I took the chicken, after it had cooked, and the man departed in sadness. So I owe Lieutenant, now Major Abernethy, one fine young chicken, which I hope to pay him for some day. After the chickens had been disposed of we sat about, listening to the firing on our front and right front.

It was evident that a stiff fight was on. In compliance with my orders to keep five hundred yards behind the Third Artillery, we now fell into column and pushed up the road through the ruined town. We had just halted, seeing some troops the required distance ahead of us, when much to our surprise we were briskly fired on from our left front. This was more than disconcerting, as it is bad business to come under fire at close range while in column. I did not know, however, that the firing line of the Third Artillery did not extend far enough to the left to cover the point from which the shots were coming. The men were at once ordered to lie down, being still in column, and Major Metcalf and I dismounted and ran out to the left into an open field to study the situation. Our appearance was the signal for an increased fire, and we could see to our front and left, not more than five hundred yards, a line of detached trenches, from which the fire was coming, and we could see the straw hats bobbing up and down. They appeared to be in the margin of a growth of woods and bamboo, and the country between us and them was perfectly level and open, being obstructed only by the low dikes of the rice fields.

That the enemy was on the opposite side of an impassable river occurred to no one. Neither of us had seen any map of the locality, and though it was known that we were approaching the Marilao River, it was thought to be a mile or more in advance. So we took the two leading companies from the advance battalion of the regiment, rushed them into the open, deployed under fire, and began the attack, advancing by rushes in the orthodox manner, until within about a hundred yards of our objective, when the charge was ordered, and we went at them with a rush. The men had raised the usual yell, and we thought that in a few seconds we would be among them, when we were brought up with a start, and the men instinctively threw themselves on the ground. We had rushed to the very brink of a river about eighty feet wide and ten feet deep. No wonder the Filipinos had stood their ground and had continued to salt us. It was a rather bad situation, as the enemy was sheltered in good trenches and our men had no cover other than rice dikes not more than a foot high. We had already had several men hit, including two mortally wounded, and I determined to withdraw the two companies from their position until a way could be found to ascertain if the river could be crossed.

Before the beginning of the advance from the Manila lines the various regiments had been provided with Chinese litter bearers. The men that we had had already shown at Tuliajan River that they were made of pretty good stuff, and now they were sent up to the firing line, only a few rods from the enemy's trenches, to bring back the wounded. They crossed the open stoically, picked up their burdens, and fell back with the two companies. It was a hard test, as they were fired on repeatedly while coming up. The two companies fell back only a short distance to a point where there was cover, and remained in line lying down. The retirement had been made without further loss and in perfect order. In the meantime the brigade commander had come up, and I explained the situation to him. He was of the opinion that I had made a mistake in retiring, though I represented that it was in no sense a retreat, but merely for the purpose of sheltering the men until a method of crossing could be found. I expressed my willingness to go back, and he consented.

The two companies that had made the attack, H and I, were now reinforced by C, and firing with great rapidity, and, fairly combing the tops of the trenches with bullets, we regained the bank of the stream without further loss. The Filipinos were kept down in their trenches by the fire poured in upon them, so that they simply could not rise up to take any aim at all. As we gradually overcame them our men rose to their feet to fire, in order to do better shooting than they could lying down. If the muzzle of a rifle appeared over the trench a score of bullets would strike the spot within a couple of seconds. In the meantime a number of us were running along the river bank, trying to find some means of crossing, and while engaged in this work I became aware of the fact that a very brisk fight was going on with a couple of trenches to our right. I did not at the time know just what troops were involved, but could see a field-piece in action right on the bank of the river, firing on a trench across the stream, and could hear the tap, tap, tap of the Colt automatic. There were

also a number of infantrymen. These latter had been
engaged in the fight for some time, but we had not known
it, being engaged with our own affairs farther to the left.
Our three companies farther down the stream had completely mastered the fire in the trenches opposite them,
but could not cross. I went over to where the artillery
and the automatic were in action, and at this time Company D of my regiment, Captain Orwig, came up to take
a hand in the fracas. Still a little farther up was a company of the Tenth Pennsylvania of Hale's brigade that
Major Bell, who was in command at this point, had
brought over from beyond the railroad. In the meantime a raft was noticed moored to the opposite bank of
the stream, about eighty yards below the trench that was
fighting Major Bell's detachment. It would be necessary
to swim the stream to get it, and I called for volunteers
to do the work. Lieutenant Hardy, Trumpeter Barshfield, Corporal Drysdale (now a first lieutenant in the
Tenth Infantry), and Privates Huntsman and Willey
stripped off their clothing and plunged over the bank into
the stream. They swam across, got the raft, and towed
it to our side. It was a gallant piece of work well done.
During this time the field-piece, the Colt gun, and Company D were pounding the near-by trench with great
vigor, while the Pennsylvania company was handling another trench a little farther up-stream.

As soon as the raft reached our side I got on it with
Lieutenant Hopkins and twenty-one men of Company C,
and we poled it to the other bank. After sending out
patrols to the front in order to give warning of a possible

counter attack from any force that might be concealed in the vicinity, we gave our attention to the trench opposite the artillery, it being the nearest. But upon reaching it we found that the men in it had already raised the white flag and had signified to those across the river their desire to surrender. This was not on account of our crossing, but because of the fact that the gun was literally tearing their shelter to pieces, while the small-arms fire made escape from it impossible. As we came in the lower end of the trench a lieutenant and a private of the Tenth Pennsylvania, whose names are unknown to me, came in at the other end, they having crossed the stream by swimming a short distance above. We found in the trench twenty-four killed, and took thirty-four prisoners, of whom twelve were very badly wounded. We broke up and threw into the river thirty-one rifles and about four thousand rounds of ammunition. The prisoners were brought across the river on the raft and in a canoe that had been found. Among the dead found here was one man who had in his chest, in a space that could be covered by one hand, five holes made by the little six millimetre bullets of the Colt automatic. Ensign Davis had served this gun in the open at a distance of about a hundred feet.

After we were all back in the United States some of the patriots of my regiment and those of the Tenth Pennsylvania tried to engage in a bloody newspaper war over the question as to who had crossed the river first, the men of one regiment or the other. I doubt if anybody could say to a certainty, as the two crossings were made from points that were not in view of each other, and probably

no one man saw them both.   It was a matter of absolutely
no importance, as the two enterprises were independently
carried on, and either would have succeeded alone.

Company D of the Twentieth Kansas had had one
man killed at this point.   Those of us who had crossed
the river now went to the two trenches that our three
companies farther to the left had overcome.   The occupants had fled, taking their wounded with them, but
had left a number of dead that we did not take the trouble
to count.

I now hoped to be allowed to ferry the whole regiment
across on the raft, a task that would have taken an hour
or so, but was directed by the brigade commander to re-
cross with the men that I had.   For some time afterward I believed that if I could have had my way we could
have rendered valuable service by marching up the stream
on its north side, rolling up the insurgents in the trenches
on that bank.   I have subsequently learned that there
was on our front a narrow but deep lagoon that would
materially have interfered with such an operation.   We
might easily have been involved alone in a very nasty
fight, so that I have no doubt that the wisest thing was
done.

We remained on the south bank for some time, awaiting orders that depended on developments in other parts
of the field.   In the meantime the First South Dakota, of
Hale's brigade, had after a very severe fight forced the
passage at another point above the bridge.   This affair,
carried out under the direction of the commander of that
regiment, Colonel A. S. Frost, was about as stiff as any-

thing that occurred in the Philippines, the regiment in question losing seven killed, including three officers, and having about twenty-five wounded. It was totally independent of the crossing effected by my own regiment farther down the stream, neither operation having any effect on the other or being aided by it. About four o'clock the brigade commander directed me to cross the railroad bridge with the regiment and deploy on the left of the Third Artillery. So we formed column of fours and set out.

As one ascends the Marilao at this point the stream makes a considerable turn to the north until opposite the town of Marilao, whence its course is easterly. Therefore, though we were right on the stream, and near the railroad, we were nearly a mile from the bridge. As we drew near we were met by the adjutant-general of the division who informed me as to the situation, and stated that General MacArthur desired that I make all possible haste in extending the existing line to the left. Hale's brigade and the Third Artillery of our own brigade were already across and in line of battle, awaiting the movement of a body of some thousands of the enemy, who could be seen coming up and deploying across the fields to the north, with the evident intention of making an attack before all the division could cross the stream. From the south bank we could see the enemy's line, which appeared to be about two miles long, and quite heavy, while behind it were troops in reserve. The ties had been removed from the bridge, making crossing it a very slow operation, but we made the greatest haste possible. The orderlies of the mounted officers managed to get their horses across by swimming them.

We had just begun the crossing, the men picking their way gingerly over the stringers, when the whole Filipino line opened fire on the troops deployed on the north bank, the distance being about twelve hundred yards. As the firing line of our troops was not more than a hundred yards in advance of the bridge, those of us on the structure naturally got our share of the bullets. The men were very quiet, and apparently somewhat nervous, as they knew that a man badly hit while on the bridge would in all probability fall into the stream. One man was killed in the crossing, and a few wounded. All of our troops that were in line were replying vigorously, the men lying close to the ground. Under such a fire it would have been folly to hold the regiment in such an exposed position until it could be properly formed. I had crossed the bridge at the head of the regiment, and found that my faithful orderly, Caldwell, had my dripping horse awaiting me, and so mounted and conducted the first few men as fast as they could run along a road which ran a few yards in rear of the prostrate and silent men of the Third Artillery, working their Krags for all they were worth, and directed them to continue the line of that organization to the left. Every man as he cleared the bridge leaped down the embankment and followed suit. It was a method of deployment not laid down in any drill book, but worked beautifully.

Just after leaving the railroad embankment I had passed two gray-haired sergeants of the Third Artillery, lying within a few feet of each other, still and calm in death, their faces as placid as if they were only asleep, and had a hurried glimpse of General MacArthur and his staff, standing near the right of the Third Artillery's line. As our right began to hook onto the left of the Third Artillery a number of the men greeted us with cheers, and cries of "Good for Kansas." It was not that they were in a pinch, but because a strong friendship had grown up between the two regiments. They were, however, naturally glad to see their exposed flank covered.

The fire of the Filipinos was of such volume that we were pretty well satisfied that they were going to crowd the attack and come to close quarters with us. Even above the roar of firing we could hear that they were yelling. Only two battalions of my regiment were able to get on the firing line, owing to a lagoon that ran at almost right angles to the line, so that one had to be held in reserve. It was now getting dusk, and the flashes of the enemy's rifles could be made out in the gathering darkness. The field that we were in was perfectly dry, and the bullets from the Mausers striking in it flicked up innumerable little spots of dust, just like the effect of big drops of rain in a dusty road at the beginning of a shower. Much as I had to think about, there went through my mind those words of Kipling, "the bullets kicking up the dust spots on the green." How bullets could make dust spots on green turf, however, I leave for the poet to explain.

I do not know just how long the fight lasted, probably half an hour after we had got on the line. It stopped as suddenly as it had begun. What had occurred, though we did not know it at the time, was that Colonel Stotsenburg with his fine regiment, the First Nebraska, forming the extreme right of Hale's brigade, had in the gathering dusk moved forward quietly, and turned the Filipino left, rolling it up and inflicting heavy loss, thus making it necessary for the enemy's whole line to fall back. As the Filipino right rested on lagoons it could not have been turned. The troops bivouacked in line of battle, and lay down to sleep where they had fought. During the day, besides its wounded who recovered, the Twentieth Kansas had lost Cook Scherrer and Privates Carroll, Hatfield, Keeny, and Wahl, killed or mortally wounded.

The necessity of repairing the railroad bridge and the much damaged track so that trains bringing up supplies from Manila could cross, as well as the construction of a bridge for our wheeled transportation, made it necessary for the whole division to remain on the north bank of the Marilao all the next day, and it was not until the morning of the 29th that we resumed the march. The day's rest and quiet had been a God-send to all, as the weather was becoming uncomfortably hot in the middle of the day, and in spite of short marches the men were beginning to show signs of fatigue, this condition being partly due to the watchfulness imposed at night. But the regiment, in common with the whole division, formed line of battle, having the First and Second Battalions on the firing line and the Third in reserve, five hundred yards in rear, and we trudged across the open fields, still having our right on the railroad. On our left was the First Montana, and across the railroad, to the right, the Tenth Pennsylvania. The Third Artillery was in reserve.

As the long irregular line of blue approached the river near Bocaue we could see trenches on the opposite bank. Soon came the crackle of the Mausers and the usual whining and zipping of bullets. We quickened our pace, and when we were within eight hundred yards the two battalions on the firing line opened up. We made the attack at a fast walk, each man stopping only long enough to take aim, and reloading as he advanced. In some respects this method of attack is to be preferred to the advance by rushes, as the shooting is much more accurate. The enemy's fire was rather heavy, but, after we opened, very wild. Major Metcalf and six enlisted men were wounded. Metcalf, as has been told, had been shot through one ear in the trenches at Caloocan, and now went to the other extreme by getting a bullet through a foot, an exceedingly painful and annoying wound. For several hours he tried to stay with the regiment, but finally gave it up and sorrowfully allowed himself to be hauled back to Manila. He recovered in time to join us at San Fernando.

The Filipinos had learned by bitter experience that it was not always best to remain too long in their trenches, especially if the ground to the rear was open, so that they could be shot down in getting away, and now, as the regiment began to yell and rush forward, they vacated. A few of us seized the railroad bridge, which they had not much injured, and several regiments crossed on it, deploying again on the other bank preparatory to continuing the advance. The loss of the enemy had been light, and we found only a few dead in their trenches and near them.

While we were forming on the north bank of this stream we could see at Bigaa station, about two miles up the track, a number of railroad trains, and could see that the enemy's troops were entraining. Our field-guns opened and created much confusion among them. As they fell back from Bigaa they burned the town, and we could see the dense clouds of smoke rolling skyward as we took up the march. Passing through Bigaa at about half-past eleven, we met with no resistance on our part of the line, though we heard some firing by other organizations. We began fondly to hope that we might camp that night in Malolos, but it was not to be. At a little after four o'clock we approached the Guiguinto River, and found the trenches on the opposite bank deserted. The railroad bridge was burning, but the fire had made but very little progress, and was put out by the men of Company B of the Twentieth Kansas, the men carrying water from the river in vessels that they found in near-by houses. The stream was deep, and the banks high and steep, so that our seizure of this bridge was a most fortunate circumstance.

Across the river for about twelve hundred yards stretched a perfectly level field from which the rice had been harvested. Beyond that was what appeared to be dense woods. There was not a sign of life anywhere, but scouts were sent out up the railroad track a few hundred yards. The large force of the enemy, concealed in elaborate trenches in the margin of the woods, held their fire until they could make it count better than by giving themselves away in order to stir up a few scouts. No one had any doubt that the coast was absolutely clear, and the crossing began immediately. The ties had not been removed from the bridge, so that this was not a matter of difficulty. The Tenth Pennsylvania and the Twentieth Kansas began crossing at the same time, the former using the right-hand side of the structure and the latter the left-hand. Two field-pieces and the Colt automatic were brought across the bridge by hand and prepared to open to the front in case the necessity should arise. For the time being all horses had to be left on the south bank.

I was standing at the north end of the bridge, talking to General MacArthur and watching my regiment cross, when we were startled by a most terrific fire opened on us. The bullets came from the north, and it was correctly surmised that the enemy's trenches were in the edge of the woods on the opposite side of the field. It was by far the best shooting that I have ever seen the Filipinos do. They were beyond the effective range of our Springfields, and knew it. They had the exact range and were using their sights, and had a good rest for their rifles over the parapet of their trench. The bullets were whipping up little dust spots all about, and actually filling the air with their various sorts of noises. Major P. B. Strong, adjutant-general of the division, standing within three feet of General MacArthur, was wounded, and dozens of bullets struck the bridge.

The two regiments crossed with great rapidity, each company, as it cleared the bridge, deploying and rushing up to the firing line. The Tenth Pennsylvania deployed to the right of the railroad and the Twentieth Kansas to the left. It was enough to warm the cockles of a soldier's heart to see the perfect coolness of these now veteran fighters under that rain of bullets to which they could make no adequate reply. Each company of the Twentieth Kansas, as it cleared the bridge, formed line at one pace interval, moved on a run by the left flank, faced to the front at a point that would make its right coincide with the left of the company that had preceded it, and then fairly flew over the ground until it came up on the firing line, when it went down flat to the earth and the men began to work their rifles with great vigor. The most of our firing was by platoon volleys, and crash succeeded crash with intervals of only a few seconds. The two field-pieces and the Colt automatic were in action, and were adding to the uproar. We soon began to advance by rushes, in order to come to close quarters. I was up on the firing line and, having occasion to look to the rear in order to see if all of the regiment had cleared the bridge, was astonished at the number of writhing forms in the little part of the field that we had crossed, and at the number of men being assisted to the shelter of the few straw stacks. The cry "Hospital Corps" was coming from all sides.

Chief-Trumpeter Barshfield and I were stooping down behind the prone men of Company G, and my attention was attracted to the difficulty one of the men, Private Birlew, was having in extracting a shell that had jammed in his piece. I was so close I could have touched him, and do not suppose I watched him more than three seconds, when I saw one whole side of his head torn open, and his face dropped down into the rice stubble, his hands clutched convulsively, and life's battle with him was over. The Filipinos had no mind to allow us to come to close quarters when they had no friendly stream to stop our rush, and when they saw that we were going to close with them, vacated their trenches, and the firing ceased as abruptly as it had begun.

I went at once toward the bridge to report to the division commander, and on my way passed one of the little straw stacks, and noticed behind it half a dozen wounded men being treated by the surgeons of the regiment who, by the way, got under fire as much as any of us. The fight had not lasted more than fifteen minutes, but the Twentieth Kansas had Privates Birlew, Dix, and Wilson killed, and Captain W. J. Watson and eighteen enlisted men wounded. Captain Watson, one of the best officers in the regiment, carries to this day, just back of his heart, the bullet received at Guiguinto. It was the last of his active service with the Twentieth Kansas, but he came back to the Philippines a year later in the Fortieth United States Volunteers, and lost a leg in an engagement in Mindanao. Having had his system sufficiently ventilated by bullets, Watson is now engaged in the peaceful pursuit of presiding over the post-office at his home town of Pittsburg, Kansas.

The troops that had fought at Guiguinto bivouacked in line of battle. The next forenoon was spent in the necessary but prosaic work of distributing rations and ammunition, and it was after two o'clock in the afternoon when we resumed the march, the Twentieth Kansas having the same relative position as on the preceding day. We were more than interested in the long and well-made trench, twelve hundred yards north of the bridge that had sheltered our assailants of the night before. If there had been any dead or wounded in them they had been removed. It is very unlikely, however, that the Filipinos had had more than a few men hit, as they had fought at long range behind excellent cover, while we had been in the open. We advanced slowly and cautiously, passing line after line of formidable trenches that must have cost an enormous amount of labor on the part of the noncombatants who had been rounded up by thousands by the insurgent leaders and compelled to work on them. During the afternoon no resistance was encountered, and at night we encamped within three miles of the insurgent capital. We would have had time to go in, but it was supposed that resistance of a serious nature would be offered, and it was not desired to bring on a fight when there was not sufficient daylight left to finish it in style.

From a strategic stand-point, Malolos was a place of no importance, but it was taken for granted that the enemy would desperately resist our occupation of his capital because of the moral effect that such a disaster would have, not only discouraging their own people, but giving the impression in foreign lands that the insurgent cause was lost, for it must not be forgotten that to the last the deluded Filipinos gave themselves "Dutch courage" by believing every ridiculous rumor of foreign intervention in their behalf. All reports agreed that the great fight of the campaign was at hand, and it looked ominous, for on our front were line after line of trenches and some formidable earthen redoubts. Scouts reported that up to this evening they were strongly held.

The next morning we were up bright and early in anticipation of an eventful day, for, fighting or no fighting, the occupation of an enemy's capital is a historical event of importance. When daylight came not a trace of life was apparent in the trenches on the front of our brigade, but the Filipinos might be playing one of their sharp tricks, trying to lure us into an incautious advance. Beginning at exactly seven o'clock there was an artillery preparation of half an hour, in which the eight or ten field-pieces with us, under the direction of Major Young, vigorously shelled the trenches and redoubts at a distance of about a mile, but without causing any stir in their vicinity. Immediately upon the cessation of the cannonade the infantry advance began, the whole Second Division being deployed on a front of over two miles. As for two days past, the Twentieth Kansas formed the right of Otis's brigade, which was on the left of the railway.

The various regiments of the division had been so reduced by sickness, heat prostrations, and battle casualties that they did not aggregate the formidable total that a week before had forced the passage of the Tuliajan. Wheaton's brigade, which had been coming up in rear of the division, guarding the line of communication, was now deployed immediately behind us as a support, so that as the two lines moved forward we numbered about

six thousand men. As the advance was to be made suc-
cessively from the right of the division to the left, Hale's
brigade got the first start, and we heard some lively firing
on its front and saw that it was carrying one or two lines
of trenches. Immediately in advance of the Twentieth
Kansas was a redoubt covering probably an acre of ground,
with flanking trenches. We were within a thousand yards
of it, when I had the regiment lie down, and sent a few
scouts to examine the work. It was a ticklish job, but
manfully done. It would be better to sacrifice half a dozen
men than five or six times that number. We watched the
scouts anxiously as they darted forward and threw themselves on the ground between dashes. Finally they made
the last rush and went over the parapet of the redoubt.
It was with great relief that we heard no firing, and soon
they were back on the parapet signalling that the coast
was clear. We then went forward rapidly, and soon
passed the work and were halted some distance beyond it
by the division commander, who was close up to the firing
line. There was still a little firing in the direction of Hale's
brigade, and a number of high bullets fired at his right
reached us, one man of the regiment being wounded.

We were now less than a mile from the nipa houses
in the suburbs of Malolos. I was on the railroad track
with the division commander, when he asked me if I would
like to take a few men and feel my way into the town.
I said I would be glad to, and took Lieutenant Ball and
about a dozen men from Company E, leaving the regiment in command of Lieutenant-Colonel Little for the
time being. Moving rapidly over to the left of the regi-

ment, our little detachment found a narrow road leading into the capital, and we went up it on the jump, now and then halting for a few seconds to peer around corners. The road soon became a street, and here we were joined by the ubiquitous Mr. Creelman, quite out of breath from his exertions in overtaking us, he having "smelled a rat" when he saw us leave. We were fired upon by about a dozen men behind a street barricade of stones, gave them a couple of volleys, and then rushed them. A minute later we were in the plaza or public square, and exchanged shots with a few men who were running through the streets starting fires. The buildings occupied by Aguinaldo as a residence and as offices and the Hall of Congress were burning. We gave such cheers as a few men could, and I sent back word to General MacArthur that the town was ours. In a few moments troops from all the regiments of the brigade, as well as the brigade commander himself, joined us.

Some time before we entered the square the First South Dakota had occupied the village of Barasoain, which is practically a continuation of Malolos, though it has, or at least then had, a separate municipal government. This circumstance caused some of our compatriots from the far north to feel irritated by the none too modest boast of a few of the men of the Twentieth Kansas to the effect that the Kansans had been the first men actually in the capital.

After all of us were comfortably seated about our own firesides in the United States the newspaper war waged over this question was only less bloody than the sanguinary long-range contest carried on by the Kansans with the men of the Tenth Pennsylvania over the Marilao affair. This is one of the weaknesses of troops having local or State pride to cater to. Circumstances had simply enabled men from these two regiments to be the first to enter Malolos and the neighboring town. As a matter of fact, the victory belonged to the whole division and the troops cooperating with it. Malolos was defended, not at Malolos itself, but at Caloocan, Tuliajan River, Malinta, Polo, Meycauayan, Marilao, Bocaue, and Guiguinto.

IV

VARIOUS considerations made it necessary for the Second Division to remain at Malolos for more than three weeks before resuming the advance along the railroad. A short delay would have been welcome, as the men had been much exhausted by the week of marching and fighting that had placed them in possession of the enemy's capital. The marches, it is true, had as a rule been short, but we were in the midst of the hot season, and the troops were not properly clothed for service in the tropics. With the exception of the Third Artillery, that had been designated as provost guard, the various regiments constituting the division were not sheltered in the buildings of the town, but were bivouacked on its outskirts, each covered by its own outposts, this arrangement being necessary in order to avoid surprise and disaster in case of a sudden attack.

Our brigade commander, Brigadier-General H. G. Otis, believing that the war was about over, resigned his commission and returned to the United States in order to attend to important private interests that he had been compelled to neglect while in service, and was succeeded by Brigadier-General Loyd Wheaton, who had heretofore been in the command of a separate brigade acting as a reserve and as line of communication troops in the advance up the railroad.

General Wheaton, who is still living as a major-general on the retired list of the army, was without doubt the most striking individual and the most interesting character among those who served in our army in the Philippines. He had served in an Illinois regiment throughout the entire Civil War, rising from sergeant to lieutenant-colonel commanding his regiment, was desperately wounded at Shiloh, and had received the Medal of Honor for gallantry at the storming of Fort Blakely, on which occasion he was the first man to enter the enemy's works, leaping sword in hand through a gun embrasure. The passage of half a lifetime since that great struggle had not abated to the slightest degree his military ardor nor his fiery valor, or caused any diminution in his restless energy. He was of slender build and quick in movement, and had a voice that could be heard above the roar of the stiffest fight. He seemed to enjoy fighting for its own sake, and had a positive contempt for danger. The only sort of man he despised was a coward, and woe unto him who in his sight showed the slightest yellow streak, for he would hear something that he would remember for many a year. General Wheaton, on the other hand, was most generous in his recognition of every gallant action by members of his command, and was very much inclined to stretch a point to give to others the credit for successes that were largely due to himself. It is needless to say that he inspired all the members of his command with a feeling of personal devotion.

The delay at Malolos was not without stirring incidents. The insurgent forces, still under the able and energetic Luna, were in heavy force on our front and right, and, despite the numerous drubbings they had received, were full of fight. Our line of communication with our base, Manila, was guarded by the Second Oregon and the Thirteenth Minnesota, there being, as a rule, one or two companies stationed at bridges and other important points. But a line of railroad is especially vulnerable, on account of the ease with which it can be damaged in a very few moments, and on the night of April 10 the attempt was made by some thousands of the enemy who had swung around our right flank for the purpose. It was a little after midnight when those of us at Malolos who happened to be awake heard the indistinct rattle of rifle fire far to our rear. Then came a few brief and alarming messages from Marilao, Bocaue, Bigaa, and Guiguinto, and nothing more, for the telegraph wires had been severed. The sound of firing became more distinct as the attacks on the various posts progressed, and as those nearer Malolos became involved. With an escort of only a few dismounted cavalrymen, General Wheaton hurried on foot down the track, picking up here and there detachments from the companies on guard at various places, and with his small force struck the enemy like a cyclone, routing him in four stiff fights. Near Guiguinto we had an armored car with several machine guns. This was pushed into the various fights by hand, and those of us listening at Malolos could distinguish the drumming of the Gatlings above the heavy and incessant rifle fire.

The insurgents had gained some minor successes before being driven off, but practically all the damage done had been repaired by daylight.

During this period our outposts were occasionally attacked at night, and we had some lively scrimmages in the darkness. On one of these occasions a very profane captain of the Twentieth Kansas caused no little merriment by falling into a shallow but unguarded well. The sulphurous remarks that reached the ears of those in the vicinity were the theme of many a subsequent camp-fire story and are still dwelt on fondly at reunions.

In the meantime all preparations were made for continuing the advance up the railroad. Our old comrades of the Third Artillery were to be left behind to garrison Malolos, so that the First Brigade was reduced to the Montana and Kansas regiments. In the Second Brigade the Tenth Pennsylvania was relieved by the Fifty-first Iowa, a regiment that had not yet had opportunity for field service. As one of the preliminaries of the resumption of the campaign, Major J. F. Bell with Troop K, Fourth Cavalry, was sent on April 23 on a reconnoissance toward the town of Quingua, on the river of that name, and became so deeply involved in an engagement with a greatly superior force of the enemy under Pablo Tecson that portions of the Nebraska and Iowa regiments were sent to the scene. The ensuing combat was one of unusual severity, the Nebraska regiment alone losing four killed and thirty-one wounded, among the former its able and gallant commander, Colonel John M. Stotsenberg, an officer who during the campaign had won an enviable reputation for dash and courage.

The division resumed operations on the next day, Hale's brigade moving out from our right flank, crossing the Quingua near the scene of the fight of the previous day, and sweeping down its right bank, carrying one line of trenches after another. The distance to be covered by this brigade was much greater than the march required to bring our own in such a position that the whole division would be in line at the Bag-Bag, the first stream up the railroad from Malolos; so that we were merely formed in column and marched out of the town to await developments. The men were allowed to fall out of ranks and lie down or make themselves as comfortable as possible, but were all held well in hand so that the march could be resumed at a moment's notice. The day was one of the hottest I have seen in the Philippines, and as there was but little shade where we were along the railroad track, we lay about fairly sweltering and listening intently to the heavy firing some miles to our right.

To me the sounds of battle have always had an absorbing interest. We were so far from the scene that the general effect was not destroyed by any uproar in our immediate vicinity. Individual shots could not be heard, and had it not been for the cloudless sky and the pitiless blazing sun one could have imagined it the rumblings of a distant thunder-storm, now rising and now falling, but always drifting toward the Bag-Bag. All day we were held in position, and bivouacked there for the night, but on the morning of the 25th Hale's brigade, having reached the desired position, resumed the march, following a cart road to the left of the railway track. General Mac-Arthur accompanied our brigade, and the armored train was pushed along the track by a number of Chinamen. This train was in command of Lieutenant C. H. Bridges, Twenty-second Infantry, and consisted of four cars, the first and last being flat cars, while the other two were box cars. The first car was to do all the fighting, and was armed with a naval six-pounder rifle and three machine guns, the others being merely to carry the impedimenta and serve as a living quarters for the personnel.

A few miles brought us to a field of young corn about a foot high, and half a mile across it we could see the railway bridge over the Bag-Bag and the brown earthworks of the enemy on the other side of the stream. Under cover of several lines of bamboo a few companies each from the First Montana and the Twentieth Kansas were deployed, those belonging to the former regiment to the right of the track, while we were on the left. A few hundred yards above the bridge the Quingua and a lagoon known locally as the Rio Chico unite to form the Bag-Bag. Hale's brigade was separated from us by the former, while the latter lay between it and the enemy, whose trenches lay along the Bag-Bag and the Rio Chico.

So far not a shot had been fired, and as we peered through the screen of bamboo across the light green of the cornfield to other fields of corn and lines of bamboo across the river it was hard to realize that in a few short moments this placid landscape would be marred by lines of madly rushing men, yelling and firing, while the air would quiver with the rattle of rifle fire, the crash of artillery, and the demoniacal drumming of machine guns. But the transformation came like a whirlwind. I was standing near Generals MacArthur and Wheaton and their staffs, just to the left of the armored train which was slowly being pushed into view. There was a spurt of flame from the long, slender muzzle of the naval gun, and a sharper and more vicious crash than we were used to from our fieldpieces, for this was a high-power gun, and a shower of earth flew from the top of the trench across the river as the shell struck and exploded. Shell after shell from the quick-firer followed in rapid succession, while the machine guns opened from the sides of the car on such portions of the trenches as they could be brought to bear on. Two field-pieces with our brigade, and the guns with the Second Brigade across the Quingua, as well as all the infantry of both brigades that had been deployed, added to the uproar.

With the first shot from the naval gun the apparently empty trenches had come to life, straw hats bobbed up and down, once more we heard the peculiar "pow," "pow" of the Mausers, and bullets zipped through the bamboos or flicked up dust spots in the dry cornfield. A private of the Hospital Corps, waiting with his pouch for the call to others in need, leaped from one of the box cars, grasped wildly at his throat, deluged with blood those who were trying to assist him, and fell dead at our feet. A normal man can hardly become so used to the tragedies of war as not to be shaken by such a spectacle.

For half an hour the uproar continued, when I received

orders from General Wheaton to seize the bridge. The attack on the structure could not be made to advantage by more than one company, so that I directed Captain Boltwood to advance his company rapidly across the cornfield, the movement being covered by the fire of several other companies and the armored train. The company selected went at its work with a vim, and closed in quickly, making the advance by rushes. Accompanied by Sergeant-Major Warner and Chief-Trumpeter Barshfield, I kept abreast of its right flank, running along the margin of the cornfield about thirty yards from the railway track. As we came to close quarters the troops supporting us had to cease their fire, and for about ten minutes the situation was interesting, to express it mildly. The men of Company K lay close to the ground just to the left of the north end of the bridge, and fought silently and hard. They had no breath left for yelling, and it was a poor time for it. Absolutely in the open, at seventy yards range, they were at a disadvantage against the men in the loop-holed trench on the other bank. But the enemy's nerve had been shaken by the severe fire he had been under for more than half an hour.

Hale's brigade was already about to force the passage of the Rio Chico, and the men of the First Montana were closing in. We could see that the farthest span of the fine steel bridge had been let down into the water, so that an attempt to rush the structure and get directly into the trenches on the other bank was not practicable. I thought it might be done by swimming around the broken span, and called on the men nearest me to come along.

Most of these were from a small detachment of Company E, under Lieutenant Colin H. Ball, that had just reported from a reconnoissance down the stream, but I was also accompanied by Barshfield and Warner and by First-Sergeant Enslow, of Company K. About ten of us ran up the embankment to the end of the bridge, and then discovered that the ties and rails had been removed, so that we had to work ourselves along the sides, a slow and tedious operation. But very few shots were fired at us, none at all after we had got half-way across, as the enemy had already begun to vacate the works. I thought it advisable to get into them at once, nevertheless, for fear that they might be reoccupied.

The bridge, including the sixty-foot span that had been dropped into the water, was a little more than two hundred feet long, but in time we reached the gap. It developed now that some of us could not swim, but it would at any rate be a good idea for some men to remain on the bridge and cover us with their fire in case the enemy should be "playing possum" or should make a counter-attack on those of us who succeeded in crossing. Taking off our shoes and leaving behind our arms and ammunition, Lieutenant Ball, Sergeant Enslow, Chief-Trumpeter Barshfield, Corporal A. M. Ferguson, of Company E, and myself swung ourselves down until we could grasp a steel rod that ran diagonally from the top of one pier to a point on the opposite one a few feet above the water, slid down this, and were soon in. As soon as I got in I reached for bottom, but could not find it, subsequent examination showing the stream to be ten feet deep at that point, so that we had to swim for it, no great task, as the distance was about forty-five feet. Although I had got into the water first, Ball beat me to the bank, being a faster swimmer, and the four of us, barefooted, unarmed, and dripping, rushed into the trench, to find in it only the dead and disabled.

The firing at this point had ceased before we entered the water, but we hastily gathered up a few rifles and cartridges to use in case of emergency, and awaited developments. At about the same time troops belonging to Hale's brigade had forced the passage of the Rio Chico above us, and as this stream in conjunction with the Quingua forms the Bag-Bag they were on the same side with us. The sharp little fight of the Bag-Bag was over in less than an hour after the naval gun on the armored train had opened the ball, and one more of the elaborately built lines of the Filipino defences had been given up to the invader.

The infantry of Hale's brigade, having crossed the Rio Chico by wading, pursued the enemy to the town of Calumpit, about two miles, and was there brought to a stand by the broad and deep Rio Grande. The engineers, having succeeded in constructing a foot-bridge over the broken-out span of the Bag-Bag bridge, our infantry crossed the next day, the artillery of the whole division having been brought across by fording the Quingua and the Rio Chico at their junction. As the position at Calumpit was so contracted there was not room for the whole division to operate, the task of forcing the passage was intrusted to General Wheaton, the division commander remaining with his brigade and exercising general supervision.

Reconnoitring parties crept cautiously forward to the river bank and seized advantageous positions, from which they opened fire on the enemy. The position was by all means the strongest that we had yet been brought against, the river being about four hundred feet wide, deep and swift, while the opposite bank was defended by fully four thousand men occupying elaborate trenches. These were so constructed as to afford excellent head cover, long slits being left for firing through, the earth being held in place by strong revetments of bamboo. The works for some distance above and below the bridge were roofed with steel rails taken from the railway. There were bomb proofs, traverses and flanking trenches, and, in fact, nothing that the cunning ingenuity of General Alejandrino, chief engineer of the insurgent forces, could conceive of had been overlooked. In addition to their infantry the insurgents had three pieces of artillery and a Maxim gun.

In an old trench we found fair shelter for the main body of the Twentieth Kansas, a few hundred yards from the river bank. The railway freight-house, a brick building, stood a hundred yards from our end of the big steel bridge spanning the river, and Company I under Captain Flanders succeeded in occupying it. We loop-holed the building and opened a blistering fire on the trenches across the river, but could make no impression, merely succeeding in drawing a hot return fire that continually peppered the building and swept the ground all about it. A piece of artillery in one of the enemy's works at the end of the bridge fired twenty shells at the building, but failed to hit it. When we captured the gun the next day it was found that the sight had been lost, which undoubtedly accounted for such bad shooting at only a little more than two hundred yards. One of these shells landed among the men back in the main position of the Twentieth Kansas, but did not get any one, and after I had gone back of the track to explain the situation to General Wheaton and was talking with him, one of them struck and exploded within a few yards of us, whereat the general merely sniffed contemptuously. Major Young, the chief of artillery, and Lieutenant Ball of my regiment had been with us, and had just started away, when the shell struck and threw earth all over them. Ball was badly wounded in the face by a bullet a few moments after.

Returning to the freight-house half an hour later, a few of us rushed the ruins of a burned rice mill right on the river bank, and a detachment from the cover of its walls continued to keep up a fire on the enemy. The First Montana, on the other side of the railroad track, was doing its share, and some of our guns, having found suitable positions, opened fire. And so wore away all of a fiercely hot day, with the popping of rifles, the occasional boom of a cannon and swish of a shell, and no end of stirring incident; but when night came to the exhausted men, with its cooling breezes, but little had been accomplished. I talked with both the division and the brigade commanders, and saw that they were deeply concerned over the situation, and thought it was up to some one to do something, and so volunteered to attempt to carry the bridge by assault with about a dozen picked men. General MacArthur at first seemed appalled by the proposition, but after a moment's hesitation gave his permission. I knew that if a dozen of us with plenty of ammunition ever got into the trenches on the other side all the Filipinos this side of Kingdom Come could not get us out before daylight, when we could cover the crossing of other troops.

It had already been ascertained that the rails and ties had been removed from the bridge, and that there was nothing left but the stringers, these being about eight feet apart. The plan was for each man to carry a strong plank and use it to bridge his way from stringer to stringer. The attack was to be covered by the fire of both regiments and all of our artillery, which were to advance to the river bank and sweep the trenches above and below the bridge. There was a suspicion, however, that even the stringers had been removed from a part of the bridge, in which case the enterprise must surely meet with disaster.

Corporal A. M. Ferguson, now an officer of the regular army, who had on several occasions shown himself equal to any emergency, volunteered for the hazardous enterprise of ascertaining the condition of the bridge throughout its length, and accompanied by Captain Flanders and myself crawled carefully to the end of the structure, where he removed his shoes and nearly all his clothing, and crawled hand over hand through the angle irons underneath the stringers. It was a perilous and exhausting task. A single slip would have meant a drop into the dark waters, forty feet below. For two long hours Flanders and I crouched at the south end of the bridge, but finally Ferguson came back with the information that at the far end of the bridge the stringers had been removed for several yards. Our cherished enterprise was shown to be absolutely hopeless, but in the meantime the requisite number of men had volunteered to assist in the assault.

I sent word to my superiors that the plan was hopeless, and with one hundred and twenty men from my regiment sneaked down the river for a mile, thinking that we might find a raft or improvise one, and by effecting a surprise get enough men across in the darkness to hold on until others could cross. Just as we were scouting for a good crossing a dog barked, there was a flash of a score of rifles on the other bank, and we were again beaten. At the same time a cannon boomed through the night to warn the insurgents to be on their guard, and a number of rockets ascended. At one o'clock in the morning, tired, disgusted, and disheartened, we dragged ourselves back to the regiment's position and threw ourselves on the ground for a little sleep. Both sides were worn out, and there was no firing until daylight.

The sun rose blazing hot on the morning of the 27th of April and the "sniping" back and forth across the river recommenced, being varied by an occasional cannon shot. Some of our men engaged in this sharp-shooting discovered close in to the bank, six hundred yards below the bridge, a small raft which the enemy had unsuccessfully attempted to burn. This find suggested a way out of the difficulty of crossing the stream. A light rope of the necessary length was obtained, but in order to be able to make a ferry it was necessary to get one end of this fastened on the enemy's side of the river. Several men volunteered for the perilous feat of swimming the stream with the rope, though they would necessarily have to land within a few feet of trenches occupied by the enemy, and from these were selected Privates W. B. Trembley and Edward White of Company B. Before leaving Malolos twenty-five Krag-Jorgensen rifles had been distributed to each company of the volunteer regiments, and now one hundred picked men armed with these weapons were selected from the whole regiment, rushed down to the river bank, and given the necessary instructions as to covering the crossing. General MacArthur had placed at the disposal of General Wheaton all the artillery and machine guns of the division, and by his orders all these were placed in readiness to assist in the enterprise.

White and Trembley stripped stark naked behind the cover of a clump of bamboos, took the end of the rope between them and plunged into the river. They were powerful swimmers, but their progress was slow, owing to the strength required to drag the rope, which was being paid out to them by their comrades on the bank. As soon as they struck the water the music began. The hundred men crouching on the bank with their Krag-Jorgensens began to sweep with bullets the top of the trench where the two were to attempt to land; just to their right Lieutenant Fleming with several machine guns, including a Hotchkiss revolving cannon, was pounding the same work. Still farther to the right, that is, toward the bridge, several field-pieces under Major Young were battering the heavier trenches near the enemy's end of the bridge in order to keep down their fire, while one field-piece in the freight-house was firing diagonally across our front and partially enfilading the trench where the two men were to make their landing.

As a melodrama the whole scene was a howling, or rather a roaring, success. The greatest lover of the sensational could not have wished for anything more thrilling. The two men battling slowly across the current, with the snake-like rope dragging after them; the grim and silent men firing with top speed over their heads into the trenches on the other bank; the continuous popping of the revolving cannon, a gun of the pompom type; the steady drumming of Gatlings and the constant succession of crashes from the big field-pieces, their shells flying harmlessly from the armored trenches on the other bank, or hurling steel rails and wagon loads of earth into the air; the thin film of smoke rising along both banks of the river, and the air filled with dust thrown up by striking shells and bullets, made a scene that could not fade from one's memory in many a lifetime. There was now being carried out one of the most difficult of military operations, forcing the passage of an unfordable river in the face of an entrenched enemy. The Rio Grande was, in fact, a vast moat for the defences on the north bank.

Finally, the two swimmers, panting and all but exhausted, dragged themselves out on the other bank at the base of the work that had been so mercilessly battered. The fire of the artillery and the machine guns on that particular trench had, of course, now ceased for fear of

hitting the two men, and only a few of the detail of infantrymen were allowed to fire, and they under strict supervision, as their bullets must clear White and Trembley
by only a few feet if the latter stood up. There was, however, no cessation of the fire on the works between them
and the north end of the bridge.

The situation of the two naked and unarmed men was,
of course, precarious, as they were separated from all
the rest of the division by a deep and swift river that had
taken all their strength to cross, while all around them
were hundreds of the enemy, who, however, were pre-
vented from molesting them by the fire still sweeping the
adjacent trenches. We could see the two men groping
about on all-fours trying to find something to which they
could tie the end of the rope. In order to see whether
there were any of the enemy still alive in the trench nearest them they made mud balls and pitched them over the
parapet. Several men dashed out and toward the rear,
but the most of them were brought down by our men on
the south bank. Finally, White and Trembly made a
noose in the end of the rope, gathered in several feet of
slack, and, astonishing to relate, made a dash for the
trench and slipped it over one of the bamboo uprights of
the work, returning then to the river bank, while we
opened fire again directly over them to prevent the occupants of the trench from cutting the rope.

The ferry was now established and we were ready for
the next move. It was highly desirable to take the arms,
ammunition, and clothing of the two men to them at
once. After White and Trembly had taken to the water

some one had found concealed under a house a very small and cranky dug-out canoe. Corporal B. H. Kerfoot, now a captain in the regular army, and Private O. E. Tyler launched this craft and started across, but upset in the middle of the stream, and had to swim out, having lost not only their own arms, but the arms and clothing of the two men on the other side, their very laudable enterprise having failed through no fault of their own.

In the meantime the raft was floated down the few yards to where the rope was tied on our side of the stream, and preparations made to ferry across enough men to drive the enemy from the end of the bridge. I realized perfectly well that according to the rules of the game a colonel should not leave the bulk of his regiment on one side of a stream and accompany a detachment smaller than a company in size, but I had initiated this enterprise and felt that I must see it through. I could not but consider the outcome as doubtful, and knew mighty well that if I should send a small force across and sacrifice it I would be damned in my home State all the rest of my life, and held up to scorn by all the corner-grocery tacticians in the country.

It was found that the raft would support eight men; so I got on board with seven others, and by pulling along the rope we had in a few moments joined White and Trembley on the other bank. In the meantime the artillery and infantry fire against the trenches near the bridge had decreased in volume, but had by no means ceased. Two men took the raft back for another load, and as two were always required for this purpose, the net gain for each trip was usually about six men. As soon as the six of us had landed we dashed into the trench near us, finding it simply full of dead and wounded men. The few who were uninjured surrendered at once. As each raft-load arrived, the men were ordered to crouch low under the cover of the river bank. Finally, I had with me Captain Orwig, Lieutenants Whisner and Hopkins, and forty-one enlisted men, every man of whom carried two hundred cartridges for his Krag.

Leaving orders for the raft to continue its trips, and for all subsequent arrivals to form in order to beat off any attack on our left flank and rear, I formed the little detachment in a single line with its right near the river and we began moving up the stream. About half-way between the spot where we had landed and the bridge a small but deep stream called the Rio Francis empties into the Rio Grande. Until we reached this we found the trenches of the enemy deserted, but the works between this and the bridge were fairly swarming with men. We opened fire straight down the trenches across the Rio Francis, enfilading them from end to end, but the occupants were well protected by traverses and the roofs of steel rails. However, they saw that if we succeeded in crossing the Rio Francis we would be among them, and having been terribly shaken by the fire poured into them from across the Rio Grande, they began to vacate, not across the fire-swept open, but along trenches leading to the rear. For a moment it looked as if the fight was won, and we tried to cross the Rio Francis, but found that it was beyond depth, though not more than sixty feet wide. Accordingly, we moved rapidly up it, marching by our left flank, and soon were in a veritable hornet's nest. We had come out from the shelter of the bamboos along the bank of the Rio Grande and were in the margin of a field of young corn about two feet high. The whole farther bank of the Rio Francis was a maze of trenches, and as the stream curved around our left flank we were getting it from two sides. The nearest trenches of the enemy were within a stone's throw, but we could not rush them because of the intervening stream.

As soon as we had broken into the open, the men had been ordered to lie flat and fire from that position, as otherwise we would have lasted about as long as the proverbial snowball in a blast furnace. We officers went down on one knee, as it was necessary to have something of a lookout, once in a while jumping to our feet for a few seconds to survey the situation. The men, though having the hardest fight of their lives, were under perfect control. We changed the front of the left flank of the detachment in order to bring a fire to bear on the trenches that were enfilading us, and as all of the trenches that we were now engaged with were of the open, standing variety, we were able to accomplish considerable in the way of keeping their occupants down.

But the situation would have been hopeless had it not been for the splendid support rendered by the artillery, machine guns, and infantry on the south bank of the Rio Grande, the fire from these troops enfilading some of the trenches that we were fighting. The shrapnel from our own guns, sweeping across our front at a distance of sometimes less than a hundred feet, caused us no little uneasiness, as a defective fuse might cause a burst short of us with disastrous results. We were not sure, either, that our own people could exactly make out our position, as the air was laden with smoke from bursting shells and with dust thrown up by striking projectiles. Had it not been for the fact that all the troops engaged on both sides were using powder that was at least nearly smokeless, our position would have been impossible. Although there were four thousand insurgent troops on the north side of the Rio Grande, the portion that we were engaged with did not probably number more than six hundred men.

The fire of the enemy had begun to lessen somewhat when a startled exclamation began to run along the line of prostrate men, as we heard directly on our front the unmistakable whirring of a machine gun, and at the same time, just past our right flank, at a distance of not more than thirty feet, the dust was being whipped up along a space four or five feet wide and sixty feet long. A dozen men cried out, "It's the Maxim," and one added the cheerful prediction, "We're goners," being immediately afterward affectionately kicked by his colonel, with an injunction to keep his views to himself. I had stood up as soon as the Maxim opened, and, by following back the direction indicated by the stream of dust kicked up, had no difficulty in locating the gun and the men serving it. It was under a stone culvert of the railway, about two hundred yards north of the bridge, and three hundred yards from our front, being completely protected from the fire of our troops on the south side of the river.

"Cease firing" was blown, and as soon as one could make himself heard the men were ordered to load their magazines, then to rise to their feet, and then the command, "Under that culvert, rapid fire." The Maxim stopped business then and there, every man in the detachment serving it being killed or disabled. It is my firm belief that, if the weapon had been played laterally instead of being held on the same spot, not a handful of us would have survived, as they had our range perfectly.

It was now plain that the enemy were rapidly vacating the trenches on our front, the most of them taking advantage of numerous trenches and "get aways" to retire under cover. I had heard firing in our rear, and looking around saw the men who had followed us on the raft and who had been deployed to protect us from rear attack were having a lively little affair of their own.

The time had come to cross the Rio Francis, and we swarmed down the steep bank, where for a moment we were out of sight of the enemy as well as of our own people on the other side of the Rio Grande. A number of the men waded out, but found the sluggish stream too deep. But there were several small "dugouts," and we piled into them and began scrambling up the opposite bank, one man taking back each one of the boats. The first one, containing Captain Orwig and several enlisted men, being overloaded, sank. The strain was now over, and at the spectacle of that gallant officer spouting muddy water like a small whale as he swam for shore, I sat down and had a good laugh. As soon as half a dozen of us were across we dashed for the end of the railway bridge, but not a shot was fired at us, the trenches being empty except for the dead and dying, and what a shambles they were in some places!

During all this time Generals MacArthur and Wheaton had been standing in the open near the freight-house closely watching the progress of events, and directing the work of the troops that had given us such invaluable support. As soon as General Wheaton saw us dash down the steep bank of the Rio Francis he had called on the nearest organizations to follow him, and had started for the bridge. They worked along the wrecked structure, holding on to the sides, and were nearly across when Orwig and I with a few men reached the north end. The place where the girders had been entirely removed was bridged over with planks and timbers. The general and his staff were the first to reach us, and there were some vigorous hand-shakings and mutual congratulations. Companies of the First Montana and the Twentieth Kansas followed as rapidly as they could work their way over the bridge, and by order of General Wheaton took up the pursuit of the enemy retiring toward Apalit. The open plain was fairly covered with them, the whole four thousand of them, minus those left dead or wounded in our hands, being in sight. They were beyond rifle range, but the pursuing troops had a lively brush with their rear guard, in which Captain W. H. Bishop, one of the most capable and courageous officers of the Twentieth Kansas, was severely wounded.

In a redoubt just above the end of the bridge we found the cannon that had made such poor practice on the freight-house. It was a bronze muzzle-loading, rifled howitzer of about three-inch calibre. A visit was at once made to the culvert under which had been stationed the Maxim that had come so near to being our undoing, but it had been removed, the wheel marks being plainly visible. On the ground under the culvert were about twenty dead and wounded men, seven of them being Spanish prisoners of war in the hands of the insurgents, they being still in the uniform of their service. One of the wounded, a corporal, told me that he and his six comrades had been compelled, under threats of death, to handle the Maxim, as the insurgents did not understand the weapon. When we had risen to our feet and opened fire four of the seven had gone down killed and three of them wounded. The corporal assured me that the gun had jammed just as we opened on them, so that after all our fire had not silenced it, though it had wiped out the personnel. The three surviving Spaniards had been hit in several places, and all died that night.

The battle of Calumpit was over, and the passage of the Rio Grande had been forced. Our dead and our own wounded, as well as the enemy's, were sent to Manila at once, while the enemy's dead were buried in the trenches they had so bravely defended. I do not think anybody took the trouble to count them. Hundreds of rifles and many thousands of rounds of ammunition had been captured. In his official report General MacArthur, a man not given to gushing even to the slightest degree, stated,

"The successful passage of the river must be regarded as a remarkable military achievement, well calculated to fix the attention of the most careless observer and to stimulate the fancy of the most indifferent." Based upon the recommendations of Generals MacArthur and Wheaton, both of them eye-witnesses of the whole affair, White, Trembly, and myself were, by direction of the President, awarded the Congressional Medal of Honor.

Several days were required to ferry across the river the artillery and trains of the division, and it was not until the morning of the 4th of May that we were ready to resume the advance. Our brigade had been in bivouac near the town of Apalit, and early in the morning we had formed in columns of fours, and were pushing up the railroad track. Hale's brigade had the wagon road to the right, and a number of lagoons made necessary a considerable gap between the two brigades. Our friends of the Second Brigade got into it first, and, as the country was perfectly open and flat, we were interested spectators of the fine fight that they were having. But in a short time our advance guard, consisting of Company H of the Twentieth Kansas, came under fire.

The country was so cut up by watercourses that effective work was very difficult. A deep and sluggish lagoon, crossed by the railway bridge, was defended on its farther bank by several hundred of the enemy in open trenches. We had with us on a hand-car one of our Gatling guns, and this weapon was placed in position and opened fire, sweeping the enemy's defences from right to left. General Wheaton, who, as usual, was on the firing line, be-

came somewhat impatient at the volume of fire delivered by this weapon, and called out to the sergeant in
charge, "Turn that damned thing faster. Are you trying
to take a nap?" whereat the thing was made to fairly
hum for a few moments, until the sergeant, a grizzled old
regular with an Irish brogue that could not have been cut
with an axe, turned about, saluted very correctly, and
said, "Sir, we are out of ammunition." The return blast
from the brigade commander was in every way worthy of
the occasion.

In the meantime Company H had deployed and advanced, under a very hot fire, to the bank of the lagoon
and had tried to rush the bridge, but found it dismantled
as usual. The men under command of Lieutenant A. H.
Krause lay down and engaged in a hard short-range fight
with the enemy entrenched on the opposite bank, and
finally drove him out, losing Private Wilcox killed and
three other enlisted men wounded.

While this affair was going on I had sent for Captain
W. S. Albright, commanding Company C of my regiment,
and was giving him instructions as to what to do with his
company when a bullet struck one of the steel rails of the
railway track on which we were standing, missing General
Wheaton less than a foot, and then buried itself in the
thigh of the unfortunate Albright. It was this officer's
birthday, and as he dropped to the ground an embarrassed
grin overspread his features as he said, "Well this is certainly one hell of a birthday present."

As the enemy vacated the trenches on the opposite
bank of the lagoon our men pushed out on the bridge and

were able to cross a few at a time, their progress being very slow owing to its wrecked condition. I had got across with two complete companies and was examining trenches abandoned by the enemy, when General Wheaton sent me orders to push up the railway track toward the Santo Tomas station and ascertain what was going on in that vicinity. We hurried forward, reached the station, which was some distance from the buildings of the town, and mighty soon found out what was doing. The insurgent commander-in-chief, Antonio Luna, had just deployed a force to make a counter-attack on those of us who had crossed the bridge, and was advancing with it in person, apparently not knowing that our small detachment had pushed up toward the railroad station. The two forces, having been screened from each other by a line of bamboo, came into contact in the open at four hundred yards range. The enemy outnumbered us about three to one, and for a few moments there took place one of the finest stand-up and knock-down fights that one would care to see. The gallant Luna himself was hit, shot in the abdomen, and we could see the riderless and terrified horses of himself and staff tearing across the fields. It was a wild five minutes. Fortunately, the scouts a short distance out on our front had given us sufficient warning, so that we had formed line before being struck.

Lieutenant W. A. McTaggart, a most capable officer, sank to the ground with both eyes shot out, but happily died before regaining consciousness. This horrible spectacle for a moment sickened me, and then I saw a corporal, shot through the brain, from one temple to the other, fall

almost across McTaggart's feet.   It should be of interest
to know that this man entirely recovered from his wound,
and died of disease a year after his muster out of the service.

Our fire soon mastered that of the enemy and the
greater portion of them fled in disorder, but their left,
consisting of about eighty men, had reached the shelter
of a roadway, and lay down in it, keeping up a lively fire
at a distance of about two hundred yards.   I saw that
Company G, commanded by Captain Howard A. Scott,
was coming up at double time, and resolved to have him
turn the enemy out of his cover by a flank attack, in the
meantime ordering the two companies with me to lie
down behind the railway track, which here was on a level
with the general surface of the ground, there being neither
cut nor fill.   Captain Scott arrived in advance of his company, and I was giving him instructions as to what to do
when I felt a most terrific blow on my left hand, in which
I was holding a pair of field-glasses.   At first I did not
realize that I had been shot, but Lieutenant B. J. Mitchell,
who for some years afterward served me as aide, picked
up the glasses, which had been hurled through the air for
some twenty feet, took me by the arm, and called a man
of the Hospital Corps.   Blood was spattering all over me,
and I had no desire to look at the offending hand, and so
held it out to the man, looking the other way in the meantime.   As he examined it, I asked, "Is there anything
left of it?"   He replied, "Clean shot," and told me to sit
down.   As I backed up against the little station building
I saw Warner, the regimental sergeant-major who had

been at my side through every fight of the campaign, reclining against the wall and looking decidedly peevish. I said, "Warner, where did you get it?" He held up his left hand, and it was a most remarkable coincidence that we had been hit in exactly the same place, barring the fraction of an inch. My hand was being bound up, and I was not yet on my feet when General Wheaton, who, accompanied by Captain H. C. Cabell and Lieutenants F. D. Webster, P. P. Russell, and E. S. Kimmel of his staff, had crossed the bridge and hurried on foot toward the sound of the firing, joined us. The general, seeing the men lying down behind the railroad track, and engaging in a fire fight with the enemy on their front, and noting the fact that I had been wounded, misunderstood the situation, thinking that the men had "flunked," and strode among them. With his tremendous voice he called out, "Get on your feet, you damned mice, lying down here, with your colonel shot. Get on your feet, and charge."

My bandage having been put on, I got up and ran toward the general to explain the situation, telling him that I had ordered the men to lie down. But it was too late. One company had risen and started forward, followed quickly by the other two, Company G having in the meantime been deployed. It was a quick dash, and soon over. The general, accompanied by his staff officers, was on the firing line, and I was a few yards to their left. The recollection of that little charge is one of the things that I treasure. The fiery old veteran discharging his revolver and calling out to the men near him to shoot faster and "burn their powder," and the general hubbub and excitement, gave us a lively minute. There could be but one result. We had covered but half the distance when the Filipinos began to break and run to the rear. They were followed by storms of bullets, but our men were so exhausted that their shooting was about the worst I have ever seen, notwithstanding which fact the enemy left on the ground a heavy toll of killed and wounded. Some of the bravest had fired until we were within fifty yards of them.

Darkness was now coming on. We gathered up our wounded and those of the enemy for transportation to the hospitals in Manila. Warner and I, not being in the habit of walking on our hands, were able to take care of ourselves for the time being, and went back to division head-quarters, General MacArthur and his staff having come up and established themselves in a field a few hundred yards to the rear. The general had heard that I had been hit, but not seriously, and as I came up with my bandaged hand, and khaki blouse drenched with blood, said very quietly, as if he were making a remark about the weather, "Well, Funston, you got it at last. I am glad it is no worse."

In the meantime ambulances were collecting to take us back to the Bag-Bag River bridge, where we could take a train to Manila. The ride was a very trying one, the road being horribly rough, and the four native horses that we had on our vehicle being very fractious. I rode on the seat with the driver, the interior of the ambulance being very properly reserved for those who were not able to sit up. Among these was Captain Dillon of the First Montana, a red-haired Irishman with a brogue that would have turned the edge of a knife. He was desperately hurt, shot clear through the body, and suffered intensely as we were jolted over the atrocious road. On one occasion we stopped to enable the driver to untangle the leaders from a clump of bamboo near the roadside, and the suffering captain called out, 'Dhriver, is the domned road all like this?" Being assured that it was, he replied, "Well, be God, I'll get out and walk," but he was not allowed to try the experiment.

But all things end at last, and at about ten o'clock at night the ambulances with their loads of suffering and groaning men reached the Bag-Bag, the wounded were carried in litters across the now partially repaired railway bridge, and placed on the train awaiting them. There was no light in the ordinary day coach that we occupied, and the heat was stifling, but finally we pulled into Manila. As the train stopped at Caloocan I was handed a telegram addressed to me as a brigadier-general. It was signed by Colonel Thomas H. Barry, now Major-General Barry, and read, "Congratulations. Shake, if your wounded hand will permit. No man better deserves the star."

For a moment I was dazed, not understanding what was meant, but it soon dawned on me that a cable had been received from Washington announcing my promotion to the grade of brigadier-general of volunteers. It had been quick work, being largely the result of the passage of the Rio Grande at Calumpit, only a week before, and was brought about by a cabled recommendation from the corps commander, Major-General Elwell S. Otis, based on the reports and recommendations of Generals MacArthur and Wheaton. I must confess that I was highly gratified, and nearly forgot the throbbing in my hand.

V

SAN FERNANDO AND THE BEGINNING OF THE GUERILLA WAR

THE ten days spent in Manila after being wounded passed pleasantly enough, as I suffered practically no pain. I was not compelled to enter a hospital, but remained in quarters, going once a day to have my hand treated. Finally I was allowed to return to duty, though I had to carry my hand in a sling for a couple more weeks. General Wheaton had been assigned to other duty, and I succeeded him in command of the First Brigade of the Second Division, which still consisted of the Twentieth Kansas and the First Montana. Major Metcalf, who had now about recovered from his wound received at Bocaue, succeeded me as colonel of the Twentieth, while Sergeant-Major Warner was promoted to second lieutenant, and I appointed him as my first aide. His wound being like mine, we recovered at about the same time. On the night of the action at Santo Tomas the Second Division had marched up the railroad to the considerable town of San Fernando, and had occupied it without further resistance.

Upon arrival at San Fernando and reporting for duty, I found that our troops were quartered in the town, but maintained all about it strong outposts, those of my own brigade being along the west and north sides of the town.

The insurgents were numerous all about us, and from time to time stirred things up. They had, out near the town of Bacolor, a Krupp field-piece of about three-inch calibre, and on several occasions let fly with it. They were using shrapnel, bursting with time fuse, but did not succeed in hurting anybody, though one burst in the quarters used by Colonel Kessler, of the First Montana. We made several attempts to capture this gun, but the enemy always saw us coming and got away with it. They also fired at the town with small arms from time to time, and managed to get a few of our people. One morning while I was lying in bed contemplating the advisability of getting up, a bullet passed through the head of the bed and assisted materially in making up my mind on that subject. In the meantime I had obtained as adjutant-general of the brigade Captain E. V. Smith, Fourth United States Infantry, who was destined to be with me in that capacity for a couple of years.

About three-quarters of a mile in front of the First Brigade's outpost line was a dry water-ditch, quite deep, and more than half a mile long. Every morning the First Montana sent out a patrol to ascertain if this ditch had been occupied by the enemy during the night. On approaching it on the morning of the 24th of May this patrol was sharply fired on and retired. I ordered both regiments to their respective outpost lines, and went there myself. As a direct attack on the ditch would result in unnecessary loss of life, it was resolved to turn the enemy out by attacking both ends of it, thus rolling up his flanks. Lieutenant-Colonel R. B. Wallace, of the

First Montana, was directed to attack the enemy's right flank with two battalions of that regiment, while Major Whitman, with two battalions of the Twentieth Kansas, was to go at the left flank, one battalion of each regiment being retained on the line as a containing force, while two guns of the Utah artillery opened fire from the same position. Major, now Major-General, J. F. Bell volunteered to guide the Kansas detachment into the best position, as he knew the ground, and in fact largely directed the fight that ensued. Owing to the nature of the country and its careful approach, this force got into position almost at right angles to the enemy's line and very close to it before being discovered, when it was briskly fired on.

Those of us who had remained on the outpost line saw as pretty a little fight as one could care for. The Kansas men advanced quickly through the tangled rice, firing rapidly, and cleared all of that part of the ditch. Of course, they had the enemy at a great disadvantage. There were picked up on that part of the field forty-eight dead Filipinos, and fifty-three prisoners, about half of whom were wounded, besides many rifles. But the regiment had not come out unscathed, as it had Privates Ryan and Sullivan killed, and Second-Lieutenant R. S. Parker, a veteran of the Civil War, and five enlisted men wounded. One of the men wounded was a magnificent big Dane, Private Sorensen. As they were carrying him off the field I passed by and said, "Well, Sorensen, you are going to get well, aren't you?" He was smoking a big cigar, which he removed form his mouth very carefully, blew a cloud of smoke into the air, and then replied very deliberately, "Yah, General, I tank so." And he did, though he had been very badly hit.

The First Montana did not have quite such good luck, being discovered in getting into position, but had a brisk little fight, losing four men wounded and killing five of the enemy who were found. It was the last time the enemy tried the trick of getting into that water ditch in the night with the intention of peppering a patrol the next morning. The main body of the enemy escaped by retreating rapidly through the town of Bacolor, and our men were suffering so with the heat, a number having fallen out, that they were pursued but a short distance.

During this time a number of minor affairs occurred, none of them of any importance, but all serving to add zest to life. One day I went out with two and one-half companies of my former regiment to reconnoitre through the town of Bacolor toward Santa Rita, being accompanied by Major Bell and the Italian attaché, Captain Vitale. We struck a good-sized outpost between the towns and had a brief skirmish with it, but this outfit had but little fight in it, and, anyway, could see that it was badly outnumbered. We chased them for awhile, but they were too fleet-footed. As a matter of fact, when it came to getting over ground, our infantry was no match for these barefooted natives.

One day General MacArthur sent for me and stated that he wished me to make a reconnoissance along the road leading north from Bacolor, and said that I could take eighty men, and no more. I asked to be allowed to have a larger force, stating that I was pretty sure to get into a hornets' nest in that neighborhood, but the general declined, saying: "If I give you a force of any size, you will bring on a pitched battle, and that is not the object. You are going on a reconnoissance and nothing else. Examine that road, and if you encounter any considerable number of the enemy, come back." Captain James Lockett, Fourth Cavalry, one of the general's aides, had overheard this conversation, and followed me out into the hallway, saying: "If you go out there with eighty men you will get hell licked out of you. I am going out to the Montana regiment, get it under arms, and when I think the firing has lasted long enough, come out and pry you loose." As long as I was limited to eighty men, I concluded to get the best in the shop, and directed the commanding officers of each of the two regiments of the brigade to have picked out from their respective commands forty of the best and steadiest men, all of them to be from among those armed with Krags. From these men were made up two "scratch" companies of forty men each. The Kansas detachment was commanded by Second Lieutenant J. C. Murphy, who had recently been promoted from first sergeant. I am sorry that I cannot recall the name of the plucky officer who commanded that from the Montana regiment. I was accompanied by Captain Smith and my aide, Lieutenant Warner, and we took with us a number of Chinese litter-bearers.

We reached Bacolor without incident, and here I left Lieutenant Murphy with his detachment, with instructions for him to get into the church tower, where he could have a good view, and watch our progress from there. If we became deeply involved, and either one of our flanks was about to be rolled up, he should come out in such a direction as to protect that particular flank, and assist in our retirement to Bacolor where, in the church or other strong building, we would be all right until the expected help came. As we were not to advance much more than a mile up the road, this was not leaving our reserve too far behind. So the remainder of us pushed to the north, along a road lined on both sides with bamboos, though the country on either side was quite open.

About three-quarters of a mile beyond the town the few men constituting the advance guard reported that they could make out a few heads above what appeared to be a short trench a few hundred yards in advance. I went up to them, and after watching for a moment concluded that the best way to find out the strength of this outpost was to stir it up, and gave the necessary order. A fine little blizzard came back, and the Filipinos stood their ground. Still, the thing did not look at all serious. The officer in command of the Montana detachment promptly deployed his men, had them take cover lying down behind a rice dike about two feet high, though he stood up through the whole fight, and opened fire. We could see that the enemy's fire was rapidly increasing in volume, and noted that his line was being extended to the right. The Lord alone knows where they all came from, as the ground literally seemed to spew them up, and soon we were out-numbered about ten to one. Their fire was furious, and as they were yelling, we knew they felt confident that they had us. All of the Filipinos, and all of us except the offi-cers and the orderlies holding their horses, were lying close to the ground.

The distance between the lines was about five hundred yards, and I had just made up my mind to charge with the men I had right into the enemy's left flank, and then trust to the superior quality of our men to roll them up. But then we noticed several hundred of them advancing in line from the north and moving in such a direction that it would further extend to the right the force that we were now engaged with. They were coming with great rapid-ity, and soon began firing, though at such a distance that their fire was for the present not much to be feared. When they joined on to the right of the Filipino line this was fully half a mile long. The enemy's left being im-mediately on our front, showed no tendency to advance, but his right had soon worked so far forward that it was on an extension of our left, and at a distance of seven to nine hundred yards was enfilading us. It was time to go. Our horses were sent to the rear, and at the same time the litter-bearers with two men who had been very badly hit. At the same time we heard volleys crashing out to our left rear, and saw Murphy bringing up his men to extend our already turned left. At the order the Mon-tana men ceased firing, filled the magazines of their rifles, rose to their feet, and at the word of command dashed to the rear for a hundred yards, then faced about and gave it hot and heavy to the Filipino line that had risen and with yells was coming for us. Those immediately oppo-site us were beaten down, but their right kept advancing. The Montana men took cover and fired rapidly while the Kansas men fell back even with it, this performance being repeated several times. The men were absolutely cool, and not one of them showed the slightest tendency to break ranks. Captain Smith, Warner, and I retired a few yards to the right of the Montana detachment, and Smith and I stooped down for a moment behind a barrel of corn in the ear that stood near a small nipa house. We were looking over the top of it when within two seconds two bullets hit the corn on the top of the barrel, knocking the grains into our faces, and a dozen bullets hit the sides of the house. Never before had I seen the Filipinos take the aggressive, and I was astonished beyond measure.

The Montana men were now down to a handful of cartridges each, though they had gone into the fight with a hundred and fifty on each man. The Kansas men still had plenty, but we could not redistribute under such a fire. How I wished for a machine gun, or for a field-piece to warm up with shrapnel the yelling outfit that was continually passing around our left flank, and to which we could not give a great deal of attention because of the troubles on our immediate front. Suddenly we noticed the Filipino line begin to give way to the rear, and looking around saw the whole Montana regiment deploying across the fields in the direction of San Fernando. As the Filipinos fell back we gave them a good salting. This ended it, as our friends, the enemy, had no intention of standing up against an equal force. I think that in the long run we would have made all right, but still we had had enough, and were heartily glad of the results of Captain Lockett's action.

Partly because of the splendid way in which the two detachments were handled by their respective commanders, and partly because the Filipino insurgent was about the worst shot ever intrusted with a rifle, our loss was astonishingly small, only two men. The enemy's shots struck everywhere from immediately in front of their own line to a mile behind us. That at least fifty thousand rounds were fired by them, I have not the slightest doubt. Our own expenditure was about seven thousand rounds. Two years later, after all the insurgent forces of central Luzon had surrendered, an officer who had taken part in the fight told us that the force opposed to us on this occasion consisted of nine hundred men, and was commanded by San Miguel and Mascardo, its loss being one hundred and two, killed and wounded. During the subsequent period of guerilla warfare, I was in a considerable number of small affairs in which we had approximately the same number of men engaged, in which we suffered more loss but did not punish the enemy near so severely as on this occasion. But these were usually short and snappy little combats at close range, in which there was not the one-hundredth part of such a quantity of ammunition expended.

One afternoon during this period a brisk attack was made on the outposts of a portion of Hale's brigade, and the firing gradually spread until it involved the Twentieth Kansas, of the First Brigade. Some time previously Colonel Metcalf had sufficiently recovered from his wound to return to duty, and he took out the regiment with Lieutenant-Colonel Little, second in command. I went with them more as a spectator than anything else. But the enemy on our front would not make a good stand, and retired after a sharp little skirmish, leaving a few dead and wounded on the ground. The Kansas regiment had four men wounded. There were a number of occasions of this kind, when we got after them, but they would not face the music. On the 16th of June, however, they took the offensive, attacking the town of San Fernando on all sides, and there resulted a fight that involved the entire division, while bullets fell in showers all over the town.

So far as the First Brigade was concerned, the first development was when Captain Howard A. Scott, of the Twentieth Kansas, who was in command of the outpost of that regiment, reported just before dawn that he had returned from a patrol half a mile to the front, and had distinctly heard commands being given and could hear men talking. I was aroused, sent the information to the division commander, ordered the two regiments of my brigade under arms and to proceed at once to reinforce their respective outposts, and then with the officers of the brigade staff went out to where the Bacolor road cut through the Twentieth Kansas outpost line. By the time we reached it there was just light enough for one to be able to see fairly well. We heard a sharp rattle of shots in the direction of an old sugar mill near Bacolor, where the Montana regiment had a strong advanced outpost, and then saw to our right front, about a mile away, a cres-cent-shaped line of battle about three-quarters of a mile long, containing about eight hundred men. We could not believe that they were actually going to charge us, but that is what they did, and did gamely, too. The line advanced rapidly, doing considerable ineffective firing, as they were not stopping to take even such aim as a Filipino takes.

The two companies on the Kansas outpost line stood up on top of their trenches in order to get a better view, and fired as rapidly as they could load and aim. They inflicted considerable loss even at this stage of the fight, but there were not enough of them for their fire to stop the advance. In the meantime the First Montana was briskly attacked. All in all, it was a very novel performance for this particular war. In a short time the line advancing on the Kansas position reached good cover, its right in a deep ditch that ran nearly parallel with our front, and its left in broken country where there was a deep road, and where they were fairly well screened by bamboos and growing crops. They kept up a brisk fire from this cover, the bullets nearly all going over our heads. The two regiments now arrived and deployed under cover, and I was just about to give the orders for a counter-stroke, when some of the enemy who had been working up a ravine got close in to our front, and a small group of the bravest dashed into the open and died to a man within fifty yards of the front of D Company. What strange fatalism possessed them one can only guess. It seemed a pity, as they certainly deserved a better fate.

A few of us with about half a company made a start

from the left of the regiment to get into the ditch, but were met by such a fire that I considered it unwise to continue and so ordered them to retire until orders could be transmitted to several companies to carry out the enterprise more effectively. On the extreme right of the line of this regiment, Major W. H. Bishop, who had recently been promoted from captain, took two companies and made a dash forward for about seventy yards into what we knew as the "sunken road." He had been getting a stiff fire from there, and found it heavily occupied. His men jumped in among the Filipinos and did heavy execution at very short range. I do not want to say just what a short section of that road looked like after it was over, but there are a good many people still living who will bear me out in the statement that it was not a pretty sight. This was not because no quarter was given, as there was nothing of the kind.

The enemy now retreated rapidly, taking advantage of several ravines, and suffered but little in his retirement. Sixty dead and thirty wounded were found in front of the Twentieth Kansas, and a dozen dead and a few wounded in front of the First Montana. Only the absolutely helpless of their wounded were left on the ground, as all who could be assisted to the rear got away. Two native priests in their robes, and with crucifixes in their hands, were lying dead within ten feet of each other. To obviate criticism, I might say that they fell six hundred yards in front of the line, that distance being so great that it was impossible to recognize and spare them. I have no doubt that their presence and exhortations on that occasion had no little to do with the unusual pluck and dash shown by this particular force.

While we were examining our own part of the field we heard hot fighting break out in front of the other parts of the division. The Second Brigade on the north, south, and east, and the Fourth Cavalry on the south-east, had good fights, but, of course, I was not a witness to any of them. General MacArthur directed me to have the Filipinos who had fallen in front of the First Brigade brought into the town and buried, instead of here and there all over the field where found. It is customary in the army, whenever you have a disagreeable job on your hands, to hunt up a quartermaster and lay it on to him. A young officer who held volunteer rank in that department had just arrived in the Philippines, and had been assigned to the First Brigade. He had transportation, tools, and Chinese coolies, and was directed to undertake the task. He had been up since early in the morning, and had been tremendously interested in his first fight, and went at his assignment with vim, but about one o'clock in the morning came into the head-quarters building, and with "tears in his voice" said to Captain Smith: "I can't get those goo-goos buried until daylight, and, anyhow, I'm no damned funeral director."

We at San Fernando were much mystified as to what the insurgents had expected to gain by so ill-timed and disjointed an attack; but two years afterward, while Aguinaldo was a prisoner in our hands and we were conducting him to Manila, he told me a good deal about it. He had ordered the attack and had arranged some of the details, though he was not present in person. For carrying out his purpose he had ordered troops from several near-by provinces, the total number concentrated being about seven thousand. It had been directed that the various organizations should surround the town during the night, but at such distances that they would not be discovered by our patrols. At 3 A. M. they were to rush over our outposts, enter the town from all directions, and set fire to every possible building, literally burning the Americans out. It was thought that the consequent confusion would enable them to deal us a finishing blow. But not a single unit reached its place at the appointed time, some of them not arriving until after daylight, while a few did not report until the fighting was over. The commanders of the various organizations thought, however, that they must do something, and as they arrived in position delivered their separate attacks, but against men on the alert, and with disastrous results. It is rather difficult to guess whether or not this lovely scheme would have worked if the plans had not miscarried. All Filipino towns are constructed of very inflammable materials, and the night of February 22, when the insurgents burned almost the entire Tondo district of Manila, shows that they were not inexpert in that particular work. At San Fernando our troops were quartered all over the town, and there can be no doubt that if a large number of fires had been started we would have had a hard time of it, principally for the reason that we would have feared to use our rifles owing to the danger of hitting as many of our own people as of the enemy. But the chances are that instead of running over our outposts the insurgents would have delayed to engage in fire fights with them, and so would have given time for their reinforcemnet.

A couple of weeks later the Twentieth Kansas and First Montana were relieved from duty at the front, the time when, according to the terms of their enlistment, they were entitled to their discharge having passed months before, and were sent to Manila preparatory to returning to the United States, and though I returned to San Francisco with my old regiment, this severed my official connection with it. It was a good regiment, considering especially all the handicaps with which it had begun its existence; not by any means the best regiment that ever fought under our flag, like several that we have all read about, but still a mighty trustworthy and reliable organization after it had had six months of training and had weeded out the most of its "weak sisters." In a year and a half of service it had had but two desertions, both of these occurring shortly after its muster-in. It lost thirty-five men from disease, fourteen of whom were victims of a small-pox epidemic that broke out in the barracks of the First Battalion shortly after our arrival in Manila. Its battle losses were three officers and thirty enlisted men killed, and ten officers and one hundred and twenty-nine enlisted men wounded.

The Kansas and Montana regiments were relieved in the First Brigade by the Ninth and Twelfth United States Infantry, commanded, respectively, by Colonel Emerson H. Liscum and Lieutenant-Colonel Jacob H. Smith. Within a short time after these regiments reported, I was under the necessity of going to Manila for the purpose of playing a prominent part in a surgical operation, and on recovery was ordered to return to the United States for muster-out of the service. Mrs. Funston and I were passengers on the transport *Tartar*, the vessel carrying all of those members of the Twentieth Kansas who had not joined some one of the new regiments being raised in the Philippines, besides a number of discharged men from various organizations. We sailed from Manila on September 3, and had an uneventful voyage. Shortly after arrival in San Francisco I was informed by the War Department that instead of being mustered out I would be retained in service. I had not expressed any wishes on the subject, but was not averse to returning to the islands, though I thought the insurrection could not last many months longer. After a visit to Kansas I returned to San Francisco, and sailed again for Manila on the same old *Indiana* that I had gone out on before, leaving Mrs. Funston with her parents in her old home, I being accompanied by my aide, Lieutenant Burton J. Mitchell. This officer, a first cousin, had been an enlisted man and officer in my old regiment, and had been recommissioned in the Fortieth United States Volunteer Infantry. He was one of those with me later in the capture of Emilio Aguinaldo.

Upon arrival in Manila I reported to General Otis, who was still commander-in-chief of the forces in the islands, and was assigned again to the Second Division, and ordered to report to General MacArthur, whose headquarters were at Bautista, province of Pangasinan, near the northern terminus of the Manila-Dagupan Railway. I was placed by the division commander in command of the Third Brigade, which was scattered all over the province of Nueva Ecija and parts of Pangasinan and Pampanga. The head-quarters was at San Isidro, in the first-named province, and the troops consisted of the entire Twenty-second and Twenty-fourth Infantry, the head-quarters and two battalions of the Thirty-fourth Volunteers, Troop G, Fourth Cavalry, and the Macabebe organization known as the Squadron Philippine Cavalry, which was really a battalion of infantry, as I never saw one of its members on a horse. A number of organizations were formed later from the loyal Ilocanos of northern Nueva Ecija. The staff assigned to the brigade consisted of Captain E. V. Smith, adjutant-general, Major W. C. Brown, inspector-general, Captain Alexander Perry, chief quartermaster, Major H. S. T. Harris, chief surgeon, and Captain Frederic H. Pomroy, chief commissary.

The war was now entering upon an entirely new phase. His forces having been broken up and scattered as the result of the hammerings they had received, Aguinaldo had directed his subordinates to return to their homes with their men and arms, and after a rest to carry on a relentless guerilla warfare against the Americans, who were now scattered all over the archipelago in garrisons ranging in size from a regiment to a company, or even less. Although all the State volunteers raised for the Spanish war had been sent home and mustered out, twenty-five regiments of United States Volunteers had been raised and were in the Philippines, as was also the greater part of the regular army. At this time we probably had in the islands as many as seventy thousand troops, distributed among some hundreds of towns. The insurgents provided with rifles were, of course, far short of this number, but their knowledge of the country, their mobility, their control over the population either through sympathy or fear, and, above all, their habit of passing from the status of guerilla soldiers to that of non-combatants really gave them an advantage that more than made up for the disparity in numbers. Aguinaldo, from his various hiding-places in the mountain fastnesses of northern Luzon, remained the actual head of the insurrection, and exercised a general control over the operations of his subordinates. To each one of his numerous "generals" was assigned the command of a district or zone, and these had under them various subordinate guerilla chiefs with their bands.

In the closing days of December, 1899, Captain Smith, Lieutenant Mitchell, and I left the railroad at San Fernando, mounted on good native ponies, and in two days of stiff riding reached the station that was to be our headquarters for the next year and a half. The country was so quiet that it was deemed safe to make the trip without escort, though we took the precaution to carry carbines in addition to our revolvers. We stopped at the various garrisoned towns en route for meals and rest. The condition of the country seemed perfectly normal, the towns being full of people and the usual work going on in the fields. There was not a sign of the war to be seen, though there had been some brisk campaigning through this region. In fact, this condition existed through the whole of central Luzon during the period of a year and a half of guerilla warfare that was soon to begin. If any one imagines that this was a desolated country, with the inhabitants fleeing to the woods and mountains for shelter, he is entitled to imagine again. The tendency of the people was to flock to the garrisoned towns for shelter from their own ruthless countrymen, they having not the slightest fear of the troops. I have no doubt that in the year 1900 Nueva Ecija raised as much rice as it ever did; at least all suitable land was in cultivation. And yet there was a nasty little war going on all of the time. It certainly was an odd state of affairs.

The garrison of San Isidro consisted of a battalion of the Twenty-second Infantry, under Major John A. Baldwin, and Troop G, Fourth Cavalry, under Captain L. M. Koehler. There were in the vicinity a number of good-sized towns garrisoned by one or more companies of the Twenty-second and Thirty-fourth Infantry. The first thing to do after arrival was to visit a number of the garrisons in this province, incidentally becoming acquainted with the country. On a trip of this kind it would not do to trust too much to the good luck that had brought us three officers through from San Fernando without escort, as there were already current reports of the appearance of guerilla bands in certain parts of the province. Accordingly, there was organized a detachment of mounted men, who not only did duty as a personal escort, but quickly developed into a fine body of trustworthy and fearless scouts. This detachment, consisting at first of only a dozen men, finally grew to be about twenty-five strong, and was made up of men selected by their various commanders on account of their horsemanship, courage, and reliability. They became known as the "Headquarters Scouts," and hereafter will be referred to by that name. Their first commander was Lieutenant E. L. Admire, Twenty-second Infantry, the non-commissioned officer on duty with them being Corporal Hull of the same regiment. They were armed and equipped as cavalry, and for the first three months of their service were mounted on native ponies, American horses being obtained at the end of that time. They were a really remarkable body of men. During the year and a half that they accompanied me on every trip or expedition of any kind, and including several "hikes" that I was not on, the aggregate of the number of miles that they marched reached such a figure that I hesitate to give it, though the facts are known to a number of officers besides myself. But I have no desire to be bothered by procuring affidavits after this is published. They were in the field more than half of the time, and always on the go. They could take care of themselves and their horses anywhere, and could whip ten times their number of Filipinos any day. I have often thought of the things that could be done with a regiment of cavalry made up entirely of such material.

A few days after settling down and getting the headquarters started going, for the brigade had just been organized, Lieutenant Mitchell and I started out to inspect the garrisons of Cabanatuan, San José, and Carranglan. We were accompanied by the Scouts under

Corporal Hull, no officer having as yet been assigned to command them. It was a most interesting ride, but devoid of adventure, as while outside of the garrisoned towns we kept moving so rapidly that persons who might have desired to attack us had no more time than that necessary to formulate the wish before we were gone. The round trip of approximately one hundred and forty miles was made in nine days, including a day spent in each of the three towns mentioned. Upon our return we heard more stories of the presence of guerilla bands, none of them large, in the vicinity of San Isidro, and after a rest of a couple of days started on a little raid with the Scouts to see if we could stir up anything. Going first to the good-sized town of Gapan, three miles east of San Isidro, we struck south-east along a country road and entered the *barrio* (small village) of Santa Cruz. The fact that the population unanimously took to their heels was regarded as a suspicious circumstance. Leaving Lieutenant Mitchell in the town with all of the Scouts except Corporal Hull, I rode with the latter to a point about seven hundred yards distant in the outskirts. Here we saw a man armed with a rifle tearing across a bare field. My first inclination was to try to ride him down, but we observed that before we could come up with him he would have gained cover in some brush that he was heading for. If we had dismounted and opened fire with our carbines we might have got him, but I hesitated a little too long. As soon as the man gained cover he turned on us, firing two shots, one of which passed between us. We could tell from the smoke as well as from the sound of the bullets that he was using a Remington instead of a Mauser. It was the first time I had heard a hostile shot since seven months before at San Fernando.

We returned to San Isidro that evening, not having had any more excitement, if being shot at by one man could be called by that name. Within the next week a couple more trips were made with the object of becoming acquainted with the country, but none of the enemy were encountered. In the meantime we had been gathering as much information as possible as to conditions in this particular province, being greatly aided by data that had already been collected by the officers of the garrisons that had been established before our arrival. The insurgent commander in this region was General Panteleon Garcia, who had commanded the brigade that was on the immediate front of the one in which I was serving at Caloocan a year before, and who had served as Aguinaldo's chief of staff for a time in the fall of 1899. Garcia, however, was ill and in hiding, and the active commander was Colonel Pablo Padilla, the man who had made the perfunctory defence of San Isidro against General Lawton's column during the previous summer. Neither of these was a man of much force and energy, and, as we shall see, both were soon captured, being succeeded by Urbano Lacuna, a man much more capable than either of them.

There were in the province about fifteen hundred rifles, but the most of these were still in places of concealment. In the mountains of Bulacan province, which was a part of the district commanded by General F. D. Grant, were Simon and Pablo Tecson, the latter a most capable chief. As the Filipinos naturally did not pay any attention to the limits of the jurisdictions of the American commanders, and as Pablo Tecson was a particularly enterprising individual, I finally had about as many fights with him as with Lacuna. The various station commanders were showing commendable energy in sending out detachments to scour the country, and there were occasional small encounters. About this time Colonel L. W. V. Kennon, commanding the Thirty-fourth Infantry, the head-quarters of which was at San José, began the organization of the Ilocano Scouts, a body of men that during the rest of the war rendered most loyal and courageous service. While many of the Ilocanos from the two provinces that are the home of those people had taken sides against us, their compatriots of northern Nueva Ecija, who were immigrants to this province, had no sympathy with the insurrection. These men were commanded largely by officers of Colonel Kennon's regiment, though there were a few detailed from other organizations. These Ilocanos were splendid marchers and fighters, and were as trustworthy as the Macabebes, and that is saying a great deal.

The large town of Gapan, which lay so close to San Isidro that the two were almost one, had not as yet been garrisoned, and information was received to the effect that a number of insurgent officers and men were taking their ease there with their families, and that there were a number of concealed arms. Accordingly, I issued the necessary orders, and one night just before daybreak the town was quickly and quietly surrounded by the garrisons of several of the near-by towns, about eight hundred men being used in the operation. The search that followed was so thorough that not a house, stable, out-house, well, or even a single room escaped. But few arms were found, but we captured a number of men who had with them correspondence that showed them to be insurgent officers. All except one were sent to Manila as prisoners of war. This one showed a letter from a captain of the Thirty-fifth Infantry, at the time provost-marshal of the town of San Miguel, province of Bulacan, to the effect that the bearer, Doroteo del Rosario, was in his employ as a secret-service man, and requesting that he be released by any persons who might capture him. The prisoner was a Filipino of the "smooth" type, being well dressed and plausible. I put him through a long examination, but he stuck to the story that he was doing secret work for the officer who had given him the letter, and this in spite of incriminating documents found in his effects. I held him, and wired the facts to the officer at San Miguel, receiving a request to release the man. This I declined to do, and in a few days received from Manila a peremptory order to turn the man loose, which I did. We shall see how I afterward met him under a flag of truce as Lacuna's adjutant, and how a year and a half later he died on the scaffold for the brutal murder of five helpless American prisoners and one of our few loyal *presidentes*.

General MacArthur desired to place a garrison in the town of Baler, in the province of Principe, on the east coast of Luzon, and hoping that this might be accomplished by a shorter march than the one by way of Pantabangan, directed me to make a reconnoissance with that end in view. So Lieutenant Mitchell and I, accompanied by the Scouts and a company of the Thirty-fourth Infantry, besides a small pack-train, struck out across country toward the mountains to the north-east of San Isidro. The region that we passed through was practically uninhabited, being for the first three days a beautiful, rolling, grass-covered plain, with trees scattered over it here and there, and occasional well-wooded creek bottoms. The fourth day was in very difficult mountains. Though very steep, they were not very high. Their slopes were covered with grass, and so slippery that it was very difficult for either men or animals to keep their feet. All of us who were mounted led our horses, and were getting along fairly well until we came to follow the summit of a very narrow "hog back," and here trouble began. It seemed impossible for the mules to keep their feet; so we took off their loads and had them carried for a distance by the men. Then ropes were passed around the animals, and with a dozen men supporting each terrified beast, we worked our way slowly along. In spite of these precautions, one mule fell five hundred feet and was killed. It is a pretty rough country where an American mule has to be held up to keep him from shooting off into space. For three days we had not seen a human being, though we had crossed a number of trails leading from the lowlands to the mountains, but on the fifth day, we being at the time crossing what is known as the Sabani Valley, where the grass was very high and dry, we were fired at a few times, and immediately afterward the small band of insurgents that had discovered and was following us tried new tactics by setting fires in the grass. This burned with great rapidity, and they made it pretty warm for us, though we were never in any danger from their polite attentions. We returned to San Isidro via Bongabong and Cabanatuan, having marched one hundred and twenty miles in eight days, some of it in bad country. The company of infantry, ninety strong, came in without a straggler. It had been ascertained that through this region there was no route to Baler.

But Baler must be garrisoned, and the march would have to be made via Pantabangan, crossing the great mountain range to the eastward of that town. It was about the middle of February when we made the start, there being the Scouts and three companies of the Thirty-fourth Infantry, besides a pack-train of more than fifty mules. Major W. A. Shunk, who was to be left in command at Baler, was in command of the infantry, and we were joined at Cabanatuan by Colonel Kennon. The march as far as Bongabong was over excellent roads, then a grilling day's work up a canyon to the little town of Pantabangan, garrisoned by a company of the Twenty-fourth Infantry. From here it was a hard pull to the summit, and we lost five mules, either killed by falls or so injured that they had to be shot; and then two days down the bed of a stream over slippery rocks brought us to the edge of the flat country on the Pacific coast, and that evening we entered Baler, all of the inhabitants fleeing except one man, and no resistance being offered. The march of a little over one hundred miles had taken ten days, owing to the great difficulties of the last half of it. The principal thing of interest was the little stone church, scarred by shot and shell and peppered by bullet marks, where a mere handful of Spanish soldiers, fifty men at the start, had for eleven long months, in the years 1898 and 1899, held out against an overwhelming force of insurgents provided with several pieces of artillery. The stubborn defence of their post by these starving men is an epic of heroism, and the reading of the simple account of it, written by the sole survivor of the three officers, makes one feel that after all it is not bad to be a soldier. It was in trying to communicate with this garrison and give them authentic information to the effect that months before the sovereignty of Spain had ceased over the Philippine Islands, that Lieutenant Gillmore of the navy and his detachment met disaster at the hands of the besieging insurgents. We gazed with interest on the wonderful trenches, redoubts, and approaches of the insurgents, and on the well that the garrison had dug in order to provide themselves with water, not to speak of the pathetic row of graves within the walls of the building. The Scouts and one of the companies of the Thirty-fourth escorted the pack-train back to San Isidro, while, leaving Major Shunk and two companies in this lonely place, the remainder of us officers returned to Manila by sea on a steamer that had arrived with supplies for the garrison, and in a few days were back at our respective stations.

Upon our return to Nueva Ecija it was learned that the insurgent bands were increasing in size and number, and that several officers, especially Major Joseph Wheeler, Jr.,

Thirty-fourth Infantry, commanding the station of Peñaranda, eight miles east of San Isidro, had had some sharp
and successful encounters with them. Within a day or
two after the return from Baler I started out with Lieutenant Mitchell, the Scouts, Troop G, Fourth Cavalry,
under Captain Koehler, and a small pack-train, and we
penetrated the mountains to the south-east of San Isidro,
learning considerable of the country, and incidentally
surprising two small bands of insurgents, with disastrous
results to them. American troops had never yet penetrated this region, and we were unexpected as well as unwelcome visitors. We were out about a week, and pretty
thoroughly "combed" a large extent of mountain country.
After our return Koehler gave his men and horses a few
days' rest, and he again took to the mountains, remaining
out another week and surprising and breaking up several
small bands, burning a barrack and capturing some arms.
This officer showed the most boundless energy in this
sort of work, and was ready and anxious to go out at
any time of the night or day. This mountain region was
absolutely uninhabited, the only people in it being the
guerilla bands that had sought there a safe place of rendezvous, being supplied with food by their friends in the
towns.

During Koehler's absence I had had opportunity to
clear off the accumulation of work on my desk, and a
few days after his return we again took to the road
with his troop and the Scouts. I had in the meantime
appointed an additional aide, Lieutenant O. R. Wolfe,
Twenty-second Infantry, and he and Mitchell accom-

panied me. In order that we might reach the mountains without being discovered, we left San Isidro just after dark, and keeping off the trails and simply depending on our knowledge of the country, were in the foot-hills, twenty-five miles from San Isidro, by daybreak. Here we captured an insurgent patrol armed with a Remington, and then concealed ourselves in a clump of woods until nightfall. In the meantime the captured man was put through a long examination, and finally agreed to lead us to the main insurgent camp, the stipulation being that if he did so he would be released instead of being sent to Manila as a prisoner of war. No violence was used on him. The man explained that he could lead us through the line of sentinels, but that in order to reach the main camp we would have to go down a very narrow canyon, where there was a strong outpost, as there was absolutely no other route. He requested that he be sent to the rear as soon as he had brought us to the outpost, in order that he might not be brought under fire. This was agreed to, and after it was good and dark we made the start, proceeding on foot, leaving the horses in the woods with a part of the troop as a guard. The guide marched ahead, his arms tied behind him by means of a picket rope, one end of which was held by a husky soldier. It was highly undesirable that he should make a quick dive into the brush, and leave us to find our way out of the mountains the best we could. The night was villanously dark, and it was raining part of the time. One could not see even the outline of a person ten feet away.

All night we kept at it, up hill and down, wading

streams, pushing our way through brush, and finally at two o'clock in the morning coming onto a fairly well-beaten trail. An hour later the sky cleared and we could make out something about the country. A little before four o'clock the man whispered to me that he was about to take us through the line of sentinels, and pointed out a low conical hill on our right, where he said was a post of two men. The hill, though only a couple of hundred yards away, could barely be made out. A few hundred yards farther on (we now walking so quietly that not the slightest sound was made) he pointed out the glow of a small fire. We were in a canyon not more than twenty feet wide, with absolutely perpendicular walls, the fire being a hundred yards from its entrance. The guide was sent to the rear, and cautiously, step by step, we advanced. The canyon was so narrow that but five men could deploy, and after a whispered consultation with Koehler it was resolved to overwhelm the outpost and then rush down the canyon in the hope of getting into the main camp before all of its occupants could get away, the guide having stated that it was on some level ground at the far end of the canyon, which was a short one.

One of the privates of the Scouts was James E. Murphy, an Arizona cowboy. Partly because he always wanted to be at the front, and partly because he had eyes like a hawk, was a splendid shot, and always cool, Murphy usually rode alone from fifty to a hundred yards ahead of any detachment of troops of which the Scouts formed a part, being what is known in military parlance as the "point," this being a precaution against suddenly

encountering the enemy while we were in close formation. Of course, when we were out with a force of any
size the point was farther in advance, and consisted of
more than one man, being a sort of advance-guard modi-
fied to suit the conditions of this sort of war. Murphy
had served in the First United States Volunteer Cavalry
in the Spanish War, and had been shot through the head
at the battle of Santiago, but had recovered, and subsequently had enlisted in the Thirty-fourth Infantry for service in the Philippines. On this occasion he was in his
accustomed place, my two aides and I being a few feet
behind him. All the remainder of the force having been
directed to halt, we four and a man of the Scouts, which
one I cannot now recall, walked quietly forward a few
yards.

During this guerilla war all of us officers carried carbines in order that we might not be entirely dependent on
our revolvers in case we should be dismounted and cut off
in any of these close-range affairs. We were now within
thirty yards of the fire, and could plainly see the two sentries standing near it, leaning on their rifles conversing in
low tones, and apparently paying no attention to keeping
a lookout. It is not pleasant to tell of having shot down
these unsuspecting sentries, but it had to be done. If we
had called upon them to surrender, they to a certainty
would have bolted into the darkness and from there added
to the fire with which we were soon smitten. And then,
too, it would have meant getting away with two rifles to
be used against us later. In this period of the war the
capture of arms was considered of much more importance

than the killing of men. The former could not be replaced, while the latter could. I gave a whispered command, two carbines cracked, and the men pitched forward,
both shot through the heart. All of us then emptied the
magazines of our carbines, firing down the canyon, as we
had seen a number of men leap to their feet. Then came
the reply, a rattle of about thirty shots. Wolfe, at my
left elbow, swung around and collapsed, falling into a hole
about six feet deep that we had not seen in the darkness,
while Murphy, at my right, sank to the ground with a
groan.

In ten seconds it was all over. In this little clash we
had suffered as many casualties as in the reconnoissance
near Bacolor, where a detachment of about equal size
was engaged an hour and had fifty thousand shots fired at
it. There are some queer things in war. Owing to the
intense darkness, an attempt of some of the men to chase
down the now flying enemy was fruitless. By the light
of brands snatched from the fire, we hastened to attend
to the injuries of the wounded. We had great difficulty
in getting Wolfe out of the hole that he had fallen into
without adding to his suffering. His case looked serious
at first, as he was shot through one lung and one arm,
while Murphy was terribly injured, one of his brawny
arms being cut entirely off at the elbow, the bullet that
struck him having evidently first hit the canyon wall and
then tumbled. We quickly applied a tourniquet, but he
had lost much blood in the meantime. Finally, we had
the two stretched out near the fire, where there was adequate light. It was absolutely out of the question for all

of the small detachments that were constantly leaving the garrisons on operations to be accompanied by medical officers, and we had none with us on this occasion.

At the first streak of dawn, which came in a short time, some of us pushed through the canyon, found and burned the now abandoned camp, and, coming back to the scene of the fight, picked up four Remington and eight Mauser rifles and about eight hundred rounds of ammunition. Trails of blood showed that the two sentries had not been the only ones of the enemy hit. I stooped down by the wounded Murphy and said: "This looks mighty bad, but I hope you can pull through." He replied quietly and calmly: "Well, General, if I can't, I think I can die like a soldier." We were thirty miles from San Isidro and five from our horses. Several men were sent back to where we had left the animals, with instructions to bring up four of the ponies. They took the direct trail to the foot-hills instead of the circuitous route of about eight miles that we had marched over during the night, and found the horses without difficulty. In the meantime, litters were improvised from poles and strips of bark, and we started on the return, each litter being carried by four men, who were allowed to change off with others every few hundred yards. Having ridden one night, been awake most of the next day, and then marched on foot all of the following night, it can be surmised that we were tired. Both the wounded were patient and cheerful throughout the trying ordeal. We followed the direct trail, and before noon met the men with the ponies, and proceeded to make what are known as pony or horse litters. Four long poles were cut, and saddle-blankets that the men had brought with them from the camp were stretched between them. Two ponies were put in each litter, one in front of and the other behind the man to be carried, the poles being fastened to the sides of the saddles. We first tried out this arrangement by having several of the men ride about in the litters, the ponies being led by men holding the bridle reins. The animals acted well, and we placed the wounded men in the litters. When we started, one of the infernal animals, the led one in Wolfe's litter, began to rear and plunge, and ended up by kicking the wounded man out. Finally, we got going, and in the afternoon reached the place where we had concealed the horses and their guard. I felt that I must remain out and attempt to hunt down the band that we had struck, but the wounded must hasten to the hospital at San Isidro, and I directed Mitchell to make preparations to take them in as soon as he and those who were to accompany him could have something to eat. As the country was infested with guerilla bands, I instructed him to keep moving, once he had started, and not to stop under any circumstances. He started on his perilous journey shortly after dark, his only escort being the Scouts, who now numbered about fifteen men. Luckily, all the ponies now in the litters behaved well.

I almost hesitate to tell of an amusing incident in connection with so sad an affair, but on the march one pretty rich thing occurred. Wolfe, who was suffering and worn out, wanted to go into camp for awhile at a point about eight miles from San Isidro. The neighborhood was an especially dangerous one, and Mitchell had his orders, and said that they would keep moving, whereupon Wolfe said: "I am your senior, and put you in arrest, and take charge of this outfit myself." Mitchell replied: "You are on sick report, and can't put anybody in arrest." The spectacle of these two lieutenants, both of them my aides, discussing this important point out there in the darkness must have been an edifying one. Finally the detachment reached its destination, most of those composing it not having had a wink of sleep for two days and three nights. That is soldiering. Wolfe recovered and returned to the United States on sick leave, but poor Murphy survived his wound only a couple of days more.

Captain Koehler and I remained out two days, and thoroughly scoured a large extent of mountain country, but, owing to the fight in the canyon, our presence was known, and the enemy abandoned the region for the time being, leaving to us only the small satisfaction of burning a few abandoned camps. On our return to San Isidro we had ridden all night, and just after daybreak of March 27 were going in single file along a trail through some high cogon grass, being at the time almost in the outskirts of one of the barrios of the town of Gapan, when I, happening at the time to be riding with the point, was surprised by seeing a man, whom from his uniform I recognized as one of our Macabebe soldiers, come running down the trail toward us. The man had both his arms bound behind him so tightly that his elbows almost touched, and he was so agitated and out of breath that he could say but little. He pointed to our right front, and gasped out in Spanish, "My companions, my companions." I correctly guessed that he and some other Macabebes had been captured and were being taken to the mountains, and that the men in charge of them, meeting us suddenly in the trail, had fled with all of the prisoners except this one who had broken away from them.

There was no time to ask questions, and I called back to Captain Koehler, riding at the head of his troop, "Right front into line and charge," at the same time pointing in the direction indicated by the Macabebe. Koehler turned in his saddle and gave the command that brought the troop quickly into line, the command to charge was given, the men drew their revolvers, put the spurs to their horses, and in almost no time were tearing through the grass. The man on the point and I joined onto the left of the line as it passed us. Soon came the popping of shots, and when it was over three Filipinos lay dead on the ground. So far we had not found any other Macabebes, but the men were still scouring the neighborhood, and a sergeant brought in two Filipinos, who from their dress and bearing I at once knew to be officers, though neither they nor any of their men that we had seen were in uniform. Accompanying them were two horribly wounded Macabebe soldiers, one of them having seven gashes across his head, face, and shoulders, and the other five. The sergeant explained that having ridden into a shallow ravine he had come upon the two Filipinos chopping with their bolos the two Macabebes, who were helpless, their arms being trussed up behind them. Captain Koehler and I and a few of the enlisted men were standing at the time in the principal street of the village. There was a hurried inquiry made in order to get at the facts in the case. After the sergeant had told his story, I repeated the gist of it to the two men, who had in the meantime acknowledged that they were officers of Lacuna's guerillas, one of them being a captain and the other a lieutenant, and asked them if they could make any denial of the facts, the reply of both being in the negative. Both of them were then asked if they could give any reason why the penalty of death should not at once be inflicted for having violated the laws of war in attempting to kill prisoners to prevent their escape. They replied that they could say nothing that would help their case. I turned to Captain Koehler, and asked: "Doesn't this come under General Orders 100 of 1863?" He replied: "If it does not nothing ever did." Two picket-ropes were called for, there was a tree near at hand, and within ten minutes after the commission of their brutal crime the two had paid the only appropriate penalty.

This recital will cause cold chills to chase themselves up and down the spinal columns of a number of good people, scattered all the way from Eastport to San Diego, so that it might be as well to state that this execution was absolutely as legal as any that ever followed trial by jury. If any one doubts this, let him peruse carefully the general order above referred to. The two men were literally caught red-handed in the commission of their crime, their persons and their clothing being spattered with the blood of their intended victims. The authorities who have discussed and elucidated the provisions of General Orders 100 agree that the accused must have been actually caught in the commission of the crime, and that the death penalty must be immediately inflicted. If I had even taken the two men to San Isidro, I could not legally have executed them, and they would have had to await the results of trail by a military commission. The moral effect of this summary action was most beneficial.

More than a year later, after Lacuna had surrendered, I discussed the matter with him, and was assured that he considered that I was justified in what I had done. The uninjured Macabebe, having in the meantime recovered his breath, explained that he and his three companions belonged to one of the companies stationed at San Isidro; the evening before they had strayed a block or two from their barracks, when they were seized by a number of men, gagged and bound, and taken to a house in Gapan, where they were kept overnight. At daybreak their captors had started to Lacuna's camp in the mountains to deliver them to him. There can be no doubt as to what Lacuna would have done to them. Shortly after leaving Gapan they had by chance run into us, and in the confusion one of the men had escaped. They led us to the house where they had been confined, and as we approached it three men leaped from the windows and started to run. They were called upon to halt, but paid no heed, two of them being killed by the fire that was opened, while the third escaped by dashing into a crowd of women and children.

In an hour more we were back in San Isidro, after five days full of excitement and tragedy. I at once reported to higher authority all the incidents of the morning, and was upheld.

VI

MORE OF THE GUERILLA WAR

EARLY in April the organization of the troops in the Philippines into tactical units, such as divisions and brigades, was changed into one on a geographical basis, the entire command becoming the Division of the Philippines, which was divided into four departments, these being in their turn subdivided into districts. General Otis was relieved, and returned to the United States, Genera' MacArthur succeeding him in supreme command, with head-quarters in Manila. General Loyd Wheaton became the commander of the newly organized Department of Northern Luzon, his head-quarters, also, being in Manila. The Third Brigade of the Second Division, my command, now became the Fourth District of the Department of Northern Luzon. Under the old arrangement the higher tactical units had become such only in name, and the new order of things was certainly much more logical.

The conditions existing in the Fourth District at this time were typical of those throughout the archipelago, and from numerous stations, scattered from the extreme north of Luzon to the shores of the Celebes Sea, there was being carried on by small detachments a most energetic war against the bands of guerillas that infested almost every locality. Naturally, conditions differed to a degree in the various provinces, depending largely on the temper of the people and the personal equation of the local guerilla chiefs.

In the district under my command, the local chieftain, Panteleon Garcia, was still in hiding, while his principal subordinate, Pablo Padilla, seemed to be losing his importance, the more energetic Lacuna making us the most trouble. It was known that the notorious Pio del Pilar, a man who had been a thorn in the flesh of both the Spanish and American authorities, was hiding in the mountains along the boundary between the districts commanded by General Grant and myself, but just what authority he exercised was not known. Becoming tired of the lean life in the *bosque*, he finally ventured into Manila, and was captured by a native police officer, who was promptly assassinated for his pains. It may be of interest to know that eleven years after this time I, as commander of the Department of Luzon, approved awarding the contract for furnishing firewood to the post of Fort William McKinley to this same Pio del Pilar. The thought of this old scamp earning his living honestly will be viewed with incredulity by many persons familiar with his past record.

During the early part of April I went out with the Scouts on several occasions, but had bad luck, not succeeding in meeting any of the enemy, though considerable was learned about the country. Lieutenant Admire had some time previously reported for duty, and was now in personal command of this detachment, and on two occasions took them out and had successful brushes with small bodies of the enemy. Major Wheeler made an expedition into the mountains from Peñaranda, had one or two fights, and burned some barracks and supplies, as did also Captain Koehler with his troop, while there were a number of enterprises carried on from various stations in the district, some of them resulting satisfactorily in punishing insurgent bands and capturing arms.

On April 22 I made another try, and started out, accompanied by Mitchell and by the Scouts, now increased to eighteen men, under Admire. Our native ponies had been replaced by excellent American horses, and we hoped to catch some insurgents in the open, and see what we could do with our new mounts. Instead of going to our old hunting-ground, the mountains, it was determined to try the flat country lying west and north of San Isidro, and just at daybreak we forded the Rio Grande, in itself a somewhat thrilling operation, and struck north through a country not known to any of us. Owing to their unreliability, we seldom used native guides, and on this march had to depend almost entirely on our knowledge as to the relative positions of the various towns that we expected to visit.

The first day was without adventure, and we spent the night at Aliaga, where there was stationed a company of the Thirty-fourth Infantry. The next day we turned to the westward, and were about five miles from that town when we had a lively little scrimmage. As there were so many trails, cutting here and there through the high grass, and as the man on the point had several times been in doubt as to what direction he should take, I was riding with him, accompanied by Lieutenant Mitchell, the detachment being about a hundred yards behind us. We were approaching a very shaky-looking bamboo bridge spanning a wide and deep ravine, when we saw two armed men start to run from its farther end. They struck out across a level field covered with short grass, and then we saw about a dozen more, all armed, emerge from the brush on its farther side, about four hundred yards distant, and advance a short distance to where they were met by the fleeing sentries, when they all formed line and opened fire. At the time they probably saw only the three of us. I directed Mitchell to fall back to the detachment, take off the six rear men, and then ride down the ravine to our left in order to protect the rest of us from a possible flank fire after we had crossed, as the ravine made so much of a curve that we might be exposed to such a fire from men that we could not get at without again crossing the bridge. Admire was directed to follow me across the bridge with the Scouts, but not to allow more than one man on it at a time. I did not like the looks of the structure, it not being wide or strong enough for wheeled vehicles, though we could see that animals had crossed it, but gritted my teeth and spurred my horse onto it. The others crossed as rapidly as they could, coming into line on my right.

To our surprise, the Filipinos stood their ground to a man, and continued to fire with great rapidity. I had taken it for granted that when they saw that we equalled them in numbers they would break, and that it would merely be a matter of running them down. As soon as

the men were in line they were ordered to draw their revolvers and charge at a gallop. It was an exciting moment, and the Filipinos did not start to run for cover until
we were within sixty yards of them, and even then they
turned and fired a number of shots in their retreat. But
they had delayed too long, and in almost no time we were
among them, our big American horses, frantic from being
the first time under fire, rearing and plunging so that we
had to think about as much of keeping our seats as of doing
anything else. I picked out as my man a fellow who I
could see was armed with a Krag carbine, paying no attention to the officer in command of them, who was retreating, revolver in hand, and whom I passed at a distance
of about four feet. Just as I passed the officer he fired
right into my face, but the bullet missed, though I was
slightly burned by the sparks. I was armed with a 45-
calibre Colt, and shot at him as soon as I saw what he
was going to do, the heavy bullet cutting his left hand
practically off at the wrist. I kept on after the man with
the Krag, who I could see was filling the magazine of his
piece as he ran. When he heard the horse close behind
him he faced about, and we had it out. My horse was so
wild that it was impossible for me to have a fair chance
at the man. I fired four times, and the plucky fellow
emptied his magazine of the five shots in it, neither of us
scoring, though the distance between us varied from only
ten to thirty feet. No doubt the plunging of my horse had
something to do with saving me, though the man had
made no attempt to take any sort of aim. My opponent
now started to run again, and jumped over a ditch about

four feet wide. I had one cartridge left in the revolver, and tried to close with him, but my crazy horse, wild with terror from the discharges in his face, would not jump the ditch, and tried to spill me off backward. The Filipino, seeing that I could not get at him, stopped and again began cramming cartridges into the magazine of his carbine, and I now noticed that the ditch between us extended only about thirty yards to the right, and quickly rode around its end to the other side. The man knew that my revolver must be about empty, and as I tried to ride down on him, faced about. By this time my hair was nearly ready to stand on end, and I made up my mind if the last shot failed to draw my carbine from its boot and throw myself off the horse on the opposite side, knowing that if I got on the ground the thing would be quickly over. For some reason my horse was now acting much better, and just as the man started to work the bolt to throw a cartridge from the magazine into the chamber I fired, and struck him over one eye, killing him instantly, the distance being about forty feet.

Being so absorbed in my own troubles, I had seen nothing of what the others were doing, though I had heard the popping of numerous shots and some exclamations and "cuss words." I looked around just in time to see the finish, one of the men leaping from his horse with his carbine and killing a man whom he had been unable to hit with his revolver. Eight Filipinos were on the ground, either killed or so badly wounded that they must have died shortly, among the former the officer, who had continued to fight even after he was so badly wounded. Six, probably nearly all of them wounded, had escaped by getting across the ditch, which none of our untrained horses would jump, and running for the near-by brush. We captured quite an assortment of fire-arms: one Smith & Wesson revolver, one Winchester, three Krag carbines, two Mausers, and two Remingtons, besides several hundred cartridges. Although the enemy must have fired three hundred shots, we had not a man or horse touched. Except for one shot fired from a carbine, all our work was done with a revolver. The Krag carbines captured were undoubtedly from among those lost by the upsetting of a raft ferry on the Rio Grande near Cabanatuan during General Young's advance through this region some months previously. In order to get rid of the captured arms we returned to Aliaga from the scene of the fight, and remained overnight, the next morning striking out across country for the town of San José, which I had visited on an inspection trip early in January.

The head-quarters of the Thirty-fourth Infantry had been transfererd to Cabanatuan, and San José was now garrisoned by several companies of the Twenty-fourth Infantry, with Major Keller in command. This officer had just received information as to the existence of a considerable insurgent camp in the mountains about ten miles east of his station, and we resolved to make a night march in an attempt to surprise it. An Ilocano guide was obtained, and we started just after dark with the Scouts and a company of the Twenty-fourth. Although we were in the midst of what is known as the dry season, a heavy rain began, and lasted all night, rendering the narrow trail through the wooded hills an abomination of mud. As is well known to many, the rank and file of the Twenty-fourth consists of negroes. It was the first time I had ever made a march with these troops, and I was very much interested in seeing how they would conduct themselves. The thing that most impressed me was their everlasting good nature during the hard work and discomforts of the night. Rain, mud, and the gruelling work up and down the steep and slippery trails seemed to have no effect on their spirits, there being such a tendency to laugh and talk and to chaff each other that it was often necessary to caution them to keep quiet. Major Keller was unfortunate in having as his mount a pony built on such lines that it was impossible to cinch his saddle so that it would not slip backward in going uphill. He was a rather stout man, past middle-age, and had a most pronounced German accent. A dozen times his saddle worked backward until it would suddenly turn, and he would be spilled off, both himself and the saddle being replaced by several of the big black fellows, after which the march would be resumed. My own saddle-girth having become loose, I dropped out of the trail to re-cinch. The men were plodding past, and probably saw me, but in the darkness mistook me for one of the Scouts, when I heard one of them say: "Sam, what do you think of this damn foolishness, anyhow?" Sam stopped for a second or two to accumulate some breath and ideas, and then responded very gravely: "De only ting dat I tinks is dat dat ole Dutch major o' ourn suttenly do like to fall offen dat rat he's a-ridin'."

Our guide did not seem to know the country any too well, and it was dawn when we cautiously approached the camp, hidden in the dense woods. The enemy was gone, and the only direct result of this march was the burning of the grass-covered sheds that had been their shelter. We went into camp here for the day in order to rest the men and horses, and give the latter an opportunity to feed, some excellent grass being found near by. During the day we were visited by another Ilocano, who said he could lead us to an important insurgent *deposito* in the hills a day's march to the south. The company of the Twenty-fourth was directed to return to its station, as we wished to go faster than men could march afoot, and just after nightfall we were off with the Scouts, the Ilocano being mounted on his own pony. Hour after hour we kept going, at times crossing grassy uplands and at others riding through gloomy forests. During a part of the night we were following trails, but usually were not. This guide certainly knew his business, but about all we could make out of it was that we were going south, which at least had the merit of bringing us nearer to San Isidro. We were fortunate in having no rain, and, the sky being clear, the darkness was not intense. About 8 o'clock the next morning the guide stated that we were within a few hundred yards of our destination. We dismounted, tied the horses, leaving them under a guard of a few men, and cautiously followed the Ilocano, every man with his loaded carbine in hand. We soon came to the foot of an absolutely perpendicular cliff about forty feet high, from the top of which hung a rattan ladder, and could make out the roofs of several sheds. We saw the head of a man looking down for a moment over the edge of the cliff, but he soon disappeared. Desiring to frighten away the guard and prevent fire being set to the stuff in his charge, several shots were ordered fired, and immediately afterward one of the Scouts went up the swinging ladder. As soon as he had reached the top I followed, the other men coming up as rapidly as possible, though no two were allowed on the ladder at the same time.

And what a find it was! There were several large sheds filled to their roofs: almost the entire records of the Malolos government, letter-press books having copies of all orders and correspondence sent out, hundreds upon hundreds of official letters and telegrams, fourteen hundred rounds of fixed ammunition for the Hotchkiss two-pounder, four thousand rounds of small-arms ammunition, five hundred pounds of powder, twelve cases of petroleum, a thousand yards of cloth in bolt, several tents, a quantity of dynamite bombs, reloading tools, box after box of official blanks and stationery, one million postage and revenue stamps, and an endless lot of miscellaneous stuff. It took us hours to sort out the find and decide what to destroy and what to bring away. We could scarcely believe our eyes as we went through it all.

In the meantime inquiry had been made of the guide as to which one of the garrisoned towns was nearest, and we were informed that two hours of fast walking would bring one to Bongabong. Accordingly, guided by this man, a few of the Scouts were sent there with a note to the commanding officer directing him to send to us any pack-animals that he might have. As luck would have it, a train of twenty-six mules was in the post, having just returned from carrying supplies to Pantabangan, and they reached us about noon. Mules are not very good at climbing rattan ladders, at least not unless they have been especially trained for that work, but we found that an approach could be made from the rear along the summit of the ridge, one end of which was the cliff that we had scaled. The guide had not brought us in that way for the reason that an outpost that we would be bound to encounter was maintained some distance out in that direction, and if shots had been exchanged with it the sentry at the sheds in all probability would have set fire to everything. The Ilocano informed us that the stuff had been here nearly a year, and it is my opinion that it was sent to this place when Aguinaldo left Cabanatuan for Tarlac, San Isidro and Cabanatuan in succession having been his capital after the fall of Malolos. It might be said here that it was at Cabanatuan that Antonio Luna, far the ablest of the insurgent generals, was killed by members of Aguinaldo's guard.

But to get back to our find. The records were considered the most important, and were loaded first, being followed by other things in the order of their value, as we could scarcely estimate how much the pack-train could carry. The barrels of powder, ammunition for the Hotchkiss and for small-arms, dynamite bombs, stationery, and a lot of miscellaneous stuff were piled in one of the sheds, and we moved several hundred yards away, leaving a soldier to start the fire. This man touched a match to the grass roof and then lit out to join us. I had never before realized how fast a man can run if the inducement is sufficient, as this gallant warrior scarcely seemed to touch the ground as he increased the distance between the blazing shed and himself. When the thing got to going it sounded like a young battle, and the explosions lasted for half an hour. As the various sheds caught fire a column of smoke rolled hundreds of feet into the air. Even after we had started on our march we could hear the explosion of an occasional shell.

We struck south, just at dark forded the Rio Grande, and shortly afterward reached the small village of Cabu, where we camped for the night. The next day brought us to Cabanatuan, and the next to San Isidro, our progress having been much delayed by the heavily laden packtrain. We had been out six days, and had marched about one hundred and thirty miles, and came in with men and horses dead tired, but so far as we were concerned we were quite happy, and if the horses felt badly about it they kept their views to themselves.

During the next three weeks I went out on several more expeditions, sometimes using the Scouts alone, and at others having Troop G of the Fourth in addition, but had rather poor luck. On one occasion we "jumped" a small band in the flat country south of Gapan, and had a little fight in which we killed one man and captured fifteen rifles and seven hundred rounds of ammunition. This force was in camp at the time, most of the men having laid aside their weapons, which they abandoned as they ran for the brush when we attacked. On May 6, while

I was absent on one of these expeditions, Captain Smith, adjutant-general of the district, learned through spies of the presence of Panteleon Garcia, commander-in-chief of all the insurgent bands in the central provinces of Luzon, in the near-by town of Jaen. With a detachment of cavalry, Captain Smith crossed the Rio Grande after dark, surrounded the house, and not only captured Garcia, but his adjutant, Hilario Tal Placido, who was afterward to accompany me on the expedition which resulted in the capture of Aguinaldo. Garcia was succeeded in command by José Alejandrino, who made his head-quarters on the densely wooded slopes of Mount Arayat, in Pampanga province. Ten days later, Lieutenant Jernigan, Thirty-fourth Infantry, with a small detachment operating from Aliaga, captured Colonels Pablo Padilla and Casimerio Tinio, the former the commander in the province of Nueva Ecija. Padilla was succeeded by Lacuna, who had heretofore been one of his subordinates.

On May 29 Captain C. D. Roberts, Thirty-fifth Infantry, whose station was San Miguel, in the Fifth District, while scouting some miles north-east of there with six enlisted men, was overwhelmed by a greatly superior force of insurgents under Tecson, three of his men being killed and one wounded, while Captain Roberts and two soldiers were captured. The prisoners were taken to the mountains, and as they were as liable to be in the Fourth District as in the Fifth, the fight having taken place about on the boundary between the two, I was directed by telegraph to hasten to that region and attempt to rescue them —quite a hopeless task, as the insurgents would naturally take every precaution to hide their prisoners far back in the mountains, and would keep going with them if pursued. I got away on the evening of the 30th with the Scouts, Troop G, and a mounted detachment of the Twenty-second Infantry. Captain Koehler was temporarily absent in Manila, and on this occasion his troop was commanded by Lieutenant Samuel A. Purviance, who had been on duty with it on many of our previous expeditions.

We hurried across the country, and just after daylight drew near to a place that we had often used on these expeditions as a rendezvous and camp-ground, which we called Stony Point. As we came in sight of this place we discovered, to our surprise, that it was occupied by an outpost of the enemy, a sentry being in plain view, standing near a big rock. In the meantime, Purviance, having been informed of the presence of the enemy, was dismounting his men, the country being too rough for a mounted charge, and soon had them deployed. A red-hot little fight followed, and lasted about five minutes. The enemy was so thoroughly screened by the bowlders that had given the place its name that there was nothing but the flashes and puffs of smoke for us to shoot at. We soon rushed the little hill and the enemy retired precipitately down its other side. When we reached the point where they had been there was not a dead or wounded man to be found, and no blood was to be seen on the grass, but we captured four ponies, with their saddles and bridles, and five hundred Remington cartridges in a sack. None of our men had been hit, but we had two horses killed.

We got several glimpses of the enemy as they crossed open places in their retreat, and fired a few volleys at them.

Orders were at once given to take up the pursuit. We had with us a few pack-mules, and not wishing to be hampered with them, they were left at Stony Point with a small guard, while the main body of us mounted and lit out at a fast trot along the trail taken by the enemy. The Scouts were in the lead, with a couple of men out as point. As we came out of a strip of woods we saw that the enemy, now increased to about fifty men, was making a stand on the summit of a steep, grass-covered ridge. We again dismounted and deployed, and after a fight in which we suffered no loss, drove them off. While firing we had hugged the ground pretty closely, only rising to our feet to rush forward a few rods at a time. I had the interesting experience of having a bullet hit the ground directly under my face and so fill my eyes with earth that for a few seconds I was blinded. When we gained the summit of the ridge we saw a force of nearly a hundred men a mile on our front, marching rapidly in the direction of Stony Point, where we had left the pack-train with its small guard. They were already nearer to it than we were, and we had to make a run for our horses and mount in haste in order to beat them to it. They saw us as we climbed the ridge up to the point, and did not attack.

We were now very short of ammunition, having no reserve on the small pack-train, which was laden with grain and rations, and besides I wanted some more troops, as the hunting seemed particularly good. So the Scouts were sent in to San Isidro with orders for a company of the Twenty-second and the remainder of the pack-train, laden with rations and ammunition, to join us. They arrived late on June 2, the company of the Twenty-second sent out being commanded by Captain George J. Godfrey. Lieutenant Admire, being required for duty with his company, had been relieved temporarily from the command of the Scouts by Lieutenant Hanson E. Ely, of the same regiment, who now came out from San Isidro with them.

On the morning of the 3d we were ready, and again left Stony Point for the grassy ridge that had been the scene of the second fight three days before. I had sent the cavalry off in another direction, and so had only the Scouts and infantry and a part of the pack-train. The ridge was again found occupied by the enemy, but in a sharp little action of five minutes Captain Godfrey cleared it, his company being assisted by the Scouts, and its recent occupants could be seen retreating rather deliberately in single file along a well-beaten trail leading into the higher mountains to the eastward. After a delay to allow the men to get their breath and refill their cartridge belts, we took up the pursuit, the Scouts under Ely being ahead, then Mitchell and myself, followed by Captain Godfrey and his company at a distance of seventy-five yards. I had directed Lieutenant Ely to push ahead and make no attempt to scout the country on our flanks, merely being careful not to march too fast for the infantry. As was inevitable in this war of small detachments operating in a country of forests, jungle, and high grass, we were taking the risk of falling into an ambuscade. If we were not willing to do this we might as well be in Manila.

The fire discipline of the Filipinos was usually so poor that they almost invariably let fly as soon as our point came in sight, not waiting for the main body, which, being thus warned, had time to deploy. But this outfit was better handled. We had just emerged from some dense woods, and were crossing a glade of about two acres, the Scouts being nearly across and the rest of us in the open, when from the margin of the woods, seventy yards to our left front, crashed out a volley from about fifty rifles, the bullets whistling all about us, but, strange to say, not hitting a man. We instinctively threw ourselves off our horses, and the infantry company very naturally went to the earth, but at the command of their captain rose to their feet, advanced their left sufficiently to face the enemy, and then at the order lay down and commenced firing. As we later discovered, the enemy was in a splendid deep trench that he had prepared months before, and he now maintained on us a very persistent fire. One of the first things noticed was that between them and ourselves was a very deep ravine which it would be impossible for us to rush across.

The combat was severe, and lasted about four minutes. All the enlisted men were lying down and fighting hard, with the exception of one who stood up among some of the officers. This was a member of the Scouts, a half-breed Pawnee Indian by the name of Bates. He was a few feet to my right, and I was perfectly fascinated by the man's coolness and the care with which he aimed every shot. He could not have been calmer if he had been shooting at a mark. Those of the Scouts in the rear of that detachment had fallen back to fight alongside the infantry, while the balance under Ely were pushing up the trail in an attempt to get onto the flank of the trench. I happened to glance along the company of prostrate infantrymen, fighting hard and silently, when I saw poor Godfrey sink to the ground, dead. How we cursed that ravine that had kept us from ending the thing as soon as it started! But now Ely had got on to the enemy's flank, and they broke back into the woods. In addition to Captain Godfrey, one man of the company, Private Ethridge, was killed. If the enemy had any loss they managed to carry their killed and wounded away, but it is my opinion that they suffered but little, if any, as they were fighting in a deep trench, and had the further advantage of being somewhat above us. For a time some of us pursued the fleeing men, but there was no hope of coming up with them, as they vanished into the depths of the forest.

It was a sad procession that made its way back to Stony Point. All who knew Captain Godfrey bitterly regretted his death, he being one of those jovial, kind-hearted men without an enemy in the world. He was a great favorite with the Filipinos in San Isidro, especially among the children, and after our return to that town I heard among its inhabitants many expressions of what I believe to have been genuine regret. It seemed the very irony of fate that one so liked by the natives should have died at the hands of their countrymen. After reaching Stony Point the infantry company marched for San Isidro with its dead, the pack-train accompanying it. I remained out a couple of days more with the mounted men, but the insurgents seemed to have vanished from the earth, except as regards one small band with which we had a futile long-range skirmish.

Heretofore our campaigning had been under the most favorable conditions as to weather, except that it had usually been very hot during the greater part of each day, but now the rains had begun and would last for six months, so that from this time on these expeditions were filled with discomfort. Not even shelter-halves, popularly known as "dog tents," were carried, and many and many a night we stretched out in the rain to get whát rest we could. Saddles were used as pillows, while each one had a saddle-blanket between him and the ground, and a rubber blanket as the only protection from the weather. And how it did rain! Often for days at a time we were drenched to the skin. Officers, of whatever rank, dressed, marched, and camped the same as private soldiers, ate the same food, bacon and hardtack, and drank the same strong coffee. It was a rough life, but we were healthy, and as hard as nails, and the experience was in many ways enjoyable. When one who took an active part in this phase of the Philippine insurrection reads of the thousands of men who were enrolled for service in the Spanish War, but who never saw the outside of the continental limits of the United States, and who are now drawing pensions because of the alleged privations and hardships of the concentration camps, he cannot help thinking that there are in this world some things that are pretty hard to understand.

From the stand-point of excitement and adventure the life that we were now leading was in the same class with tiger-shooting, as it required initiative and acting quickly when the occasion arose, and was by no means devoid of the element of personal danger.

One of the unique features of this period of the war, at least so far as the Fourth District was concerned, was the pleasant social relations between the officers of the American garrisons and the better class of the people in the towns. Often we would come back to San Isidro from a raid into the *bosque*, and that same evening attend a *baile* or other social function given at the home of some prominent resident. While we never had any fear that our host, whoever he might be, would be so treacherous as to take advantage of us on such an occasion, we realized that it was not impossible that some over-zealous leader might seize the opportunity to make a "ten strike" by swooping down on the town, surrounding the house that we were in, and carting all of us that he had not killed out to the mountains and giving us an opportunity to admire the scenery for a few months. So we habitually came to these affairs with our revolvers and an ample supply of cartridges. Of course, it would be bad form to appear armed in the parlor or ballroom, so that we always festooned the hat-rack with a collection of belts and holsters, each one weighted down by a big weapon. On a certain occasion at the home of Señor Sideco, who lived only a block from the building used as district head-quarters, I was late in arriving, and as I hung my contribution on the hat-rack took the trouble to count those already there, and found that mine was number seventeen, which was the exact number of officers present.

As hosts, the more cultured among the Filipinos are most agreeable. The Malay (and all pure-blood Filipinos are Malays) is a rather reserved but courteous and hospitable man, having little sense of humor, and being much averse to anything in the way of "horse-play." Our sometimes rough but good-natured and really kind-hearted soldiers did not much appeal to them, but the relations between them and the officers of the garrisons were often quite cordial.

In the Fourth District we were quite fortunate in the way the war was carried on. This was not due to any particular merit on my part, being largely because of the policy pursued by the most prominent among the insurgent leaders who did me the honor to keep things stirred up in my own particular parish. It was well known to all of us that Aguinaldo was a man of humane instincts; but he was not always fortunate in the selection of his subordinates. It is a fact beyond dispute that Alejandrino, who succeeded Garcia in command of the "Centre of Luzon," carried out a most relentless policy in his treatment of those of his unfortunate countrymen who were so unlucky as to incur his displeasure, and the scores of executions by our own military authorities of men who had carried out his orders are matters of record, the instigator of these hideous crimes saving his own skin by avoiding capture, and finally surrendering after the government had all but stayed its hand. But while Alejandrino had in many of the provinces subordinates who thought

as little of burying a man alive as of killing a chicken, Lacuna and Pablo Tecson (for there were three of the Tec-
sons) were of a different stamp, and though they did not
hesitate to destroy property, were chary when it came to
taking life unnecessarily, both of them being in addition
quite humane in their treatment of such Americans as
fell into their hands. Teodoro Sandico, who carried on
some perfunctory operations on the northern part of
Neuva Ecija, while a nonentity as a military leader, was
not a bad sort of fellow personally, and treated well the
few prisoners of war in his power. Tagunton, one of
Lacuna's subordinates, was, however, a monster of cruelty, and we shall see how, in the course of time, he "got
his."

On June 5 a detachment of the Thirty-fifth Infantry,
operating from San Miguel de Mayumo, in the Fifth District, had struck in the mountains east of that place a
force of some four hundred men under Pablo Tecson,
and had been pretty roughly handled, leaving one of its
wounded in the hands of the enemy. Upon hearing of
this reverse the department commander ordered General
Grant, commanding the district named, to take steps to
drive the enemy from his position, and I was directed to
gather up from my own command as many men as I could
without losing too much time, and report with them to
General Grant at San Miguel. By drawing on San Isidro
and several of the near-by garrisons, I got together eight
hundred, and with these and our pack-train reached the
rendezvous thirty-six hours after receiving the telegraphic
order, but it required some quick work and a strenuous

night march. With the troops that General Grant had with him we now reached the quite respectable total of thirteen hundred men, infantry, cavalry, and artillery, and proceeded with them toward the mountains.

On the second day after leaving San Miguel we reached the scene of the reverse to the detachment of the Thirty-fifth. But Tecson was too shrewd to fight a force of such size, and, as he afterward told me, was so far away with his main body that he could barely hear the reports of our mountain guns in the affair that followed. He had left behind a delaying force of forty men under Captain Claro, and this plucky fellow held on for quite a time, having his men distributed along the summit of a steep ridge in deep rifle-pits, the only ones I ever saw in the Philippines. If he had bunched his men up in a short trench he undoubtedly would have suffered loss, though most of the firing was at twelve hundred yards range; but these excellent pits, so far apart that they made most unsatisfactory targets, so protected his men that he came off unscathed, as he and Tecson both personally assured me a year later, when, all the insurgents in the region having surrendered, we were fighting the battles over again. Besides, immediately after Claro vacated the ridge I personally examined the position, and could not find a drop of blood. When Claro fell back he burned the large number of sheds that had been the barracks of Tecson's force, sparing the one in which was lying the wounded prisoner taken in the fight of the 5th. During the most of the time that we were out on this expedition the weather was atrocious, and on the night following the fight we slept out in one of the worst rain-storms I ever saw anywhere.

We had been back in San Isidro only a day or two, and men and horses had not yet had time to rest, when about noon of the 14th a telegram was received from Major Wheeler, of the Thirty-fourth, commanding the garrison of Peñaranda, stating that he had been informed by one of his spies that Lacuna with four hundred men was in the *barrio* of Papaya, about two miles from Peñaranda, and that he intended to burn the latter town that night. Major Wheeler was going after him immediately with the force at his disposal, but feeling that some mounted troops would be necessary in order to make a successful pursuit after the expected fight, I directed him to await my arrival. Troop G and the Scouts, the latter again under the command of Admire, were ordered to saddle immediately, and we took up a keen trot for Peñaranda.

Besides the officers on duty with the organizations named, I was accompanied by Major H. S. T. Harris, chief surgeon of the district, Captain Smith, my aide Mitchell, and Lieutenant D. C. Lyles, Thirty-fourth Infantry, all of whom had at one time or another participated in a good many expeditions. Reaching Peñaranda, we found that Major Wheeler was ready to march out with one company of his command under Lieutenant L. L. Dietrick, an officer who had already quite distinguished himself in the work of hunting down guerilla bands. There was also a detachment of eighteen mounted infantry, who were directed to report to Admire, who was then ordered to follow the south bank of the stream known as the

Rio Peñaranda until he reached the small *barrio* of Callios, across the stream from Papaya, where he was to await developments. The remainder of us crossed the river and pushed rapidly forward to Papaya, and were informed that Lacuna had gone toward Callios. For a time I feared that Admire and his small force might suddenly run into Lacuna and have a hard time of it before we could reach him, but shortly one of the Scouts came up with a message from that officer to the effect that he had located the enemy and was keeping him under observation.

Lacuna, thinking that he had only Admire's few men to deal with, had formed line of battle in partially open country, and was awaiting an attack. I detached Lieutenant Purviance with twenty men of the cavalry to watch a certain ford, and the remainder of us hurried southward. In less than an hour we had joined Admire, and the situation was explained to us. The march was continued along a road well screened by trees, so that our approach was not observed. Major Wheeler had charge of the advance, having the company under Dietrick, the cavalry being held in rear in order that it would be at hand to charge when needed. The infantry, joined by Admire's men, who had dismounted, was deployed, and broke into the open, being greeted by a fierce rifle fire from the grass on its front and left front. The men were ordered to lie down, and at a distance of three hundred yards a savage little fire fight took place, and lasted a few moments. Some of the enemy, however, taking advantage of inequalities of the ground, were quite close in on our left. I had dismounted and tied my horse to a tree, when I noticed a puff of smoke from the grass under a bush not seventy yards from the left front of the prostrate company. It would take too long to get a soldier to attend to the matter, so I stepped over to my horse, drew my carbine from its boot, and fired three of the shots in the magazine at the base of the bush, aiming each one very carefully. After the fight was over I went to the spot, and found a dead Filipino, with his Remington still in his hands. He had been hit in the head and in the shoulder.

Major Wheeler was ordered to close with the enemy and did so with great vigor, his men firing as they advanced, and at the same time Koehler, having formed line behind a narrow screen of trees, broke into the open in a mounted charge against the enemy's left. As the infantry company advanced it was hotly fired into from the left by a group of insurgents, who were attended to by Captain Smith, who took a few men and drove them out of a shallow, brush-filled ravine. The Filipinos stood their ground well, and fought hard though ineffectively, and the dismounted men were almost among them before that portion of the line struck by them gave way, the most of them, including the majority of their wounded, reaching the brush and escaping. A considerable number, however, were driven into the open by the charge of the cavalry, which then kept up the pursuit as long as there were any to be found. My big black horse had been making such frantic efforts to pull up by the roots the tree that he was tied to, that I began to fear he might succeed, and being a warm advocate of forest conservation,

I mounted just as the advance started, and thereafter the most of my efforts consisted in trying to keep the brute from jumping clear off the island of Luzon. Major Harris's horse also bolted with its rider just at the beginning of the fight, and had the bad taste to run under a tree with our energetic *medico*. Major Wheeler's horse was killed, while those of Admire, Mitchell, and Lyles broke loose and escaped into the woods, being eventually picked up by the enemy. Some months previously Mitchell had ordered from the States a fine rain-coat, and this was the first time he had taken it out, it being tied on behind his saddle. For the next year this coat served to protect Lacuna from the rigors of the climate of his native country, and when he finally surrendered he brought it in with him. For some time the subject of rain-coats was tabooed in Mitchell's presence.

The fight that had just ended was from our standpoint about the most successful that we had in the Fourth District. Not including those who were run down by the cavalry in the pursuit, and whom there was no opportunity to count, we found twenty-two dead, and took sixteen prisoners, all of them wounded, besides capturing a considerable number of rifles. After his surrender Lacuna told me that he had had four hundred men in the fight, and that of these forty-four were killed or died of their wounds. First Sergeant O'Brien, of Troop G, a fine old soldier of many years' service, was killed in the mounted charge, and a man in the infantry was wounded. O'Brien was hit first through the arm, and called out to Captain Koehler, "Captain, I'm shot," the reply being,

"Don't fall; stick to your horse," but an instant later he was shot through the heart, and pitched to the ground, dead. Our loss had been small in numbers compared with the punishment inflicted on the enemy, though I would rather have foregone it all than pay for our success in the death of such a man as Sergeant O'Brien.

Some years previously there had arrived at an infantry post in the States a young recruit by the name of Paul Draper, he having enlisted in order to win a commission from the ranks. For a time there was a tendency on the part of some of the rougher men of the company to which he belonged to make life a burden for Draper and to impose on him generally, but he found a friend and protector in one of the non-commissioned officers of the company, the same O'Brien who on this day died in the fight at Callios. In time Draper became an officer, and O'Brien, his term of service having expired, re-enlisted, this time in the cavalry, and became a first sergeant. Since then their paths had not crossed until Draper, as an officer of the Twenty-second Infantry, was on duty with the company garrisoning the town of San Antonio, and O'Brien was stationed at San Isidro, only three or four miles distant. Whenever Draper came over to San Isidro he hunted up the old friend of his "rookie" days and had a chat with him. One day Draper, while superintending the construction of a raft ferry on the Rio Grande, fell into the river and was drowned, his body being recovered and interred in the cemetery at San Isidro. The day after the fight at Callios all of us officers from district head-quarters, Troop G, and many officers and men from various organizations stood bareheaded in a howling storm of wind and rain while Lieutenant Purviance read the burial service and the body of Sergeant O'Brien was lowered into the grave next to that of the officer that he had befriended and protected in a quiet garrison on the other side of the world. Certainly, all the romance is not contained in the pages of novels.

At this season rain-storm followed rain-storm in such quick succession that the streams were so swollen as to be unfordable except at a few places, the mountain trails became quagmires, and all the elements seemed to conspire to make it impossible for us to continue the active campaign that so far had been waged unless we were willing to break down every man and horse in the command, and be satisfied with meagre results, as the Filipino is at home in mud and water, and in this aquatic game had every advantage over our soldiers. The plucky little Macabebes under Major Batson and such able subordinates as Captains J. N. Munro, F. H. Cameron, and others, and our Ilocano allies in the north part of the province, were about the only ones of our troops who could keep in the field to advantage. The not unnatural result was that the insurgent leaders began to think that we could not follow them into the mountains, and so became more aggressive. Lacuna, by great effort, and by obtaining help from Pablo Tecson, concentrated more than seven hundred well-armed men, made the foolish mistake of dividing them into three detachments, and on the night of the Fourth of July savagely attacked the garrisons of Peñaranda, Gapan, and Manicling, all east of San Isidro at distances varying from three to eight miles.

We at San Isidro, hearing the heavy and continuous firing, could not spare troops to help out the other towns, as it was thought that our turn would come next; but I felt no uneasiness as to the result of these attacks, having confidence in our now veteran troops and their commanders. Peñaranda and Gapan came out all right after sharp fighting, but suffered some loss, while the struggle at Manicling was a hard one. This small town had not heretofore been garrisoned, having, in consequence, become a rendezvous for insurgents; but on this very day there had arrived a detachment of forty men of the Twenty-fourth Infantry, commanded by Lieutenant E. B. Mitchell. The new garrison had not as yet had time to construct anything in the way of adequate protection, when a force outnumbering them eight to one, commanded by Lacuna in person, made a determined effort to get them. Lying close to the ground behind some improvised shelter, the negroes fought long and hard. Lieutenant Mitchell was badly wounded early in the fight, but continued to exercise general control, being ably seconded by First Sergeant Washington, a fine-looking old soldier, who was killed in an engagement a few weeks later. Unable to make any impression, Lacuna finally gave it up, having inflicted on the garrison a loss of one enlisted man killed and one officer and one enlisted man wounded.

The incidents of this night settled it with us; and, mud and quagmires notwithstanding, we again had to take the field. A few scouting expeditions, made under the most trying conditions, and the work of Major Wheeler's spies informed us that Lacuna had established himself in a rainy-season camp far back in the mountains, and, now that he thought we could not go after him, contemplated a series of raids into the lowlands. Accordingly, there was organized a column consisting of the Scouts, now under Lieutenant Richard C. Day, Thirty-fourth Infantry, whom I had taken on as the second aide to which I was entitled, Troop G of the Fourth Cavalry under Koehler, a battalion of the Twenty-second Infantry under Captain J. F. Kreps, two companies of the Thirty-fourth under Major Wheeler, and the so-called squadron, really battalion, of Macabebes under Major Batson, in all about eight hundred men. I was accompanied by nearly all of the district staff, and we had the complete pack-train laden with rations and ammunition. A short time previously I had applied for and received a Vickers-Maxim mountain gun, throwing a twelve-and-a-half-pound shell, and this weapon was now taken out for the first time. There was no artillery organization in the command, but several of the Scouts were given instruction in caring for and handling the gun. The concentration of the various elements going to make up this mixed force was made at Peñaranda, and before dawn of July 16 we marched from there toward the mountains again to try conclusions with the redoubtable Lacuna.

Before long Major Batson with three-quarters of his command and Captain Koehler with his troop were detached and ordered to the southward, the former to bar Lacuna on the only trail to the south, while with the main body I marched straight into the mountains toward the insurgent camp. A little before noon the advance-guard came under a long-range fire, and we began deploying for action, Captain Cameron, commanding the only company of Macabebes left with the main body, being sent forward to develop the enemy's position and strength. Lacuna retired from his camp, and on the summit of a steep, grassy ridge immediately behind it formed a line of about four hundred men. The temptation to try out our new gun was too strong, and the Vickers-Maxim was taken from the backs of the mules carrying its various parts, set up, and loaded. I had a vague recollection of having once been an amateur artilleryman, and so did the aiming. The first shrapnel exploded a short distance in front of the line, being followed by two more. But the insurgents would not stand for the shells, and the line began to retreat. In the meantime the several organizations were getting into position and opening fire, and everything was coming our way, when an officer who throughout almost the whole war had rendered gallant and efficient service, made a grievous error of judgment, and, overcome by a desire to get into the fight immediately, ruined everything. Lacuna escaped after having suffered trifling loss. The officer who blundered had done so well heretofore that I could not bring myself to take the action usual under such circumstances. So we contented ourselves with the doubtful pleasure of burning twenty-six grass-roofed buildings used as barracks, and destroying some supplies, and then camped near the ridge where Lacuna had made his brief stand. Our only loss during the day was two Macabebes wounded.

The next morning the force was split up and sent in various directions to clear out the whole mountain country. I went with Koehler and his troop, and we struck Lacuna's trail and hung to it, up hill and down, across raging streams and through dense tropical forests until we were in the country of the Ilongotes and Negritos, doubtless where no white man had ever been, coming very close to the divide that separates the drainage of the Rio Grande de la Pampanga from that of the Pacific slope of the island. But we had to give it up, as we were practically out of rations, and there was no grass for the horses.

On this trip we came across the first real human habitation that we had ever seen in the mountains of this region, passing a small house surrounded by an acre or so of cultivated ground, while a few chickens and pigs were running about. The owner of this place was without doubt one of the class of people known in the Philippines as *remontados*, men who for one reason or another have fled from civilization, and with their families begun life anew in regions where the hand of the law is not apt to reach them. If there was any one thing understood by our soldiers during this period of the war, it was that they were not allowed to take anything from the inhabitants without payment, and as the proprietor of this establishment had not tarried after he saw us coming, commercial transactions even to the extent of buying a few chickens or some green corn were quite out of the question.

A couple of hours after passing through this place we had gone into noon camp, and Koehler and I were sitting on the ground waiting for our bacon, hardtack, and coffee to be brought to us, when the former sniffed the air, and said: "I smell chicken cooking. I'll bet it's that little cuss Albright." The unfortunate Albright was sent for, and approached looking exactly like a boy who has been caught with an arm up to the elbow in one of his mother's jars of peach preserves. "Albright, have you been stealing chickens again?" "Yes, captain." Then a long and judicial silence, ending in an order for the recently deceased bird to be brought up for inspection, in order, I suppose, to establish a *corpus delicti*, as the lawyers would say. The sizzling fowl was placed on the ground before us, then another judicial silence, followed by the dictum: "You know the orders about looting. You are fined one broiled chicken." The enterprising soldier walked away, glad to have got off so easily, but in the meantime the fragrance had smitten our nostrils and we could feel our rectitude fairly oozing out of us. Koehler broke the painful silence by saying, "It would be a positive sin to leave that for the ants to eat, and it won't do to let the man who stole it have it. We must do our duty"—and we did, but I could not help feeling a bit sneaking as I got away with my part. Seven years later I was the guest of Major H. C. Benson, Fourteenth Cavalry, then superintendent of the Yosemite National Park, on a fishing trip, and recognized among the soldiers on duty with the small pack-train we had with us the same man who on the occasion described had so inadvertently contributed to my lunch. I said: "Hello, Albright, is there anything doing here in the ckicken line?" He grinned sheepishly, and said it was a poor country for chickens. A peculiar coincidence was the fact that the man in charge of the pack-mules on this fishing trip was the same old chief-packer Gayler, who had hustled along the mules on this very expedition in the Philippines.

This brings us logically to a few words about·the men who handled the pack-mules that accompanied us on nearly all of the more extended of these "hikes." They were Americans of the type so familiar to those of us who have lived or travelled in the more isolated portions of our own West. They were civilian employees of the Quartermaster's Department, and had been obtained in those States and Territories where the pack-mule is still in vogue. They were not pretty, as a rule drank whenever they could find anything potable, swore large, round oaths, and ate with their knives; but if it should ever fall to me to pick out a lot of men who would stand by until the finish, I would not ask for better. Mr. Gayler, who had charge of them, was quite an elderly man, but vigorous and full of life. He was a mild-mannered person, never swore, and would only take a drink when he considered it necessary to do so in order to keep going. At first these packers were armed only with revolvers, but finally carbines were obtained for them, whereat they were greatly pleased. They had been much disappointed because of the fact that they had always been taking care of the pack-train while the soldiers did the fighting, but at least once they got their chance. On one of our expeditions to the mountains, which one I am not absolutely sure, Sergeant Frank White, of Troop G, had been ordered to go into San Isidro with a detachment of twelve men, and escort out to

Stony Point the pack-train with a lot of rations and ammunition. He was half-way back with his convoy, the
whole train of fifty-six mules and the necessary number
of packers, when he was attacked by a very considerable
number of the enemy. The affair soon became a running
fight across a rolling prairie country with a little scattered
tree growth here and there. Sergeant White handled his
small detachment very well, acting as a rear-guard for the
pack-train being hurried toward its destination; but the
attack was pushed so vigorously that it soon came to a
"show down," and the soldiers had to have help. This
was the chance of the packers, and leaving the train in
charge of a couple of unwilling men, they dismounted,
for the man who could fight on a mule has yet to be
born, and, carbine in hand, got into the fray. Acting in
conjunction with the soldiers, they literally chased those
Filipinos off the earth, and that night, having reached
Stony Point, kept the most of us peaceful and unwarlike
old gentlemen awake by violent arguments as to which
one had done the most killing. Their only loss was one
of the mules killed, but they saved his saddle and cargo.

But to get back to the other detachments that after
the recent fight had been sent in various directions. I
had directed Major Wheeler to go straight south through
the mountains, in the hope that he might get onto the
trail of those of Tecson's men who had assisted Lacuna in
the late operations. Wheeler was joined by Major Batson with Munro's company of Macabebes, and after a
brisk fight, in which he had one man wounded, pushed
still farther to the south, having with him now only two

short companies, C of the Thirty-fourth and F of the Twenty-second, the former under Captain George E. Gibson and the latter under Lieutenant David L. Stone, the Macabebes having separated from him and gone in another direction. On July 22, six days after our all but fruitless fight on the headwaters of the Peñaranda, he struck Tecson, who was awaiting him in a carefully prepared position. The combat that ensued was the most severe that occurred in the Fourth District, and was ended by an assault on a steep, grassy ridge, led by Major Wheeler in person. The fight was a desperate one, our men being greatly outnumbered, but the summit was reached and the enemy driven from it in disorder. Our troops suffered a loss of two enlisted men killed and Captain Gibson and five enlisted men wounded. Nearly two days and nights of the most gruelling work were required to get the wounded in to San Isidro. Captain Gibson was a Scotch Highlander, with a "burr" to his accent that was the delight of all of us who had ever listened to him. Although he finally recovered, his wound was of the most terrible nature, a Remington bullet having struck him under one eye and ploughed its way through his face and one shoulder, coming out in the small of his back. He had been one of our most capable officers, and his loss was keenly felt by all of us. The Filipinos, however, restrained any emotions they may have experienced, as Gibson had served long as provost judge of the district, and had given malefactors something of a taste of what military law means.

Our long-drawn-out raid into the mountains had the

effect, for the time, of relieving the garrisoned towns from the affairs which we usually referred to as attacks, these incidents usually consisting in a force of Filipinos taking shelter behind natural cover at night and indiscriminately shooting into a town until the local garrison could get under arms and chase them off. It is a fair guess to say that for every one of our own men hit in these performances half a dozen Filipinos—men, women, and children—suffered death or injury. The fragile houses in which most of the inhabitants lived offered less resistance to a bullet than would a board fence. The situation of the people who had taken refuge in the garrisoned towns was in many ways pitiable. We knew that every one of them who was even suspected of having money was contributing to the insurgent cause, we having a secret service that it would be hard to beat under the circumstances, and more than once some prominent resident was invited to visit head-quarters, told the amount of his latest contribution and the date thereof, and then allowed to go, it being known that the most of the people were acting under compulsion.

It must be remembered that the insurgent bands were not recognized as operating under the orders of anything in the way of a real government, and that, as they were carrying on an irregular warfare against the only constituted authority, they were in theory merely bandits, or, to use the legal term, war rebels, and as such were not entitled to treatment as prisoners of war. In the eyes of the law persons contributing to the support of these bands or giving them aid and comfort were as guilty as those who were in the field. In actual practice our enforcement of the drastic provisions of military law was very mild except in cases where it was proven by trial before military commission that the accused had been guilty of murder or other crimes of violence. In these instances the death penalty was not infrequently imposed. The American people in general have no conception of the horrors of that period of the Philippine insurrection that began early in 1900, when the only thing that approached a responsible native government had been broken up, and the power of life and death over their unfortunate countrymen passed into the hands of the leaders of the guerilla bands. There can be no doubt that during the period of the war referred to the number of persons—men, women, and children— the most of them innocent of wrong-doing from even the insurgent stand-point, who were brutally and senselessly murdered far exceeded in the aggregate the total of the men in arms killed by our own troops during the same time, as the figures reached into the thousands. This is not mere personal opinion, but is a matter of common knowledge among those who served in the Philippines in those days. If one wants to feel the cold chills creep over him, let him read the general orders of the Pacific Division for the years 1900 and 1901, in which are reviewed the findings and sentences of the military commissions that tried such of the culprits as could be caught and against whom evidence could be obtained. It is a record of monstrous and savage cruelty, and though nearly three hundred men paid the penalty on the gallows, and many more were sentenced to terms of imprisonment, only a small proportion of the victims was avenged. Even in Nueva Ecija, we did not entirely escape these atrocities, though, owing to the personalities of the principal insurgent leaders in that province, their number was not great. A little ten-year-old boy, son of a prominent man who had had the temerity to show some leaning toward the Americans, was kidnapped by Tagunton's men, and by order of that chief *flogged to death*, while the wife and daughter of a member of the municipal police of San Isidro were tied together and thrown alive down a well, where they perished.

With us now, in spite of mud and rain, the war went merrily on. It was a sort of process of attrition by which we hoped in time to wear the insurgent bands down to nothing. Our losses were not great, and every rifle captured from the enemy lessened his power just so much, for while men could be gathered up from the fields and forced to fight, the weapons lost to us could not be replaced. On August 1 Lieutenant F. W. Alstaetter, Corps of Engineers, while making an examination of the road between San Miguel and San Isidro, was overwhelmed by Lacuna. Alstaetter had three enlisted men of his own corps and an escort of eleven men of the Fourth Cavalry. Outnumbered more than twenty to one, he put up a long, hard fight, surrendering after his last cartridge was gone, having suffered a loss of one man killed and three wounded. Lacuna, with the humanity that usually distinguished him in dealing with captured Americans, sent the dead man and the three wounded into San Isidro, carrying the others as prisoners into the mountains. Within a couple of weeks the enlisted men were released, but he still held the officer. It was only a short time, however, until the opportunity presented itself to bring about his release.

A concerted movement of the garrisons of half a dozen towns was made with the object of clearing of insurgents the flat country between the mountains and the Candaba swamp. The operation was greatly interfered with by bottomless mud and swollen rivers, but some good little fights were had, nevertheless. In one of these Lieutenant-colonel Manuel Ventus, one of Lacuna's subordinates, was wounded and captured, being placed in our hospital for treatment. As soon as he was near recovery I wrote Lacuna stating that while I could not arrange an exchange of prisoners with him, I promised to release Ventus if he would do the same with Alstaetter. A few days later the latter was escorted to our outposts by a couple of insurgents and Ventus was released at the same time, but was allowed to remain in the hospital until his recovery. For months we had known of the presence with the insurgents of this region of an American negro named Fagan, a deserter from the Twenty-fourth Infantry. This wretched man was serving as an officer, and had on two occasions written me impudent and badly spelled letters. It was mighty well understood that if taken alive by any of us he was to stretch a picket-rope as soon as one could be obtained. Fagan was prominent in the fight in which the detachment above referred to had been captured, and appropriated Alstaetter's West Point class ring, declining to give it up on the eve of the latter's release. We shall see how in the course of time we got not only the ring, but Fagan's head in a sugar-sack.

The horses of Troop G of the Fourth Cavalry, that had served so long and efficiently in the Fourth District, had become so worn out that it was necessary for that organization to go to Caloocan to refit and remount, its place being taken by Troop A of the same regiment, commanded by Captain George H. Cameron, with Lieutenant C. S. Haight second in command. Captain Cameron, however, had to be relieved shortly, having been appointed regimental adjutant, and was succeeded by Lieutenant John Morrison, Jr., a splendid officer, who within a few months was to make the great sacrifice. In order partly to make up for the lack of cavalry, so necessary in this sort of war, horses had been obtained some months previously, and at all garrisons there had been organized small detachments of mounted infantrymen, these proving most useful. That from the portion of the Twenty-second Infantry stationed at San Isidro was commanded by Lieutenant Raymond Sheldon, a young officer of great energy, and rendered especially notable service. And still the hard work went on without cessation, there being scarcely a garrison that did not have some of its troops in the field at all times. Many and many a swift night march was fruitless, as was also many a well-laid plan to surprise the enemy, but we had occasional successes.

On October 13 I went out on a short raid with the Scouts under Day, and Troop A under Morrison, Major W. C. Brown going along for the excitement, Mitchell because he was my aide, and Dr. Pease in order to mend our hurts. We had a brisk little fight with an equal force of the enemy, driving them with some loss, and having

Private Robinson of the Scouts wounded. Ten days later I started out just after dark with the same two organizations. We plodded along through the sodden fields, keeping off all trails and roads, and just after daybreak were about fifteen miles south-east of San Isidro, when the man on point reported that we were approaching a small group of houses. These little isolated hamlets were always apt to yield something during the rainy season, when the insurgents, like ourselves, were not averse to sleeping under cover. We trotted quietly into this one, when Gantzhorn, of the Scouts, who was in the lead, was fired at from the window of a small nipa shack at a distance of not more than six feet, but was not hit. Gantzhorn had his revolver in hand, and returned the fire, hitting in the neck the man who had shot at him, killing him almost instantly. In an instant men began to run from the houses, some of them stopping to fire, but the most of them thinking only of gaining the brush. One man, who from his appearance we knew to be an officer, dashed down the bank of a ravine and through water up to his waist, while Gantzhorn and I emptied our revolvers at him. The former then plunged his horse over the bank of the ravine, fully fifteen feet, but I had not the nerve to do it. The fleeing man was none other than the long-sought Lacuna himself, and months later he told me that it was the closest call he ever had. Once into the jungle, he was safe, and escaped. He had been spending the night here accompanied by a small escort. In the house that he had fled from we captured much of his correspondence, and, most important of all, the stamped paper on which were afterward written the bogus letters over Lacuna's signature that were to be the undoing of the famous Aguinaldo, the king bee of them all. In this affair we suffered no loss, but killed two men and took five prisoners, three of them wounded, and also captured six rifles, some ammunition, and four ponies with their equipment.

For some time three of the officers stationed at San Isidro and several others in various towns of the district had had their wives with them, and I had sent for Mrs. Funston to come out from the United States. Accompanied by her sister, she arrived in November, I going to Manila to meet the two and escort them to San Isidro. The American women who lived in San Isidro in those days had some experiences that in these times do not ordinarily fall to those of their sex, as the town was fired into on several occasions by bands of marauders, and one time a portion of it was burned.

On the night of December 5 we started out on one of our endless expeditions, I having with me the Scouts under Day, Troop A of the Fourth under Morrison, Major H. S. T. Harris as surgeon, and Mitchell. It was a dark and rainy night, and we steered by compass, having information from one of our spies as to the exact location of Tagunton's band. We swung in a curve, first north-east, then gradually to the south-east and south, just at daybreak striking a tributary of the Peñaranda near where it emerges from the foot-hills. We crossed the stream to its south bank, and then hurried down it, straight west in the direction of San Isidro, thus having made a wide circle of the enemy, and were coming in on his rear. Just an hour after striking the stream we approached the unsuspecting enemy, and dismounted for the attack, as the country was so close that a mounted charge was impossible. We had to dash straight across the stream under a hot fire, as they discovered us as we were dismounting. We killed four men and captured two wounded, besides getting five rifles and some ammunition. In this fight I got a fairly good look at the notorious Fagan at a distance of a hundred yards, but unfortunately had already emptied my carbine. First Sergeant Alexander and Sergeant Schwartz, of Troop A, were severely wounded, the former receiving from the War Department the Certificate of Merit for his gallantry on that occasion. Sergeant Schwartz was within ten feet of me when he was hit, and as I heard the bullet strike him, I saw him throw his hands over his face, and, as the blood gushed through his fingers, whirl clear around, and fall face downward between two rows of growing sweet-potatoes. Thinking his eyes had been shot out, I had not the courage to go to him, as such spectacles are too much for me. But it was not so bad, the bullet having, however, gone clear through his head. In time he completely recovered.

For a time now I had bad luck, and did not succeed in getting any good fights out of the enemy, though out nearly all the time; but various other officers in the district made up for it, and struck the insurgents some hard blows. On one occasion Captain J. F. Kreps, of the Twenty-second Infantry, Mitchell, and I, with an escort of a dozen mounted men of the Twenty-second, were nosing about in the country south of Peñaranda, and had a little fight

in which we killed one man and wounded several, and
had one of our own detachment wounded, though not
severely.   On January 17 of the new year, 1901, we suffered a great loss in the death of Lieutenant Morrison,
who, operating in the country south-east of Peñaranda,
struck a much superior body of the enemy, and was
killed in the fight that ensued.   A sergeant, who succeeded
to the command, dispersed the Filipinos, and brought in
the body of the unfortunate officer.

Twelve days later we evened up some scores by killing the monster Tagunton, who had shown such heart-
less savagery in dealing with his own countrymen.   With
Major Brown, Lieutenants Mitchell and Sheldon, and Dr.
Chamberlain, I had gone out with twenty-five mounted
men of the Twenty-second Infantry to scout the country
along the Malimba River, some miles south of San Isidro.
About two o'clock in the afternoon we were riding quietly
through some high cogon grass, following a fairly good
trail, my orderly and I being some yards ahead of the remainder of the detachment, when the former called attention to a saddled pony on the opposite side of a ravine,
some thirty feet deep and fifty wide.   Brown, Mitchell,
and Sheldon joined us, and for a moment we sat on our
horses, peering through the grass to see if we could make
out anything.   But we were discovered by some one on
lookout, and a rifle cracked from the opposite side of the
ravine, being followed by quite a fusillade of shots.   We
instinctively drew our revolvers, and began shooting at
the several men who could now be seen.   Major Brown
was armed with a Colt automatic pistol, a weapon that

had just been invented, a few having been sent out to the Philippines for trial under service conditions, and he and my orderly, Private Ward, gave their polite attentions to a bulky individual who was making frantic efforts to mount the pony that had first attracted our attention. The frightened animal was jumping about, and the man was hardly in the saddle when he slipped out of it. Just before reaching this point Mitchell had noticed a practicable crossing of the ravine, and now rode down there with a few men and got onto the other side.

In the meantime a number of the detachment had dismounted and begun firing. It was soon over, as the only ambition of the enemy seemed to be to get away. We had no loss, and the enemy did not suffer much in numbers, as besides the big officer, wearing the shoulder-straps of a lieutenant-colonel, there was one other man dead, while two wounded were found on the ground. From descriptions that we had of him, we were quite sure that the big fellow was the noted ex-bandit who for some time had been an insurgent officer, but the proof was not positive. A good-natured dispute had arose as to who had killed him, it being between Major Brown and Ward, but Dr. Chamberlain, who was examining the body and had noticed a lump over the left breast, settled it with his pocket-knife, bringing to view the steel-jacketed bullet of the automatic. It was a good shot, through the heart at seventy-five yards, and Major Brown received many bouquets from all of those present. The pony that the Filipino officer had attempted to mount had escaped, and was tearing around. All efforts to catch him being futile, he was shot, in order that we might be able to examine the contents of the pair of saddle-bags that we could see flapping up and down, and in them were found dozens of letters addressed to Tagunton, and other papers that established beyond doubt the identity of the dead man. There was also a photograph of one of the most prominent of our fellow-countrymen, and written underneath it in Spanish the words, "The friend of the Filipinos." Of course, this picture had not been sent to Tagunton or any one else by the smiling gentleman whose wholesome visage was there portrayed, it having been clipped from a newspaper, but still it gave us a good laugh, and we needed laughs in those days, for they came mighty seldom. Don't think I am going to say whose photograph it was. It being now in the possession of Major Brown, it would obviously be discourteous to him for me to do so. He can tell if he wants to.

We were exultant over the result of this little scrimmage of a few minutes. Had we killed either of those good fighters and decent men, Lacuna or Pablo Tecson, it would not have been much of a satisfaction, and the only fly in our ointment was the fact that Tagunton had the privilege of dying a soldier's death, instead of stretching hemp, as he deserved. With the exception of the few moments' fusillade at the time of the capture of Aguinaldo, I have not heard the whistle of a hostile bullet since that day on the Malimba River, ten and a half years ago.

VII

THE CAPTURE OF EMILIO AGUINALDO

IT was the 8th day of February, 1901, and in the room that served as an office in the head-quarters building at San Isidro, I was going over the morning's work with the adjutant-general of the district, Captain E. V. Smith, when there arrived a telegram that for the moment disturbed our equanimity—a brief message that was to have no small part in the making of the history of the Philippine insurrection. It was signed by Lieutenant J. D. Taylor, Twenty-fourth Infantry, commanding the company of that regiment that constituted the garrison of the town of Pantabangan, about sixty miles to the north-east, at the foot of the western slope of the massive mountain range that separates the great central plain of Luzon from the Pacific coast of the island, and was to the effect that a small band of insurgent soldiers had voluntarily presented themselves to him, and that the man in command had stated that he was the bearer of despatches from Emilio Aguinaldo to certain subordinates in central and southern Luzon. The letters addressed to Baldomero Aguinaldo, Alejandrino, Urbano Lacuna, Pablo Tecson, Simon Tecson, Teodoro Sandico, and other insurgent leaders were in cipher and so could not be read, and evidently signed fictitiously, though in a handwriting that seemed to resemble that of Aguinaldo.

For more than a year the exact whereabouts of the elusive chieftain of the insurgent Filipinos had been a mystery. Rumor located him in all sorts of impossible places, but those best qualified to judge thought that he was somewhere in the great valley of the Cagayan, in the northern part of the island, or in one of the extensive mountain ranges on either side of it. Probably few if any of those in high command among the insurgent forces knew where he was, as he was taking every precaution against treachery, or the disclosure of his hiding-place by the capture of correspondence, having gone so far as to forbid that the name of his temporary capital should be put on paper in any of the letters sent out by himself or staff. A few trusted men saw that letters to him reached their destination.

The period of guerilla warfare that had succeeded the heavier fighting of the earlier days of the insurrection had now lasted more than a year and a half, and it must be confessed that from our stand-point the results had not been satisfactory. Scattered all over the Philippines we had more than seventy thousand troops, counting native auxiliaries, and these in detachments varying in size from a regiment to less than a company garrisoned every town of importance and many places that were mere villages. Through the country everywhere were the enemy's guerilla bands, made up not only of the survivors of the forces that had fought us earlier in the war, but of men who had been recruited or conscripted since. We had almost worn ourselves out chasing these marauders, and it was only occasionally by effecting a surprise or through some streak of good fortune that we were able to inflict any punishment on them, and such successes were only local and had little effect on general conditions. These guerillas persistently violated all the rules that are supposed to govern the conduct of civilized people engaged in war, while the fact that they passed rapidly from the status of peaceful non-combatants living in our garrisoned towns to that of men in arms against us made it especially difficult for us to deal with them. It was realized that Aguinaldo from his hiding-place, wherever it might be, exercised through their local chiefs a sort of general control over these guerilla bands, and as he was insistent that the Filipinos should not accept American rule, and as he was still recognized as the head and front of the insurrection, many of us had long felt that the thing could not end until he was either out of the way or a prisoner in our hands.

Therefore it was but natural that the telegram from Lieutenant Taylor should have created no little excitement, though as I now recollect the circumstances I do not believe that it occurred to any one of us that we would be able to do more than transmit the information for what it might be worth to higher authority, the plan which afterward worked so successfully being evolved later. It was directed that the leader of the surrendered band, with the correspondence that he had given up, be sent to San Isidro with all possible speed. With an escort of soldiers he arrived in less than two days, and proved to be a very intelligent Ilocano, giving his name as Cecilio Segismundo. After being well fed he told me the story of his recent adventures. During this recital he looked me squarely in the eyes, answered all questions frankly and apparently without reserve, and seemed to be telling the truth and keeping back nothing. This conversation was carried on in Spanish, which the man spoke quite well.

According to his story he was one of the men attached to Aguinaldo's head-quarters and had been with him many months, his principal duty being such errands as the one that he had now been sent out on, that is, carrying official mail between the insurgent chief and his subordinates. On the 14th of January, accompanied by a detachment of twelve armed men of Aguinaldo's escort, he had left with a package of letters to be delivered to Urbano Lacuna, the insurgent chief in Nueva Ecija province, who was to forward to their final destinations those that were not meant for him. After a terrible journey down the coast and through mountains he had in the vicinity of Baler encountered a small detachment of our troops out on a scouting expedition and had lost two of his men. It subsequently developed that this was a detachment of the company of the Twenty-second Infantry garrisoning the town of Baler, and was commanded by Lieutenant Parker Hitt. After this encounter Segismundo and his little band had made their way across the pass through the mountain range to the westward, and finally, twenty-six days after leaving Palanan, had reached the outskirts of the town of Pantabangan. Here, foot-weary and hungry, he communicated with the local *presidente*, or mayor, who had formerly acted in the same capacity for the insurgent government that he was now filling under American rule. Segismundo not unnaturally thought that this man, like practically all of the Filipinos who in those days took office under us, was a double dealer, but this one was true to his salt. He told Segismundo that he was in the service of the Americans, and strongly counselled him to present himself to the commander of the local garrison, give up the correspondence in his charge, and in fact attach himself to the chariot of progress and be an *Americanista*. I don't suppose the loyal *presidente* put it just that way, but that is what he meant. Segismundo was loath to take so radical a step, and with his band remained in hiding in the woods. It took much diplomacy on the part of Lieutenant Taylor, the *presidente* at first acting as go-between, to get him to surrender, but he finally did so. Lieutenant Taylor deserved the greatest credit for the excellent judgment he used in the whole matter. Of course, any attempt to capture the band would have spoiled everything, as the most of them would probably have escaped. Segismundo then went on to tell of conditions at Palanan. Aguinaldo, with several officers of his staff and an escort of about fifty uniformed and well-armed men, had been there for several months, and had been in constant communication with his various subordinates by means of messengers. The residents of the town and most of the soldiers of his escort were not aware of his identity. He passed as "Capitan Emilio," and by those who did not know him to be Aguinaldo was supposed to be merely a subordinate officer of the insurrection.

So far we had no evidence beyond the word of Segismundo that the man who had sent him on this long journey was really Aguinaldo, and it was not impossible that the man himself might be mistaken. Our attention was now given to the surrendered correspondence. All the letters were addressed to the persons for whom they were meant, but those not in cipher contained little of importance. What there was, however, tended to bear out Segismundo's story. All official communications were signed by what were evidently fictitious names. A number of personal letters from soldiers of Aguinaldo's escort to their friends and families helped us some, as two or three of them referred to "Capitan Emilio," and one or two to the "Dictator," and stated that the writers were still with him. Not one of these referred in any way to the town of Palanan, so that we were entirely dependent on Segismundo's word so far as that place was concerned.

The cipher letters completely balked us for many hours. They seemed to be made up of a jumble of letters of the alphabet, making words in no particular language. Captain Smith, Lazaro Segovia, the versatile and courageous Spaniard who for nearly a year had done such excellent secret-service work for me, and I took off our coats and even other things, in fact, stripped for action, and with pencils and pads of paper seated ourselves around a table and racked our brains, while Patterson, our negro soldier cook, from time to time brought in copious libations of hot and strong coffee in order that we might be able to keep awake, for daylight became darkness, and dawn was at hand before the peerless Segovia, whose knowledge of both Spanish and Tagalo now stood us in such good stead, found the key word of the cipher, which was in the latter language, having done it by ransacking his brain for every word in that Malay dialect that he had ever heard of. Among us, we then slowly unwound the mess, and mess it was when there are taken into consideration the difficulties of reducing a cipher and of rendering it through two languages to get the letters in which it was written into English. When it was over, tired and sleepy as we were, we had left enough energy to be wildly enthusiastic over the result, for it was realized that there had been laid bare the plans of the one man who, for what seemed to be a long time, had been the head and front of the insurrection against the authority of the United States. Before we had finished it was nearly noon, and despite Patterson's administrations of hot coffee we were nearly done for. We had been without sleep or food for twenty hours. Some of the cipher letters were signed "Colon Magdalo" and others "Pastor," this apparently depending on to whom they were addressed, but from their context these communications could come only from one who was recognized as the leader of the insurrection, as they gave positive orders to officers of the highest military rank. But besides that I had once heard that Aguinaldo had used "Colon Magdalo" as a *nom de plume*. The body of all of these letters had evidently been written by a secretary, but the handwriting of the signatures very much resembled several of Aguinaldo's that I had seen in captured correspondence.

Not one of the communications, either official or personal, intimated the name of the obscure town in which Aguinaldo had taken his refuge. Two, those to Lacuna and Baldomero Aguinaldo, stated that the trusted messenger knew the name of the town where he had his head-quarters. The most important letter, and the one that was the final undoing of its writer, was to his cousin, Baldomero Aguinaldo, then in command of the insurgent bands operating in Cavite province just south of Manila.

This directed the person to whom it was addressed to proceed at once to the "Centre of Luzon," and, using this communication as authority, to supersede in command José Alejandrino, who evidently was not giving satisfaction to his chieftain. As soon as he had established himself in command, Baldomero was to direct his subordinates, that is, Lacuna, Mascardo, Simon, and Pablo Tecson, and possibly one or two others, to send him detachments of men until the aggregate should reach about four hundred.

These were to be made up of picked troops, and might be sent by whatever routes their respective commanders thought best. A letter to Lacuna contained nothing of importance, but was of interest for the reason that for more than a year the troops under my command had been trying to break up the guerilla bands that recognized him as chief.

After translating the letters we went to bed, but I had great difficulty in sleeping, as plans began to evolve themselves. About four o'clock I got up and sent for Segismundo. I thought the best way was to go at him boldly, now that he had apparently cast his lot with us, and told him that I was going to capture his chief and expected him to help in the operation. He had already told me that the trail leading eastward from the valley of the Cagayan was so carefully watched by outposts that any advance from that direction would be discovered days before it could possibly reach Palanan. Some months before a company of our troops had, after a most trying march, entered Palanan from that direction, but Aguinaldo, his staff and escort, had leisurely retired to the mountains in the vicinity, taking with them all their archives and records, and compelling all the inhabitants to accompany them. As we learned afterward, this was a company of the Sixteenth Infantry, commanded by Captain Cochran. According to Segismundo, the trail along the coast to the south was so carefully watched by the Negritos and Ilongotes, primitive savages, that the same conditions existed. In reply to a question as to whether an expedition from the sea, landing at night on the beach about seven miles from Palanan, would have any chance of success, he stated that the presence of any vessel off the coast would to a certainty be reported, and that, even if such an expedition succeeded in landing, it would be discovered before reaching Palanan. The prospects did not seem any too bright, and I went to bed to sleep it over. In the meantime I had taken into my confidence Captain Smith, Lieutenant Mitchell, my aide, and Segovia, and had discussed the matter with them. By morning I had thought out the general features of the plan which was eventually to succeed, and on asking Segismundo whether it was in his opinion practicable, he replied in the affirmative. There were now all sorts of details to work out, and in these matters I had much assistance from those who had been taken into my confidence. We knew exactly where Aguinaldo was, at the obscure and isolated village of Palanan, a few miles from the east coast of Luzon and very near the north end of the island. We knew that he would be expecting reinforcements from the guerilla bands in central Luzon, he having sent orders to that effect. It was settled beyond the possibility of a doubt that no force the nature of which was known could get even within several days' march of him. So the only recourse was to work a stratagem, that is, to get to him under false colors. It would be so impossible to disguise our own troops that they were not even considered, and dependence would have to be placed on the Macabebes, those fine little fighters, taking their name from their home town, who had always been loyal to Spain and who had now transferred that loyalty to the United States. As it would be absolutely essential to have along some American officers to direct matters and deal with such emergencies as might arise, they were to accompany the expedition as supposed prisoners who had been captured on the march, and were not to throw off that disguise until there was no longer necessity for concealment.

This plan was briefly outlined in writing and sent to the department commander, General Wheaton, who was stationed in Manila. This officer ordered me to Manila for immediate consultation, and approved the project, as also did the division commander, General MacArthur. The latter was to arrange with Admiral Remey, commanding the Asiatic Station, for a small naval vessel to transport the expedition to the east coast of Luzon. After a few days in Manila I returned to San Isidro to complete the plans.

As mentioned in the last chapter, when, during the preceding October, with a detachment of scouts and Troop A of the Fourth Cavalry, I had "jumped" Lacuna's camp, though that individual escaped we had found ourselves in possession of all his personal effects, besides much correspondence, records, and his official stationery. This last had been kept and now proved to be of the utmost value.

In order to pave the way for the bogus reinforcements, which were supposed to be those from Lacuna's command, it was considered essential to have them preceded by letters from that individual. In fact, had this not been done the expedition would without a particle of doubt have met a disastrous end. Aguinaldo himself afterward told me that it was the supposed letters from Lacuna that threw him entirely off his guard and caused him to welcome the supposed reinforcements. The stationery captured in Lacuna's camp had at the top of each sheet the words *Brigada Lacuna*—in English, Lacuna's Brigade—they having been put on with a rubber stamp. It would be necessary, if we were going to utilize supposed letters from Lacuna, to imitate his signature, which was without doubt known to Aguinaldo. In captured correspondence we found several examples to serve as models, and had at hand the man to do the work. Nearly a year before an insurgent officer by the name of Roman Roque had voluntarily presented himself to me, and since then had been employed at district head-quarters as interpreter and clerk.

He was an expert penman, and I set him to work practising on Lacuna's signature. I, of course, did not inform him as to the object of this work. The faithful Roque kept at it with such success that in a few days his work could not be distinguished from the original. After he had reached this degree of perfection, one of the bogus signatures was placed at the foot of each of two of the sheets of the stamped "*Brigada Lacuna*" writing-paper. The bodies of the two letters were not to be filled in until we were at sea.

It was now necessary to make up the personnel of the expedition. Captain Smith was exceedingly anxious to be taken along, but the nature of his duties was such that he could not be spared from San Isidro. I selected as one of the officers Captain Harry W. Newton, of the Thirty-fourth United States Volunteer Infantry, now a captain in the Coast Artillery Corps. Captain Newton had had some experience at sea, and, besides, while stationed at Baler about a year previously, had made a boat expedition from there to Casiguran, a town that we would necessarily have something to do with. Of course, I took along my efficient aide, Lieutenant Mitchell. Segovia and Segismundo would be very necessary, and in fact proved invaluable. But it would be necessary to have some Tagalos, as Lacuna's force, from which this detachment was supposed to come, was made up entirely of men of that race. The selection of these men was a very delicate matter, as they would have it in their power to ruin us by disclosing our real character. As will be seen, they were absolutely faithful. But I would never again take such a risk, as I believe that we could have succeeded without them. None of them was informed as to what we were going to do, they merely being told that I wanted them to accompany me on an expedition. One of the men was Hilario Tal Placido, who was to be the supposed chief of the expedition, he being personally known to Aguinaldo. He had been badly wounded in a fight with the Twentieth Kansas at Caloocan in 1899, had been captured with his chief, General Panteleon Garcia, in the town of Jaen, by Captain Smith, in May, 1900, and had been released after taking the oath of allegiance. He had on several occasions shown that he was friendly to the Americans by giving me information of value. The other two Tagalos were young men, Dionisio Bató and Gregorio Cadhit, both former insurgent officers. The former had been captured and the latter had surrendered, both having voluntarily taken the oath of allegiance. All of us went to Manila ready to sail.

General Wheaton had selected as the main part of the expedition Company D of the First Battalion of Macabebe Scouts. This organization contained about one hundred men and had seen much service in the field. The two officers on duty with it were Captain R. T. Hazzard, of the Eleventh United States Volunteer Cavalry, and his brother Lieutenant O. P. M. Hazzard, of the same regiment, the latter now an officer of the regular army. A weeding out of the Macabebe company so that we would have in it only men who could speak Tagalo, and so pass themselves off as belonging to that race, and the leaving behind a few who it was thought might not be able to make the long march anticipated, brought the number actually embarked down to eighty-one. Of course, it was absolutely essential for them to discard everything in the way of their equipment as American soldiers, or any attempt to pass themselves off as insurgent troops would have been worse than futile. So before sailing we obtained a sufficent supply of the clothing of the country, the most of it being second-hand material, as it would not do for the men to look neat. Even if it had been thought advisable to do so, it was considered unnecessary to clothe the Macabebes in insurgent uniforms, as the time when the great body of insurgent troops wore uniforms had long gone by. There was also obtained from the Manila arsenal a sufficient number of Mauser and Remington rifles with the necessary quantity of cartridges, all of this being material that had been captured in the field. An insurgent company armed exclusively with Krags would indeed have been a most unusual sight. Admiral Remey had designated the gunboat *Vicksburg*, Commander E. B. Barry commanding, to carry the expedition, the object of which even he did not know. The clothing and arms that would enable the Macabebes to pass off as insurgent troops were quietly placed on board at night. The greatest secrecy had been maintained, as, outside of Generals MacArthur and Wheaton, two or three officers of the district staff left behind at San Isidro, the officers who were to go on the expedition, Segovia and Segismundo, not a single man had been informed. I felt that it was incumbent on me to tell all to Mrs. Funston, who had accompanied me from San

Isidro, and all through the long three weeks that we were absent from Manila the poor woman had to keep her council. During this time she was the guest of our old friends, Captain and Mrs. George P. Ahern.

At last everything was ready. No precaution had been omitted, and nothing was forgotten. On many occasions while in Manila I had been in consultation with Generals MacArthur and Wheaton, and when I made my last call on the former, just before sailing, he said: "Funston, this is a desperate undertaking. I fear that I shall never see you again." At the same interview he told me that some days before he had received from the War Department by cable an order to return me to the United States for muster-out of the service, but had cabled for and received permission to retain me for a short time for some special duty. Of course, as a volunteer officer, I was subject to muster-out any at time, but this, coming at the time that it did, filled my heart with bitterness, and nothing but a feeling of the loyalty that I owed to my division and department commanders made me willing to go on with the apparently thankless and all but hopeless task.

On the night of March 6 the *Vicksburg* slipped out of Manila Bay, and steered south in order to pass through the straits of San Bernardino.

There was no longer any occasion for secrecy and Commander Barry and the other officers of the vessel soon knew the object of the expedition that they were transporting. The next morning, having Segovia to assist me in order that everything would be well understood, I sent for Tal Placido, Bató, and Cadhit, the three ex-insurgent officers with us, and told them that we were going after their old chieftain, and that they would be expected to play their part, as they had all of them without compulsion taken the oath of allegiance to the United States. If they were faithful they would be well rewarded, if not, there would be but one penalty and that would be inflicted, if it was the last thing done. They seemed thunderstruck but soon regained their composure, promised to do their part, and did it. They even showed no little interest and enthusiasm as we outlined to them the complicated plan which it was hoped might bring success. As they were to have important parts to play, it was necessary to confide in them fully and give them complete instructions as to what they were to do. Next came the Macabebes. No one who ever served with them would doubt their loyalty, even to the last extremity, but many of them were men of not a great deal of intelligence, and so they had to be instructed very carefully and thoroughly. This work was done mostly by Captain Hazzard, Lieutenant Hazzard, and Segovia. The little "Macs," as we called them, were quite enthusiastic over the whole proposition. Their first sergeant was Pedro Bustos, a little shrivelled old fellow who had spent his life since boyhood in the native regiments of the Spanish army, and had been decorated for gallantry in the wars with the Moros of Mindanao. He had not an atom of fear in his whole system, and when I asked him if they would stand by us until the end, he replied: "I cannot speak for the others, but I am a soldier of the United States." It was not necessary to make any further inquiries from him. Day after day the instruction of the Tagalos and the Macabebes went on, and they were often tested to see how well they knew their parts. According to the elaborate yarn that they had been instructed in, they constituted one of the companies of Lacuna's force operating against the Americans in the province of Nueva Ecija. Some time in February they had started on the march to the northward. In the course of this they had crossed the mountains between Pantabangan and Baler, and on this part of their journey had encountered a party of ten American soldiers making maps of the country. They had succeeded in surprising these men, and after a brief fight had killed two and wounded three, all of whom they had left on the ground. The remaining five had surrendered, and they had brought them along as prisoners, as they could not detach men to take them back. They were drilled over and over again in the story of this fight and march until all of them seemed to know it by heart. The Macabebes were further instructed that they must at once begin to communicate with each other in the Tagalo dialect, and not use their own under any circumstances until the job was finished. This would, of course, be absolutely necessary after we had landed and got into touch with people who were still insurgents, as they would know mighty well that there were no Macabebes on their side of the war. In the meantime every vestige of their equipment as American soldiers was taken from them and stored on the vessel, and they were rigged out in the lot of nondescript clothing obtained in Manila, and armed with the job lot of Mausers and Remingtons from the Manila arsenal. There were,

however, ten Krag carbines, supposed to have been captured from the unfortunate mapmakers. In their new rig
the Macabebes did not know whether to feel sheepish or
to take a humorous view of the situation. When he saw
them Hilario Tal Placido's fat sides shook with laughter,
and he assured me that they would pass as real insurgents.

One of the things that Segismundo had impressed on
me was that if any steamer approached the east coast of
Luzon, even as far south of Palanan as a hundred miles,
Aguinaldo would soon be informed of the fact by runners,
and would be on the lookout. For this reason it was determined to call at some port on the east coast of Luzon
and obtain several large *bancas*, native sailing boats. We
were to be loaded into these some thirty miles at sea and
then cast adrift, the *Vicksburg* immediately getting out of
the way, so that her smoke could not be seen from shore.
We were to run in to the coast at night, land through the
surf as best we could, and then begin the march northward. Even if the *bancas* should be seen they would not
cause alarm. Accordingly, in a couple of days the *Vicksburg* called at the town of Antimonan, on the east coast of
the province of Tayabas, and I sent Lieutenant Mitchell
ashore with the necessary funds, but no *bancas* were to be
had except a few that were too small for our purpose. So
we sailed for the island of Polillo, and there were more
successful, obtaining three that among them were large
enough to hold all of us, each of them having two masts
with the necessary sails. These boats were taken in tow
of the *Vicksburg*, and on the 12th of March, six days
after leaving Manila, we headed to the north-west, bound

for the mouth of Casiguran Bay. Two Macabebes were placed on each boat to steer them and to clear the towing lines in case they should become fouled. They had provisions and water for two days. The wind had been rising and soon began to blow a gale. The sea ran very high; the first of the two *bancas* was swamped, and went down, the two men on it crawling along the rope to the second. By four in the afternoon the sea had increased to such an extent that it was necessary to lower the ship's boats and rescue the six men, who were hanging on to the two remaining *bancas*. The *Vicksburg* was rolling and pitching fearfully, and it looked to the most of us like a hopeless job. But the gallant men of the navy went at it in fine style, and in two hours of gruelling and dangerous work had accomplished their task. Shortly after the rescue the last of the *bancas* went down, and the tow-ropes were cut. So that was one part of the game that did not work. It was now necessary for us to change our plans to the extent of landing in the ship's boats at night, trusting that before daylight the vessel would be far enough away from shore to prevent her being seen.

The time had now come when it was necessary to write the two bogus letters from Lacuna to Aguinaldo, these to be on the sheets of paper that bore at their head the stamp of the former and his imitated signature at the foot. I made out a rough draft of what I wanted said, but left the actual composition and writing to Segovia, as his knowledge of Spanish was much more comprehensive than my own. One of them was dated February 24, 1901, at Buloc, a locality in the mountains of eastern Nueva

Ecija, and acknowledged receipt of Aguinaldo's two letters of January 13 and 14, and at the same time thanked
him for his confirmation of his, Lacuna's, appointment as
brigadier-general, made some time previously by Alejandrino. There was also some news as to how the campaign was progressing, and some "airy persiflage" about
the things the writer was doing to the hated invader. The
second letter, dated February 28, stated that the writer had
received orders from Baldomero Aguinaldo, who had just
assumed command of the "Centre of Luzon," to send one
of his best companies to report to the Dictator. It should
be noticed that the first of these letters referred to the
two communications received from Aguinaldo, giving their
dates as well as making reference to their contents. The
second was in the line of what Aguinaldo would expect
as the natural result of his letter to his cousin, Baldomero
Aguinaldo. This latter letter said that the force was in
command of Hilario Tal Placido, whom the Honorable
Dictator doubtless recollected as one of his former officers.
He had been some time previously compelled to take the
oath of allegiance to the Americans, but on orders from
Lacuna had returned to active service. (This was put in
for fear that Aguinaldo might have heard that Tal Placido had taken the oath.) According to the same letter,
the second in command was the gallant Spaniard, Lazaro
Segovia, who had shown himself so much addicted to our
cause. (Segovia chuckled as he wrote this.) The other
two were Dionisio Bató and Gregorio Cadhit. And then
there was some mere rubbish, just to fill in space down
to the bogus signature. These letters were held until

the opportunity should come to send them in advance of us.

Fortunately for us, the weather was thick and squally, and at one o'clock on the morning of the 14th, the *Vicksburg* having very carefully approached the coast, with all her lights screened, we were landed in the ship's boats. We were inside the entrance to Casiguran Bay, and so fairly well protected, with the consequence that we had no surf work. The darkness was intense, however, and it was raining, so that we did not feel particularly comfortable or cheerful. It would have been impossible to carry out the plan of deception if we had landed with a supply of the food ordinarily used by American soldiers, so that we brought ashore one day's ration of rice. All of us Americans were dressed as private soldiers of our army, that is, in campaign hats, blue shirts, khaki breeches, and leggings. As I looked our crowd over the next morning I thought that we were a pretty scrubby-looking lot of privates. There is a lot in clothes, after all. In going ashore one of the Macabebes accidentally cut himself so badly with his bolo that we had to send him back to the ship, and another got "cold feet," and hid himself in the hammock nettings. It is a safe guess that life was a burden to him after his exultant comrades returned to their native village. So it happened that eighty-nine of us, counting Filipinos and white men, landed on that dreary coast. I do not recall that we had any particular emotions or sensations, as we were too busy trying to make ourselves comfortable. All realized the hazardous nature of the undertaking, and without any agreement having been entered into on the subject, it was thoroughly understood that we would never be taken alive. Loyalty to our Macabebe comrades, who could not expect quarter, marked but one course for any men who made even a pretence at being soldiers.

The several hours until dawn were passed in simply sitting about and trying to keep out of the rain as much as we could. With the first daylight we made a short march in order to find fresh water. Here, with no little difficulty, fires were built, and some rice was boiled in vessels that we had brought along for the purpose. At seven o'clock we began the march. For a while it was not half bad, despite the fact that we had not had a wink of sleep during the night. Our progress was slow owing to the nature of the beach, for it should be understood that we were following the west side of Casiguran Bay, and there were no trails through the woods. We had landed at about the same point that a force coming across-country from Nueva Ecija would have struck the beach, and this was a part of the game.

Everything was now in our favor, as we felt positive that our landing had not been discovered. I very much doubt whether a straight line drawn from the point of our landing to the town of Casiguran would show the distance to be greater than ten miles; but we could pay no attention to straight lines, as some of them would lead through water up to our necks or over considerable ridges. In other words, we had to follow the sinuosities of the coast. We waded about a dozen streams, none of them over hip deep, but the greatest nuisance was the fact that during the greater part of the march it was high tide, which, owing to the fact that the mangrove bushes came down to the water's edge in dense masses, compelled us to wade pretty well out in the bay. Our salt-water wading during the day aggregated certainly five miles, and naturally added greatly to our fatigue and discomfort. About noon we discovered a small *banca*, capable of holding half a dozen men, in the mouth of a small creek. It was very desirable to send word of our coming to Casiguran, not only that the inhabitants of the village might not be alarmed by the approach of an armed force, but that supplies might be collected for us. It must be remembered that this was a town that recognized no authority except that of the insurgent government, and no Americans had ever been in it except the few who had been with Captain Newton on his coast expedition from Baler in a futile attempt to rescue a Spanish friar, held prisoner by the insurgent officials. As soon as we discovered the *banca* we concocted another letter. This was addressed to the *presidente* of Casiguran, and was written by Segovia. This communication stated that the writer was in command of a body of insurgent troops belonging to the command of Lacuna and on their way north to report to the "Dictator." It was requested that the recipient would immediately send a guide to meet the column, and have all arrangements made for the housing and provisioning of the force. After the letter had been got up I invited my corpulent friend Hilario to sign it. This he did without batting an eyelash. I doubt if he ever read it. We sent this missive by Segismundo, he being accompanied by

Gregorio Cadhit and two armed Macabebes. The last-named men had their instructions as to what they were to do in case of treachery. But Segismundo and Cadhit seemed to enter into the spirit of the thing, and took a lot of satisfaction out of fooling their former compatriots. The four men sailed straight across the head of the bay, delivered the letter to the *vice-presidente*, the *presidente* being absent, and then became the guests of the village. Really, there were some ridiculous features about the whole business. In the meantime the little column had resumed its march. At four o'clock the guide sent out by the *vice-presidente* of Casiguran met us, and we knew that so far all was well, or he would not be "among those present." We had to make a considerable détour around the head of the bay, and then entered a forest along a fairly good trail. Naturally, there was much excitement in the little town of Casiguran, and crowds of people came to meet us. Of course, they thought that they were greeting some of their own victorious soldiers bringing in prisoners that they had captured. The village band was pressed into service, and we entered the town in great style. We had had a hard time in impressing on the Macabebes the fact that as soon as we came in contact with insurgents they must treat us as real prisoners. This was a terribly hard thing for these men to do, as from their long service in the Spanish army, as well as the few years they had spent in our service, they regarded a commissioned officer as a being almost sacred. By considerable cussing on the part of the officers of the company as well as by Segovia it was finally drilled into them that they were to obey orders regardless of their personal feelings. Among those who met us as we entered the town was the badly fooled *vice-presidente*. He was a man of good appearance and address, and seemed somewhat solicitous regarding the welfare and comfort of the supposed American prisoners. I am glad to be able to state that the general attitude of the people of the town toward us was not hostile. Of course, we were a great show, being the first Americans they had ever seen, for all of them had fled when Newton's boat expedition reached the town during the previous year. They crowded around us, and there were some black looks, and some remarks not of a complimentary nature, but in general there was nothing in their conduct to criticise. Finally, we entered the plaza, the local band exuding some lively, if not very inspiring, music. The whole situation was so ludicrous that it was with difficulty we could keep from laughing, despite the peril of our position. The *vice-presidente* had directed that a number of buildings be vacated in order that the recently arrived patriots and their prisoners might be properly sheltered. I had impressed it on Segovia that it would be necessary for him and me to be so situated that we could communicate without difficulty, and he accordingly informed the *vice-presidente* that, as he was personally responsible for the safe-keeping of the prisoners, he wished to be near them. This was arranged without difficulty. We were confined in a room in the municipal building, our guards being our own Macabebes, while Segovia, Segismundo, and the Tagalo officers were accommodated in a room across the hallway. In the meantime, Segovia and Tal Placido had been talking with the *vice-presidente*. This official informed them that the march to Palanan would have to be made under great difficulties unless we could wait several days until he could collect a sufficient quantity of cracked corn to furnish us with food for the journey. We now learned to our surprise that rice is not raised to any extent in the vicinity of Palanan, but that the people subsisted almost entirely on cracked corn, fresh fish, and sweet-potatoes. For reasons that will occur to any person of reasonable intelligence, the last two named were out of the question for a long journey. The *vice-presidente* thought that in four or five days he might be able to collect enough corn to see us through the nearly a hundred miles of uninhabited wilderness that still lay between us and our goal. But it had already been arranged with Commander Barry of the *Vicksburg* that he was to reach Palanan Bay on the 25th and, if he did not find us awaiting him on the beach, land a force and march to the town to ascertain if possible what had become of us.

We Americans were lying on the hard floor, talking in low tones as to the possible outcome of the adventure that we were now hopelessly committed to, when Segovia sneaked in, lay down by my side, and, speaking Spanish in whispers, made me acquainted with the situation. There was one comforting thing, and that was that our disguise was evidently perfect, as nobody seemed to suspect our real character. As to the question of food, we discussed the matter among ourselves, and it was unanimously agreed to push on after a stay of two days, trusting that our luck would not desert us.

In the meantime the Macabebes were being entertained by the people of the town. It can scarcely be imagined what uneasiness we felt lest one of them should have his tongue loosened by some of the *bino* that was being passed around, and ruin everything. But they simply filled up the yokels of Casiguran with wonderful yarns of their service under Lacuna in far-away Nueva Ecija, with the story of their great march across the mountains, the capture of the American soldiers now in their hands, and, in fact, most anything that would make the people proud to associate with them. The next day, the 15th, was spent in our prison, resting as well as the hard boards that we were lying on would permit. One most disquieting piece of news, fortunately false, that we received here was to the effect that the well-known insurgent general, Tinio, had joined Aguinaldo with four hundred well-armed men. The story did not seem at all improbable, and we did not know that there was nothing to it until we were within eight miles of our goal. The Macabebes, who also heard the story from their Casiguran friends, who thought they were telling them something pleasant, were badly worried, as it looked as if we would be outnumbered five to one; but we succeeded in convincing them that by means of a surprise we could win. Everybody in Casiguran and the surrounding country came to see us, among them being some of the Ilongotes, the most treacherous and cruel of all the head-hunting savages of Luzon. The Macabebes, supposed to be rigidly guarding us, laid it on pretty thick in telling how they had captured us. Once I saw a sergeant, whose eye I had caught, start to laugh, but he got a look and a shake of the head that brought him to his senses. It would be essential, in order that Aguinaldo and those with him might not be alarmed at the approach to Palanan of an armed body, to send word to him in advance. So Segovia and I concocted another letter, supposed to come from Tal Placido, stating that the writer, in accordance with orders from his chief, Lacuna, was on his way to join him with a company of troops under the command of Captain Lazaro Segovia; in crossing the mountains he had surprised a small detachment of American soldiers, had killed two, wounded three, and was bringing five prisoners, as he could not detach men to send them back. As the main body of the two bogus letters from Lacuna were in the handwriting of Segovia, we had Tal Placido copy as well as sign this missive. In the meantime, the *vice-presidente* obtained two of his townsmen and an Ilongote to carry this letter and the two supposed ones from Lacuna. They started on the morning of the 16th and beat us to Palanan by two days. The second day of our captivity passed without especial incident. The guileless *vice-presidente* had all of this time been working like a beaver to hustle enough cracked corn to at least start us on our journey, and succeeded in obtaining about four hundred pounds, which might be considered a rather short four days' ration for our force. There was also a small quantity of dried carabao meat and half a dozen live chickens. Of course, these last would have to be eaten very soon. Early on the morning of the 17th, a gloomy and rainy day, we started on the last and longest leg of our fateful journey. We were told that the march was usually made in a week, and that but one white man, a Spanish friar, a generation before, had accomplished it. In order to carry our food supplies and cooking-pots, twelve men of the town were obtained, with an Ilongote to act as guide. The *vice-presidente* and a number of the principal men of the town accompanied us for a couple of miles, finally saying *adios* and *buen viaje* to all, including the "prisoners." I wonder what this simple and really good-hearted fellow thought when he found how he had been tricked. Of the numerous ones that we made fools of, he was the only one that I ever had the slightest qualms about. I hope he is gifted with a sense of humor. The first half-day lay along a muddy trail through the woods to the sea-beach. Here the rascally Ilongote deserted us, but one of the Casiguran men said he felt confident he could act as guide. The presence of these men made it necessary for us to keep up the deception on the march and in camp, as the slightest word might send one of them scurrying ahead to Palanan, and the poor Macabebes were under the necessity of continuing to converse in the Tagalo dialect.

From here our course generally followed the beach, though we were occasionally compelled to make détours over mountains because of cliffs coming down to the sea. The most of the beach was soft and deep sand, though we had two days over bowlders of every size from a watermelon to a freight car. I do not believe it necessary to go too much into the details of that horrible march, as it is not pleasant reading. The rain never ceased pouring, and from the morning we left Casiguran we were drenched to the skin for a week. We waded more than sixty streams, some of them mere brooks, but others so deep and swift that we had to put our hands on each other's shoulders and go in up to our armpits. The food, soaked through and through, became a soggy and fermenting mass. The usual programme was to start at daybreak and march until ten o'clock, then stop for breakfast, resuming the march about one o'clock, and keep it up until darkness, when we would have the second and last meal of the day, exactly a duplicate of the first. From the start we went on half rations, and in a few days were ravenous with hunger. Of sleep we could get very little, as our bed was the bare ground, and we were exposed without shelter to the never-ending torrents of rain. Of course, the building and maintaining of fires for cooking was a matter that taxed to the utmost the ingenuity of our Macabebes, used as they are to taking care of themselves under all sorts of conditions. To eke out our food supply, a few small fish were caught in their hands by the Macabebes, and they scraped limpets from the rocks and gathered snails. All of these things, however, could not help out much with the now one hundred and one of us including the Casiguran men. The snails, limpets, and small fish were stewed up with the corn, and made a revolting mess. One funny thing happened, and gave us all a much-needed laugh. It was a pitch-dark night and the Macabebes had just set before us on this occasion a stew-pot containing this delectable mixture. Mitchell, who was ravenously hungry, drew a fish about three inches long, and had downed it before he realized it had not been dressed. Then and there his gorge rose and he became violently "sea-sick." We laughed at him so much that his temper rose perceptibly. On the night of the fifth day out of Casiguran we lay down supperless. Segovia had developed a terrible abscess in one of his feet, but the plucky Spaniard never faltered. (When we finally got on board the *Vicksburg*, the surgeon opened up his foot and gave him relief.) All day of the 22d we stumbled along in a half-dazed condition, marching the entire day without food. Our men were scattered for a mile along the beach, some of them so weak that they reeled as they walked. It was plain that the end was at hand, but we were approaching our destination. It seemed impossible that the madcap enterprise could succeed, and I began to have regrets that I had led all these men to such a finish, for it must be remembered that we still expected to have to fight Tinio with his four hundred men, and it did not now seem that there was any fight left in the outfit. Every mile during this afternoon we expected the crackle of rifle fire from some cliff.

About five o'clock we saw a man ahead of us along the beach, evidently watching us. The crisis was at hand, and Segovia went to meet him, while we made some attempt to close up the column. We breathlessly watched Segovia and the man while they were talking, and saw the latter hand the former a letter. Segovia came limping back down the column, and as he passed us Americans said in Spanish, "It is all right. We have them." What a load it lifted off our minds! We were now within ten miles of our quarry. The letter, which

Segovia opened and read at once and then passed to me, was from Simon Villa, Aguinaldo's chief of staff, and was addressed to "Lieutenant-Colonel Hilario Tal Placido." Although it showed that our ruse was working and that our real identity was not even suspected, there was in it one thing that disturbed us greatly, this being an order that the five prisoners would not be brought into Palanan, as they might find out that the "Dictator" was there, but would be left under a guard of ten men at the place known as Dinundungan. Just think of living in a place with such a name as that! We had in some way to circumvent this plan, and succeeded, though it brought us nearer to disaster than any other thing connected with the expedition. We marched two miles farther up the beach and reached Dinundungan, which was not a town but merely the name of a locality, it being the point where a trail from Palanan, eight miles distant, reaches the beach. Here we found an old Tagalo in charge of a few Negritos just completing a couple of small grass-roofed open sheds, one of which was for the prisoners and the other for their guard. It was already dark, and again we lay down supperless to bed, if one could call the water-soaked ground by such a name. In whispers we discussed the situation, and before going to sleep had worked out our little scheme. But we had to have food, or the march of eight miles would be out of the question, so Hilario wrote a note to Villa reporting his arrival at Dinundungan, and stated that in the morning he would resume the march to Palanan, but that food was necessary, as his men were so weak from hunger that they could go no farther. The orders directing that the prisoners be left where he then was had been received, and would be complied with. This letter was sent to Palanan by one of the Negritos, and by daylight a sufficient quantity of cracked corn to give us all a fairly satisfactory meal had arrived. This incident was the basis of the charge afterward made and harped upon by certain people in the United States, that being in a starving condition we had begged Aguinaldo for food, and then violated his hospitality by using the strength thus given us to capture him. We had simply fooled him into supplying us, as he thought he was rationing his own troops. Had we, disclosing our identity, asked for quarter, and that food be furnished us, and had then turned on him, the case would have been entirely different. I would be very much interested in seeing the results of a surgical operation performed on the skull of a man who cannot readily see the radical difference between the two propositions. I do not think that even "sweetbreads" would be found.

At last, morning came on the great day, nine days after we had landed from the *Vicksburg*, and we set to work to pull the wool over the eyes of the old Tagalo who had constructed the sheds, and who knew that the prisoners were to be left with him. It was taken for granted that if we boldly disobeyed the instructions he would light out to Palanan with the news. An attempt to seize him was considered too risky, as some of the Negritos might get away and give the alarm. So we again had recourse to the pen, which certainly is sometimes mightier than the sword. We picked out one of the most intelligent of the Macabebe corporals as the man who was to be left in charge of us with a guard of nine men, and gave him his instructions. A letter to him from Segovia was then prepared informing him that a messenger from Palanan had been met on the trail with a letter from the chief of staff revoking previous instructions relative to the prisoners, and directing that he immediately follow with them. At eight o'clock the main column left on the trail to Palanan, leaving us with our guard. In about an hour two of the Macabebes came running down the trail and very ostentatiously handed to the corporal a note, which he showed the old Tagalo, who was able to read it, it being in his dialect. The old fellow merely remarked that he did not see why they had put him to so much trouble if they did not intend to use the shelters. This disposed of him, and with our guard we set out along the trail, the two Macabebes who had brought the bogus letter accompanying us.

Fortunately, we now had with us only our own people, and were relieved from the trying necessity of watching every action for fear it would arouse suspicion in the minds of the Casiguran men, who were with the main body. The trail led in a north-westerly direction and was very muddy, as the sunlight seldom reached the ground in those dense and gloomy woods. Despite our breakfast, we were very weak, and were six hours in covering the eight miles. Of the Americans, Mitchell and I were in the worst shape, the Hazzards and Newton standing it better. I had to lie down flat on the ground every few hundred yards to get a rest of a moment or two. We crossed and recrossed many times by wading a small branch of the Palanan River. About half-way to the town we were disturbed by meeting a Macabebe sergeant and one of the privates coming back along the trail as rapidly as they could. The two men were out of breath, and simply motioned frantically to us to get off the trail and hide in the woods. This we did, and they joined us. The sergeant quickly explained that some real insurgent soldiers were on the way to Dinundungan to take charge of us, in order that all the men of our party might be able to come to Palanan. Soon we heard the men come splashing along laughing and talking. They passed within thirty feet of us, as we lay close to the ground, almost fearing to breathe. If they had met us in the trail or discovered us in our hiding-place it would have all been off then and there, as they would have insisted on taking charge of us and conducting us back to Dinundungan. A fight would have been the result; the firing would have been heard in Palanan, and the least that could happen was that the quarry would escape. For we now knew, having been so informed by the old Tagalo at Dinundungan, that the story of Tinio having reached Palanan with four hundred men was a myth, the only troops there being about fifty men of Aguinaldo's escort. Anyhow, this was the closest call the expedition had, and it owed its salvation to the quick-witted Segovia. The main body that he was with had met the detachment in the trail, and upon inquiry had learned from the non-commissioned officer in charge his instructions. Detaining the man in conversation for a moment, he managed to step aside and whisper to one of the sergeants to hurry back down the trail and warn us.

We resumed our march, having had a fine scare. It was not desirable to catch up with the main body, as we correctly presumed that some officers might come out from Palanan to meet it, and see that the orders regarding the prisoners were not being carried out, so that we kept some distance behind it until we realized that we were approaching the town, and then hurried on as much as possible.

The main interest now centres in the adventures of the main column, the one by which the actual capture was made. About a mile outside the town it was met by a couple of insurgent officers, who escorted them the remainder of the distance. About three o'clock they approached the Palanan River, here about a hundred yards wide and quite deep, and saw the town on the other side. The only way to cross this stream was by means of a rather good-sized *banca*. Hilario and Segovia crossed with the first load, leaving instructions for the men to follow as rapidly as they could, form on the oposite bank, and then march up to Aguinaldo's house, where they would find him. The boat was to be sent back to await our arrival. Segovia and Hilario now had a most trying half-hour. They called on Aguinaldo at his head-quarters, and found him surrounded by seven insurgent officers, all of them armed with revolvers. Outside, the fifty men of the escort, neatly uniformed and armed with Mausers, were drawn up to do the honors for the reinforcements that had made such a wonderful march to join them. Segovia and Hilario entertained those present with stories of the march from Lacuna's head-quarters, and were warmly congratulated on having made it successfully. Segovia took his position where he could look out of one of the open windows and see when the time had arrived. Finally, the Macabebes under Dionisio Bató and Gregorio Cadhit marched up, Segovia stepped to the head of the stairway outside the house, for they were in the second story, and signalled to Gregorio, who called out, "Now is the time, Macabebes. Give it to them." The poor little "Macs" were in such a nervous state from their excitement over the strange drama that they were playing a part in that they were pretty badly rattled. They had loaded their pieces and were standing at "order arms," as were the men of the escort facing them on the other side of the little square. They fired a ragged volley, killing two men of the escort and severely wounding the leader of Aguinaldo's band, who happened to be passing between the lines when fire was opened. Aguinaldo, hearing the firing, and thinking that the men of his escort had broken loose to celebrate the arrival of the reinforcements, stepped to the window, and called out, "Stop that foolishness. Don't waste your ammunition." Before he could turn around Hilario had grasped him about the waist and thrown him under a table, where he literally sat on him, and Hilario was a fat man. I had given the most positive orders to the effect that under no circumstances should Aguinaldo be killed, and that no lives should be taken unless it was absolutely necessary. But as Segovia dashed back into the room several of the officers started to draw their revolvers, and he opened fire on them, hitting Villa three times, who was tugging to get a Mauser automatic pistol out of its holster, and also wounding Major Alhambra. Villa surrendered, as did Santiago Barcelona, treasurer of the so-called republic. Alhambra and the other officers leaped from one of the windows into the river, the house standing on the bank, and escaped by swimming. As Hilario grasped Aguinaldo, he had said, "You are a prisoner of the Americans," so that the fallen "Dictator," as he now called himself, had some sort of a vague idea of what had happened to him.

In the meantime we Americans with our supposed guard had reached the river, jumped into the *banca* waiting for us, and had paddled across in frantic haste. Running up the bank toward the house, we were met by Segovia, who came running out, his face aglow with exultation and his clothing spattered with the blood of the men he had wounded. He called out in Spanish, "It is all right. We have him." We hastened into the house, and I introduced myself to Aguinaldo, telling him that we were officers of the American army, that the men with us were our troops, and not his, and that he was a prisoner of war. He was given assurance that he need fear no bad treatment. He said in a dazed sort of way, "Is this not some joke?" I assured him that it was not, though, as a matter of fact, it was a pretty bad one on him. While naturally agitated, his bearing was dignified, and in this moment of his fall there was nothing of the craven. He is a man of many excellent qualities, far and away the best Filipino I ever was brought in contact with. It was well known that he was a man of humane instincts, and had done all he could to prevent the horrible atrocities committed by some of the guerilla bands that now made up his forces; but under the circumstances his control over them was limited. The wounded Villa was more inclined to stand aloof, but we dressed his wounds, thereby mollifying him somewhat. Barcelona was as mild as could be. There was some difficulty in getting under control the wildly excited Macabebes. A lot of them insisted in throwing their arms about us.

Aguinaldo's escort in their flight had dropped eighteen rifles and about a thousand rounds of ammunition, and these we now gathered up. It was regrettable that two of these men had been killed, but there was no help for it. The escort had to be surprised and quickly scattered. If we had sent our cards to them, told them who we were, and invited them to retire, as some lady-like persons in the United States afterward insisted that we should have done, it would merely have exposed our own men to a volley from them, and it scarcely could have been less fatal than the one that they received from us. The lives of these two men were of small moment counted against those that would have been lost had the insurrection continued. Few men have died to better purpose.

We supposed prisoners now took command. Aguinaldo, Villa, and Barcelona were confined in a room in the house and made as comfortable as possible. We posted guards all about the building and searched it thoroughly, finding great quantities of the correspondence of the insurgent government, showing that Aguinaldo had all of the time been in touch with his subordinates, even with those in the far-away Visayan Islands. We recaptured the two bogus letters from Lacuna and the one from Hilario at Casiguran. We had now no further suffering from lack of food, as we found cracked corn, rice, sweet-potatoes, and chickens. The inhabitants of the town had fled to the last man, woman, and child, so that we merely helped ourselves. There was no destruction of property and we left the town in as good shape as we found it. Lieutenant Mitchell had a small camera, carried on the march for him by one of the Macabebes, and took some interesting photographs. Aguinaldo, whose gameness and general bearing won our hearts, wrote and handed to me a brief note congratulating me on the outcome of the perilous expedition. In fact, the pleasantest relations were soon established between captors and captured.

We had made careful estimates of the distance marched each day, estimating at the rate of a mile and a half per hour, certainly conservative enough, and found that since landing from the *Vicksburg* we had covered one hundred and ten miles: twenty from the point of disembarkation to Casiguran; eighty-two from there to Dinundungan, and eight from the latter place to Palanan. It could not be less and might be ten or more miles farther.

The *Vicksburg* was not to be in Palanan Bay to take us on board until the 25th, so that we were compelled to wait over one day, but owing to our condition, this was a godsend. We spent the day in resting, sleeping, and eating. One of us American officers remained in the room with the prisoners all the time, day and night, this being at their request because of a wholesome fear of their hereditary enemies, the Macabebes. Early on the morning of the 25th we set out for the beach at Palanan Bay to meet the *Vicksburg*, the direction being north-east. The distance was two miles less than that over the trail to Dinundungan, being only six miles. But there was such a multiplicity of trails leading in all directions that we lost much time, as we had no guide, and none of the prisoners knew the way. Many of the Macabebes suffered severely from their bruised feet, and Segovia had a hard time of it. But all things end some time, and at noon we again saw the Pacific, and far out on it a wisp of smoke, the *Vicksburg* coming in. We had brought from Palanan a bed sheet to be used in signalling, and when the vessel was two miles out Captain Newton wigwagged the message, "We have him. Send boats for all." Soon came the reply, "Well done." Finally she anchored and we could see the boats being lowered.

It will be remembered that in the firing at Palanan the leader of Aguinaldo's band had been badly wounded. It was considered only right to take him to Manila for treatment, and he had been brought down the Palanan River in a canoe by two of the Macabebes, they being furnished with a pass by Villa in order to protect them in case they should fall in with insurgents. They arrived about this time, the place where we had reached the beach being not far from the mouth of the river. The surf was very ugly, but the boats came bucking through it, Commander Barry being in the first one. One of them was upset and we had great difficulty in getting into them, and were all drenched, but that was nothing. The greatest difficulty was with the wounded man.

As we rowed alongside the crew cheered time and again. We were soon on board and en route for Manila, sailing around the north end of the island. The prisoners were treated with the greatest courtesy, being entertained in the officers' messes, and sitting about on deck whenever they desired. On the morning of the 28th we entered Manila Bay with all our lights screened, as it was desired to keep the return of the expedition secret. At six o'clock I left the *Vicksburg* in her steam-launch, being accompanied by Lieutenant Glennon, executive officer of the vessel, Lieutenant Mitchell, and the three prisoners. We steamed into the mouth of the Pasig River and up through the city to the Malacañan Palace, the home of the division commander, where we all went ashore. General Mac-Arthur was just rising, and came out in a wrapper to meet me. He shook hands, looked at me in a quizzical way, but did not ask a question. I said, "Well, I have brought you Don Emilio." The general could scarcely believe it, and asked, "Where is he?" I replied, "Right in this house." As soon as he could dress the general came out and greeted cordially all of the three. We all sat down to breakfast, but Aguinaldo was not very talkative, being apparently somewhat overcome. But the general put him at his ease finally, and told him that he would immediately send for his family, whom he had not seen for a long time. The general got off his official despatch, and then the news was made public. To say that the city was wild with excitement mildly expresses the condition. It was now the opinion that the war that had wasted the country for so long a time was at its end. In the meantime I had hurried to tell the news of my return to the poor woman who for three long weeks had waited in an agony of suspense. A few days later General MacArthur sent for me, and as I entered his office said, with a very serious look on his face, "Well, Funston, they do not seem to have thought much in Washington of your performance. I am afraid you have got into trouble." At the same time he handed me a cablegram announcing my appointment as a brigadier-general in the regular army. The other officers, all of whom had splendidly done their parts, were also given commissions in the regular army, while Segovia, Segismundo, the three Tagalos, and the Macabebes were given appropriate rewards in various sums of money.

VIII

CLOSING DAYS

AFTER his capture and delivery to the division commander, Aguinaldo was held as a prisoner, but under such conditions that he suffered no hardship or humiliation, there being assigned to him as a residence a very respectable house only a few doors from the Malacañan Palace, the home of General MacArthur and his personal staff. Here he was allowed to see any of his friends who might call, and to confer with them in private, and besides had the company of his family. A guard of a few men was maintained over the building, more to protect him from possible assassination than because of a fear that he would attempt to escape. I called on him a few times, and he expressed the keenest appreciation of the treatment accorded him, he evidently having expected something entirely different. While his ideas on the subject of the ability of his countrymen to maintain a stable and responsible government seemed rather vague and inchoate, his dignity of manner and his attractive personality made a most favorable impression on all who came in contact with him. Finally, entirely of his own volition, and not under pressure of any kind, he issued a manly and well-written proclamation advising his subordinates to give up the struggle that had wrought such harm to the country, and to accept the sovereignty of the United States.

While a few surrenders of importance had already been made, the end of the war was by no means in sight, though the unceasing military operations against the guerilla bands all over the archipelago had had the effect of greatly reducing the number of those in arms against us. But now they came tumbling in, and within six weeks only two leaders still remained in the field: Lucban, in Samar, and Malvar, in Batangas; but the former was soon captured, while the latter was polished off by General Bell, and in time came in out of the rain.

Within a week after returning from the Palanan expedition I had returned to San Isidro, and deemed the time more than propitious to open up negotiations with Lacuna. Accordingly, there was written him a somewhat lengthy letter, in which was set forth a statement of conditions as they then existed, the surrenders of several prominent insurgent leaders being cited, and a copy of Aguinaldo's proclamation being enclosed. Lacuna sent in reply a letter which, while rather non-committal, indicated that he was willing to consider any reasonable proposition. Several more communications passed back and forth, with the result that an agreement was made to the effect that all hostilities in the Fourth District should at once cease. Lacuna was to be allowed to concentrate at Papaya, the little *barrio* of Peñaranda that we knew so well, all of the members of his widely scattered bands that he could get together, I giving a guarantee that in the meantime our troops would be confined to their garrisons and that we would attempt no operations. The faith that Lacuna had in the promises of the Americans was shown by the fact that during this period of the concentration of his troops he did not even maintain outposts.

At last a personal interview in order to discuss the terms of surrender was arranged, and one day about the middle of May, accompanied by several members of the district staff, my two aides, and a dozen men of the Scouts, I rode out through Gapan and Peñaranda to Papaya. The curiosity of all of us to see and talk with the man who had made things so warm for us during the past year made us quite impatient to cover the ten miles. Without even a white flag, and without having out a man as point, we rode quietly into the insurgent camp, information as to when we might be expected having been sent in advance. We dismounted, the men of the Scouts holding our horses and their own, and were met by an officer whose face was strangely familiar to me, though it was impossible to place him. We were conducted to a rather large, grassroofed shed, the guard of some twenty men coming to "present arms" in very good style, and at last were face to face with Lacuna. He shook hands with all of us, introduced us to a number of officers who were with him, and then had some coffee and cake brought in. Naturally, for a time nothing was said about the object of our visit. We found him to be an apparently full-blood Malay, very dark, of medium stature, and possessed of the quiet dignity of his race. He was a man of about middle-age, and had enough knowledge of Spanish to be able to speak the language fairly correctly, so that we understood each other without difficulty. On this occasion he was in the uniform of his rank, but it was evident to all of us that these articles of clothing had but recently been prepared for the occasion.

While these mild and harmless social pleasantries were going on I from time to time caught the eye of the good-looking and well-dressed officer who had first met us. Finally, I strolled over to him, and said in Spanish, "I have seen you before. Where was it?" and he said, with the greatest calmness, "Why, I am Timoteo Dhalan, adjutant of this force, and at the same time I am the American spy Doroteo del Rosario, and I am the man that you captured at Gapan more than a year ago, and who presented to you a letter from the provost-marshal of one of the American garrisons, this resulting in my release." And then it all came back in an instant, and I realized that the supposed American secret-service man that I had released under peremptory orders was this same individual.

But it was not very long before we got down to business. I explained very carefully to Lacuna that all of his officers and men would be allowed to surrender provided they turned in all arms and ammunition in their possession and took the oath of allegiance to the United States, and that all crimes against their own countrymen would be overlooked. It might be best to explain that in doing this I was carrying out the orders of higher authority, which was also the case when it came to the question as to what steps would be taken against any persons whom subsequent developments might show to have been implicated in the murder of American prisoners of war, it being made plain that they could expect no immunity. While this discussion was going on I noticed that my smooth little friend was taking considerable interest in it, and suspected that his solicitude was due to the fear that some crime that he had committed might be found out. Lacuna himself yielded the point, having nothing to fear; and then came up the question of Fagan, the negro deserter from our army, who was serving as an officer with the force concentrated at this point. It was made clear that this man could not be received as a prisoner of war, and that if he surrendered it would have to be with the understanding that he would be tried by court-martial, in which event his execution would be a practical certainty. Lacuna recognized the fact that any other solution was out of the question, and it was finally agreed that with the exception of Fagan all of his men were to march to San Isidro, deliver up their arms, and take the oath of allegiance to the United States, after which all would be released, but that any who should later prove to have been guilty of killing American prisoners would have to stand trial. The terms were then reduced to writing and signed by both of us.

A few days later, on the 19th of May, Lacuna and his force marched through Peñaranda and Gapan to San Isidro, where they formed line on the public square. All the Americans, including the few ladies, were present, while the streets were packed with natives. It was a brief ceremony, and in a few moments three hundred and seventy-nine serviceable rifles and several thousand rounds of ammunition were stacked on the ground. With the exception of seventy-five rifles that Lacuna had not yet had time to get in, but which were delivered within the next two weeks, these were all that remained of the fifteen hundred with which the insurgents of Nueva Ecija had begun the guerilla war less than a year and a half before. A few moments later we went over to district head-quarters, where I administered the oath to Lacuna, the others taking the obligation later in the day. Really, there was something pathetic about it all, for as soldiers we could not but have some appreciation of the game men who had stood out against us so long, and who had suffered such heavy losses at our hands. Lacuna had been the last of the insurgent leaders within the limits of the Department of Northern Luzon to give up the struggle, and General Wheaton, the department commander, sent the following despatch:

"THE CHIEF OF STAFF, DIVISION OF THE PHILIPPINES:
    "Lacuna having surrendered with all his officers and men to-day, I report that all insurrectionary leaders in this department have been captured or have surrendered. This is the termination of the state of war in this department so far as armed resistance to the authority of the United States is concerned."

It seems to be the usual thing for the cessation of military operations to be followed by an era of good feeling, so far as concerns the men who have been fighting each other, and conditions in Nueva Ecija were no exception to the rule. Americans and Filipinos met at many social functions, and the attitude of the whole population was exceedingly friendly. Pablo Tecson, Sandico, and other former chiefs came to see me, and we spent many hours in pleasant reminiscence. It is a great pity that the feeling of those days could not last. It is hard to place the blame with certainty. The fault was not with the army, and certainly not with the honest and highly efficient civil government that soon replaced military rule. But there arose soon a particularly noisy, pestiferous, and illogical band of native agitators, mighty few of whom had possessed the courage to face us on the field of battle, and these were aided and abetted by a number of contemptible persons among our own countrymen.

The departure for the United States of General F. D. Grant, commanding the Fifth District, and of Colonel J. M. Thompson, commanding the Sixth District, resulted in the consolidation of those two commands with my own, San Fernando, Pampanga, being designated as headquarters. I was assigned to the command of the new district, and prepared for final departure from San Isidro. Including native auxiliaries, the new command contained more than fifteen thousand troops; but the war was over. On the journey from San Isidro I was accompanied by Padilla, Lacuna, Alipio Gonzalez, *presidente* of San Isidro, and a number of prominent residents, and the journey of two days was made without incident. I could not but feel pleased at the compliment of having so distinguished an escort, but a sarcastic officer of my staff said that it was because they were glad to be rid of me. However, I would rather take the other view of it.

The work at San Fernando was largely of a routine nature, being connected with supply and discipline. Our "hiking" days were over, but there were still a few scores to settle. After the surrender of Lacuna, Fagan had for a time disappeared, but now he began to be heard from, he having in some way obtained two or three rifles and, with a couple of unreconstructed natives, taken to the *bosque*, whence he had made a, few forays for the purpose of committing robberies. I made a trip to Manila to discuss the matter with General Wheaton, and came back with the authority to offer a reward of six hundred dollars for Fagan, dead or alive. Whatever he had been before, he was now a bandit, pure and simple, and entitled to just the same treatment as a mad dog; which is what he got. A proclamation, written in Spanish and Tagalog, offering a reward of six hundred dollars for the head of David Fagan, American negro, deserter from the United States army, was posted in every town in Nueva Ecija, and at Bongabong was read by one Anastacio Bartolome, a Tagalog who for years had made his living as a deer hunter. Having heard rumors of the recent movements of Fagan and his companions, and not being averse to earning an honest penny, Anastacio took to the woods with one companion, and two days later found Fagan, two Filipino men and three women in camp on the beach of the Pacific coast of the province at the place known on the maps as Dingalan Cove. The party was just sitting down to a dinner of camotes and fish, and invited the visitors from Bongabong to join them. The opportunity for Anastacio to carry out his plan not being favorable at the time, he accepted. He knew Fagan by sight, having himself been an insurgent soldier, and so was sure he had the right man. The meal being half finished, he gave his companion a look; the two sprang to their feet, and in a few strokes beheaded the three men, sparing the three screaming women. Fagan's head, the only one of importance, was brought to Bongabong and delivered to Lieutenant R. C. Corliss, Thirty-fourth Infantry, commanding the company of Ilocano Scouts constituting the garrison of that town. With the head were brought in three Remington rifles, two revolvers, Fagan's two commissions, one as first lieutenant and the other as captain, signed by both Alejandrino and Lacuna, and Lieutenant Alstaetter's West Point class ring, taken from him by Fagan at the time of his capture, a year before. Only a short time later Lacuna told me that we got the right man, though there was never any doubt on the subject, as all of the colored soldiers who had been captured had been in one way or another accounted for. Anastacio received his money in less than two weeks, and it was more than he could have saved in many years of following his useful but not very lucrative occupation; and Fagan was at least one American traitor who got what was coming to him. Let us hope that after his return to his home Anastacio did not bet all of his winnings on the wrong bird.

We had not been in San Fernando very long when there began to be noised about rumors of the presence of a white bandit operating in the country thereabouts. This was more than interesting, being without precedent in our times in the Philippines, and the matter was looked into. Finally, the suspected man was arrested, and proved to be George A. Raymond, a recently discharged soldier of the Forty-first Infantry. The evidence against the accused was worked out by Captain George H. Cameron, of the Fourth Cavalry, and his unwinding of the whole thing was a piece of detective work that in itself would make a chapter. Raymond, having already been discharged from the army, was not subject to trial by court-martial, and so was sent before a military commission, which is the same thing, only worse. This particular body was presided over by Captain A. C. Macomb, Fifth Cavalry, and it did its work in mighty few hours, fewer, in fact, than the number of weeks that the same case would have dragged along in one of our ridiculous trials by jury at home. Military commissions, though governed by the rules of evidence that prevail in civil courts, and while at all times guarding the rights of the accused, pay no attention to technicalities, and brush to one side everything that it may be sought to bring in to obscure the main issue, which, after all, is whether the accused is guilty or not. If I should ever do anything very naughty, I should very much dislike going before one of them, but if innocent of the charge, would ask nothing better. Once the sentence of a military commission has been approved by the superior military authority on the ground, there is no appeal except to the President of the United States; and he is liable to be on the other side of the world. Raymond was convicted of murder, robbery, and another crime that cannot be mentioned here; and on the 27th day of September ten thousand Filipinos packed the public square at Angeles to see a white man die on the scaffold. A kindly old native priest did the decent thing, and stood at the side of the wretched man until it was over, though Raymond had never had anything to do with his church or any other. Raymond, despicable criminal though he was, had the good taste not to lower the prestige of his race in the way he met death, and, defiant to the last, went to his doom with sullen courage. If they had ever had any doubts as to whether the stern and implacable justice administered by our military commissions knew either race or color, the natives should have been convinced by this incident. But there were other examples; for just a week before, Harry Cline, an American employee of the Quartermaster's Department, had been hanged at Fort San Antonio, Abad, Manila, for the brutal and senseless murder of a native boy; and it was during the period that a civilian scout, a white American, who at San Fernando needlessly shot a native prisoner in his charge, was sentenced to imprisonment for twenty years.

Among the prisoners confined in the guard-house at San Fernando was one Manuel Gonzalez, an insurgent lieutenant, awaiting trial on the charge of breaking a parole, he having returned to the field after being once captured and released. The surrenders of the numerous insurgent bands, with the return to their homes of the men constituting them, and their consequent release from the control of their superiors, now began to have the effect of assisting us in unravelling some of the mysteries of the past two years. On the 30th day of October, 1900, a detachment of ten men of the Thirty-fifth Infantry, acting as escort for José Buencamino, the newly elected *presidente* of San Miguel de Mayumo, while he was on his way to that town to assume his duties, was ambushed near the Maasim River and Buencamino and five of the soldiers captured, never again being heard of alive. Several circumstances now brought to light pointed to the guilt of Gonzalez, the prisoner at San Fernando, in making way with the six missing men. I had him brought over to my head-quarters, and Segovia and I took him in hand. No violence was used nor threatened, nor were promises held out, but hours of a grilling cross-examination, catching him in innumerable lies, finally broke the man down, and he told everything. He had personally superintended the execution of the six men, but had acted under written orders from the then local guerilla chief, Timoteo Dhalan. And now it was clear why this man, when he surrendered with Lacuna, being at that time his adjutant, had shown such solicitude as to what proceedings might be taken against insurgents implicated in the killing of prisoners of war. Gonzalez gave the names of the sergeant and five other men who under his personal direction had done the bloody work, and told all the ghastly details. Buencamino had been separated from the American prisoners, and was killed with a dagger, while the five soldiers, Privates Hickman, Smith, Jarvis, Dane, and Wilson, of the Thirty-fifth Infantry, with their arms tied behind their backs, were conducted into the high grass bordering the Candaba swamp, where the helpless men were stabbed to death, their bodies being left unburied. Segovia, Lieutenant

Mitchell, and I mounted our horses and in two days reached Baliuag, where we were joined by Lieutenant Robert I. Rees, of the Third Infantry. The sergeant and five privates implicated in the confession of Gonzalez were quickly captured, and being examined separately, and confronted with our knowledge of the facts, confessed everything. It was important now to find the letter that would be essential in order to convict Dhalan, as the unsupported word of Gonzalez would not be sufficient, the other men captured having no knowledge of the orders under which Gonzalez had acted. Gonzalez had told us that the document was probably in the house of his mother in a small village near Baliuag, but he did not know just where, as nearly a year had passed since he had seen it. The house was found with some difficulty, but Gonzalez's mother either did not know where the document was or would not tell, though she was assured that it could in no way injure her son, he already having confessed. The building, a nipa structure of a few rooms, was searched so thoroughly that the fatal letter was found concealed in one of the hollow bamboo door-posts. It was directed to Lieutenant Manuel Gonzalez, and was signed by Timoteo Dhalan, the date being November 1, 1900, and gave the most explicit orders as to the execution of Buencamino and the five Americans. A long search in the cogon grass along the edge of the great swamp in the hope of finding the skeletons of the murdered men was futile, though months afterward they were all found by Lieutenant Rees, and given burial. Dhalan was quickly arrested and brought to San Fernando. The "smoothness" that marked him on the occasions of our two previous meetings did not forsake him now; nor did that plausibility that had enabled him so completely to pull the wool over the eyes of one of our officers that he had been employed as a spy under the name of Doroteo del Rosario at the same time that he was an insurgent officer in active service. Major George H. Paddock, Fifth Cavalry, was president, and my aide, Mitchell, judge-advocate of the military commission that met at San Fernando in our head-quarters building to try the cases. I was called as a witness as to previous meetings with Dhalan and the finding of the letter to Gonzalez. The latter, Sergeant de la Cruz, and the five privates who had done the actual killing went on the stand in succession and told the sickening story, hiding nothing. Lacuna was introduced as an unwilling witness for the prosecution for the purpose of identifying the handwriting of the letter as being that of his old adjutant. When the question was put to him, he being asked if he recognized the penmanship of the letter as that of Dhalan, he hesitated, looked helplessly around the room, and finally in a barely audible voice answered, "I do." It was an intensely dramatic and very painful moment, and all of us felt keenly sorry for the old guerilla chief, placed in the position of having to take his choice between committing perjury or assisting in weaving the web about a former staff officer. But we were not altogether dependent on the testimony of Lacuna, for a number of undisputed specimens of the handwriting of Dhalan were available for comparison. On the 8th of November, Timoteo Dhalan, *alias* Doroteo

del Rosario, and Manuel Gonzalez met death on the
gallows at Baliuag, the former before that day having
made a complete and full confession. If one could consider Dhalan apart from the shocking crime for which he
was responsible, it would be easy to regret his fate, for he
was a rather likable man of attractive personality. Sergeant de la Cruz was sentenced to death, but this was
commuted to imprisonment for life, while the five privates
were allowed to go without trial.

Brutal as was the crime for which these men were punished, it was a mere misdemeanor compared with the one
for which the insurgent *commandante*, Francisco Braganza,
was hanged at Nueva Caceres just a week later, this being
the chopping to death with bolos of *one hundred and three*
Spanish soldiers, prisoners of war, in order to prevent
their rescue by the American troops. Had the military
authorities relentlessly punished all the crimes that were
now brought to light, there would have been a gallows set
up in nearly every town in the Philippine Islands; but
considerations of policy and possibly the fear of a not very
discriminating public sentiment at home stopped the work,
and after the hanging of some three hundred Filipinos and
half a dozen Americans the military commissions ceased
their functions, and left unavenged the deaths of thousands
of helpless Filipinos who in those terrible years had suffered martyrdom at the hands of their own people. After
all, it is better that this course was taken, for had we been
strictly logical, and held every man to an accounting for
his deeds, there would have resulted one of the most painful chapters in modern history.

But it is pleasant to turn from such a distressing theme. We officers on duty at district head-quarters at San Fernando had our home and office in the same building, the finest residence in the town, and life was quite agreeable, especially as we were now often able to go to Manila, and to entertain friends from there, the trip to the capital requiring a railroad journey of only a few hours. Lieutenant Day, having been appointed treasurer of Nueva Ecija province, had been mustered out of the service, and had remained in San Isidro, so that I had taken as the second aide, to which I was entitled, Lieutenant Thomas E. Merrill, Second Artillery. It was during these days that Mitchell conceived the idea that his social standing would be improved if he had his own private vehicle, and so, having in some way saved up eighty dollars, he purchased a *carromato*, and at the same time the necessary harness. After he had done this it suddenly occurred to him that he had no horse to place between the shafts, and without a horse the new purchase was liable to be of but little use. Captain Smith was the owner of a very fine native pony of unusual size, and of light roan color, the name "Willie Grow" having in some way been attached to him. I knew Willie quite well, and in fact had ridden him on several expeditions. When Mitchell confessed his plight to the effect that he was the possessor of a *carromato* and harness, but had no horse, Captain Smith said, "Why, why not use Willie?" The brigade adjutant then retired for his *siesta*, but from the window of my room I watched the proceedings. The fact that Willie was a saddle-horse, and never in his life had been decorated with a harness, added interest to the obsequies. Willie stood still while he was being hitched up, but looked insulted and peevish. Mitchell got in, and somewhat impatiently said to the driver, "Why don't you make him go? Touch him up." Willie went, straight through a high board fence, distributing Mitchell, the native driver, the harness, and the fragments of the *carromato* impartially over the landscape, and calmly went to cropping grass.

In September I had to take a hurried journey to Manila for the purpose of undergoing a most serious surgical operation, and spent the next three months in the First Reserve Hospital. Mrs. Funston had returned to the United States in May, so that I could not have the benefit of visits from her during this trying time; but General Chaffee, who on July 1 had relieved General MacArthur in supreme command, General Wheaton, and many other friends among the officers called frequently to cheer me up and help to pass away the dreary weeks. Finally the long siege was over, and I was ordered home, not to return to Manila for more than nine years. While coming out on my third trip in February, 1911, it brought back vividly the long-ago days when I was a filibuster, to see lying in the harbor of Honolulu the same old *Dauntless* on which I had made the trip to the coast of Cuba nearly fifteen years before. And these closing lines are written in my quarters in Manila, in the very house which was once the home of Don Valeriano Weyler, not unknown to fame as a somewhat energetic suppressor of insurrections, and the commander-in-chief of the Spanish forces in Cuba during a part of the War of Independence. All of which brings up musings as to the queer things that are sometimes brought about by the turns of the wheel of fortune.

THE END

INDEX

445